Descriptive Statistics and Probability Theory

First published in 1972, in *Descriptive Statistics and Probability Theory* the numerical work- the selection of numerical data-is used as a basis for developing the statistical theory. Other starting points could have been chosen but a beginner will readily understand this sort of work and hence be able to 'get the feel of' statistics, untroubled by the learning of fresh concepts.

From this numerical work emerges the 'need' to introduce counting techniques, permutations, combinations and the binomial theorem. In a similar way the necessity for probability is shown and the basic ideas are developed intuitively. A final short chapter shows how these ideas can be formalised within an axiomatic system. In all cases, simple intuitive ideas are taken as a starting point and then discussion leads to the final formalization. As concepts are introduced the language of statistics is developed. A large number of examples is used and they are all worked in full detail. Occasionally the reader is placed in a problem situation and invited to attempt his own individual solution before reading on to match his own attempts to other solutions. It is hoped that motivation of this sort will lead the reader to develop greater sensitivity than would otherwise be the case. This is an important read for students of statistics, mathematics and economics.

Descriptive Statistics and Probability Theory

Robert A. Barks

Routledge
Taylor & Francis Group

First published in 1972
by Hutchinson Educational

This edition first published in 2025 by Routledge
4 Park Square, Milton Park, Abingdon, Oxon, OX14 4RN

and by Routledge
605 Third Avenue, New York, NY 10158

Routledge is an imprint of the Taylor & Francis Group, an informa business

A Library of Congress record exists under ISBN: 0091125103

ISBN: 978-1-041-07689-6 (hbk)
ISBN: 978-1-003-64175-9 (ebk)
ISBN: 978-1-041-07691-9 (pbk)

Book DOI 10.4324/9781003641759

Descriptive Statistics and Probability Theory

ROBERT A. BARKS

HUTCHINSON EDUCATIONAL

HUTCHINSON EDUCATIONAL LTD
3 Fitzroy Square, London W1

London Melbourne Sydney Auckland
Wellington Johannesburg Cape Town
and agencies throughout the world

First published 1972

Dedicated to Leslie Lackie

Printed in Great Britain by litho on smooth wove paper by Anchor Press, and bound by Wm. Brendon, both of Tiptree, Essex

ISBN 0 09 112510 3 (cased)
0 09 112511 1 (paper)

Contents

Introduction

What is statistics?

One major difficulty in giving an explanation of statistics to a beginner is the difficulty of language. The ideas of statistics are expressed in statistical terms and any explanation must use these terms. Hence the beginner, unfamiliar with the language of statistics, will find it impossible to understand the ideas. Another difficulty is that statistics is now such a vast science that a simple explanation is just not possible.

In these circumstances it might be best for the beginner to consider a problem, typical of those presented to a statistician, see how he sets about solving it, and then consider some generalisations that can be made from the ideas that come out of the actions of the statistician. We follow this line of thought in the following paragraphs.

If a statistician is presented with a problem, what does he do to get an answer to it? Let us consider the following problem:
A washing powder manufacturer is considering expanding his production so that he can offer his two products *Brand A* and *Brand B* in a town where hithertoo they have been unavailable. What increase in production must he make so that he can meet the demand in this new town but at the same time not manufacture too much?

Presented with this problem the statistician first of all has to decide what information – or *data* as it is called – needs collecting. He then has to arrange for the collection of that data in the most efficient and accurate way possible. Next he must organise this data into some appropriate order and then, having done this, he is in a position to analyse it – i.e. find out what it tells him – and then from this analysis he makes predictions with varying degrees of certainty.

Let us see how this follows through in the case of the washing powder manufacturer. A typical process and reply would be as follows:
Stage 1: Decide to sample 200 households in the new town. This means that 200 households will be contacted in some way and asked their opinion about the two powders *Brand A* and *Brand B*.

Stage 2: Decide to knock on doors until 200 'volunteers' agree to help. They will be asked to test both powders on consecutive wash days and then to answer the questions:
If these powders, *Brand A* and *Brand B*, were available in the shops along with the powder that you normally buy, would you buy (i) *Brand A*; (ii) *Brand B*; (iii) Your usual powder.
Brand A is delivered to the 200 households in time for a washday. The following week, *Brand B* is likewise delivered and then, after the second washday, the replies to the question – i.e. the data – is collected.
Stage 3: After collection the raw data is sorted into the three groups (a) those who would prefer to buy *Brand A* (b) those who would prefer to buy *Brand B*, and (c) those who would prefer to buy their normal powder.
Stage 4: The data is analysed and the results (hypothetical) are arranged as follows:

Those who would prefer to buy *Brand A*	Those who would prefer to buy *Brand B*	Those who would prefer to buy their *normal powder*
60	50	90

The statistician now sees that 60 out of 200 of the households sampled would prefer to buy *Brand A* if they could get it, that is 30%. Similarly 50 out of 200 shows that 25% of the household sampled would prefer to buy *Brand B*. Finally 90 our of 200 shows that 45% of the households sampled would return to their normal washing powder.
The statistician now argues that if this sample is a good sample, then 30% of the households of this town would switch to *Brand A* if they had the opportunity, 25% would switch to *Brand B* if they had the opportunity, and 45% of the households would not buy this manufacturers product.
Supposing now that there are 10 000 households in this new town then by applying these figures the statistician would give the following:
Answer: If you make your two washing powders available in this town then you can expect that

between 2750 and 3250 households will buy *Brand A*
between 2250 and 2750 households will buy *Brand B*
between 4250 and 4750 households will not buy your washing powder.

Although this is a simplified version of what happens the main outline is correct and although this is a typical process and reply it is by no means the only one. The following remarks show how different methods might have been employed at different stages.

Stage 1: Although in this example a sample of 200 was taken, samples of other sizes could have been used instead. We therefore have to find some criterion which will enable us to decide what is the best sized sample to take. Briefly it can be said that the sample must be large enough to be representative of the population. To take the absurd case of a sample of one is illustrative. If the one person in the sample had elected to turn to *Brand A* then this would signify the 100% of the sample had decided to switch to the new powder. The inference from this is that 100% of the population, i.e. the whole town, would switch to the new powder – obviously an invalid conclusion in practical terms. Samples of two, three and four give similar lugubrious results.

From this it can be restated that the sample must be large enough to be representative of the population.

Two other factors are also important in deciding the size of the sample – time and money. The larger the sample the better the final picture of the population but the larger will be the cost and the longer will be the time over which the collecting of the data will be spread. These considerations have made statisticians develop techniques for getting the maximum amount of information out of samples, especially if they are small. Considerations of this sort are usually taken into account and dealt with in the section of statistics known as *sampling theory*.

Stage 2: Interviewers have to be engaged and instructed in interviewing householders and persuading them to take part in the tests of the washing powders. They have to cover different parts of the town and interview people of differing ages, family size, and so on so that a good cross section of the population of the town is obtained in the sample. If, for example, all the people who volunteered to help were over 60 years old and living in one part of the town, then most certainly a *biased sample* would be obtained and so the sample would not reflect the opinion of the town as a whole. If the sample is not representative of the town population as a whole then any conclusions based upon it will be invalid. If, for example, the sample showed 30% of the town would switch to *Brand A* and the manufacturer geared his production on this information, and then it was found that only 12% of the town were buying *Brand A* , then there are obvious difficulties for the manufacturer.

In summary, we have to be fairly sure that the sample will be representative of the population for it to be a *good sample*.

Different sampling methods can be used at this stage. For instance, instead of knocking on peoples doors, the interviewers could be instructed to stop people in the streets of the shopping area of the town, and request their assistance in the tests.

There are also methods available without using interviewers. One consists in writing to people and asking for a reply of willingness to be returned. This method is much cheaper than the use of interviews but the replies are not certain to come back either in time, or, at all.

Considerations of this sort are usually taken into account in the section of statistics known as the *design of the experiment*.

Stage 3: When a sample is taken from its population it may be examined in two ways. First of all it may be considered in isolation and put into order without reference to the population. This process of putting in order and describing the results is known as *descriptive statistics* because the information is only described. No conclusions about the population are drawn at this stage.

Secondly, and this brings us to *Stage 4*, the sample may be considered in relation to the population from which it is drawn. This consideration is concerned with what may be *inferred* about the population from the information provided by the sample. This process of inferring is known as *statistical inference*. If it is a representative sample of a certain size then there is much that it can tell us about the population.

Answer: It should be noted that in this example the answer is given so that the manufacturer can know what minimum and what maximum number of households he can expect *in all probability* to buy his product. This is typical of a statistical reply – statistical techniques are applied to situations involving an element of *chance* or *uncertainty* and so predictions can only be made within certain limits. These limits and how accurate they are will be further explained in the text but it gives an opportunity to give a warning. Statistics does not claim to be 100% accurate. It is accurate only within the limits of the techniques used and these limits should always be stated by the statistician and looked for by the reader.

As prediction are made only with varying degrees of probability we shall see later that the *theory of probability* occupies a central position in statistics.

We are now in a position to give some sort of answer to the question '*What is Statistics?*', and in the light of the above, we say that *Statistics is the science which deals with the collection, processing, and analysing of raw data for the purpose of drawing inferences and making predictions.*

In order to learn statistics it is necessary for the beginner to concentrate on the various stages as outlined above one at a time. The reader is urged to return and re-read this introduction whilst devoting the major part of his time to the study of one of the stages. This will help in locating the position of the individual stages in the overall scheme of statistics.

It is interesting to look at the history of statistics and see how it grew into what it is today. The word 'statistics' itself gives the clue to the origin of statistics. Originally it was applied to numerical data collected by the state – and hence stat(e)istics. The word 'statistics' was not used in the middle ages but the survey for Doomsday Book was a statistical survey.

Present day statistics has two facets – statistical calculations and the mathematical theory behind these calculations – and these two facets have entirely different origins. Let us look at the origin of statistical calculations. In past times it was found convenient to count and record measurements of various items in order that the possessor of these items may better manage his affairs. The early kings and rulers took an interest in the possessions of their subjects in order that they might know what taxes to impose or what resources they might call upon in time of war. This supplying of information to the state can be called the forerunner of present day statistical calculations. It was purely counting, measuring and recording. The other aspect of present day statistics – the mathematical theory of statistics – traces its origins back to less distant times. In the sixteenth and seventeenth centuries, games of chance were popular with the wealthy and one of the most ardent of these, Chevalier de Mere, wrote to the French mathematician Blaisé Pascal (1623–1662) about a point that puzzled him. This letter sparked off correspondence between Pascal and other mathematicians of the day and this correspondence is usually considered the origin of modern *probability theory* upon which is based the *mathematical theory of statistics*. Thus we have have two distinct starting points for statistics and had these two essentially different activities not interacted then we would not have statistics as we know it today. Fortunately they did interact – figures obtained by calculations suggested theories, and abstract theories produced by mathematical deduction alone have been found to have practical application. This is a familiar pattern not only in statistics but in other branches of science as well. The number of famous mathematicians who have made contributions to statistics since these early days makes it impossible to mention them all individually but anyone interested can find the details in the literature of statistics.

This brief introduction to statistics is concluded by pointing out that statistics has invaded practically every sphere of human endeavour and is particularly applicable to any sphere where there is an element of chance or uncertainty.

Exercise

1. A shoe manufacturer wishes to ensure that he makes the sufficient variety of shoe size so that he may cater for all types of feet but not to make too many of any particular size. Discuss how he should tackle the problem and show the various stages of investigation.

2. What properties must a sample have in order to be described by a statistician as a *good* sample.

3. Look up the meaning of the following words and phrases: Probable; possible; likely; equally likely; chance; random; scientific; technique; method; population; sample

4. Can you think of any more methods of sampling other than stopping people in the street or knocking on householders doors?

1 Graphs

1.1 Preliminary Remarks

In the Introduction, we saw the various stages in the solution of a statistical problem and it would be possible to learn statistics by studying the various stages in the order stage 1 through to stage 5. However, experience has shown that a study of stages 1 and 2 – which really come under the heading of *techniques and methods of sampling* – is better undertaken with prior knowledge of stages 3 and 4, and we therefore start by considering raw data and its organisation.

When a statistical investigation is undertaken and the raw data collected, the first problem which presents itself is the organisation of this raw data into a readily comprehendible form. Experience has shown that if the data is put into picture form then the essential details are much more readily grasped and understood. Putting the data into picture form is called *graphing the data,* and the resultant representation is called the *graph* of the data. Many different types of graphs have been developed and the main ones are given in the following sections.

1.2 Pie Graphs

Raw data: In a class of 36 pupils, 20 had brown eyes, 8 had blue eyes, 4 had hazel coloured eyes, and the remaining 4 had eyes that could not be put into the above three categories.

Source: Form 3a, *X* Junior School, *Y* Town

Before graphing raw data it is always convenient to put it into tabulated form as follows:

Tabulated form:

Brown eyes	20
Blue eyes	8
Hazel eyes	4
Others	4

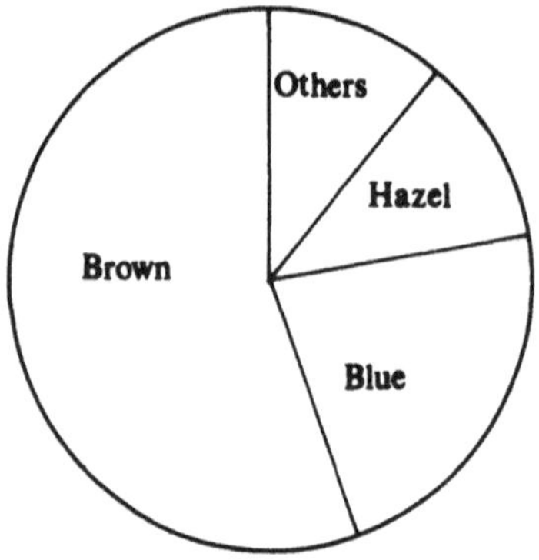

Fig. 1.2(a). Pie graph to show the colour of the eyes of the students in Form 3a, *X* Junior School, *Y* Town

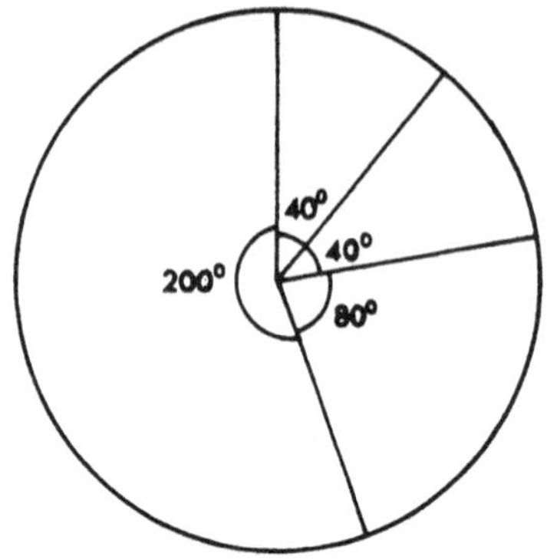

Fig. 1.2(b). Diagram to show the angles which correspond to the pie graph

Individual items of the data are expressed as a fraction of the whole data, and the central angles of the graph are the corresponding fractions of 360°.
For example, *Blue eyes – 8*: This information, expressed as a fraction of the whole data, becomes $\frac{8}{36} = \frac{2}{9}$. Two ninths ($\frac{2}{9}$) of 360° is 80°, hence the corresponding central angle is 80°. This is shown, together with the others, in Fig. 1.2(b).

Radial or horizontal labelling may be used, the criterion to follow in deciding is clarity. The number of divisions must not be large or clarity will be lost. It is difficult to give a general rule as to the maximum number of divisions because of different factors which may be present in any individual graph (for example, the size of the graph, use of colour or shading, printed or hand-written characters and so on) but in most cases the number of divisions should not exceed 6 or 7.

In a pie graph the relation of the individual items to the whole is readily seen.

1.3 Pictograms

Raw data: In 1954, the average number of hours of Bright Sunshine per day was as tabulated below:

Aberystwyth	3·8 hours
Buxton	2·5 hours
Douglas	4·0 hours
Felixtowe	4·1 hours
York	3·1 hours

Source: The Meterological Office

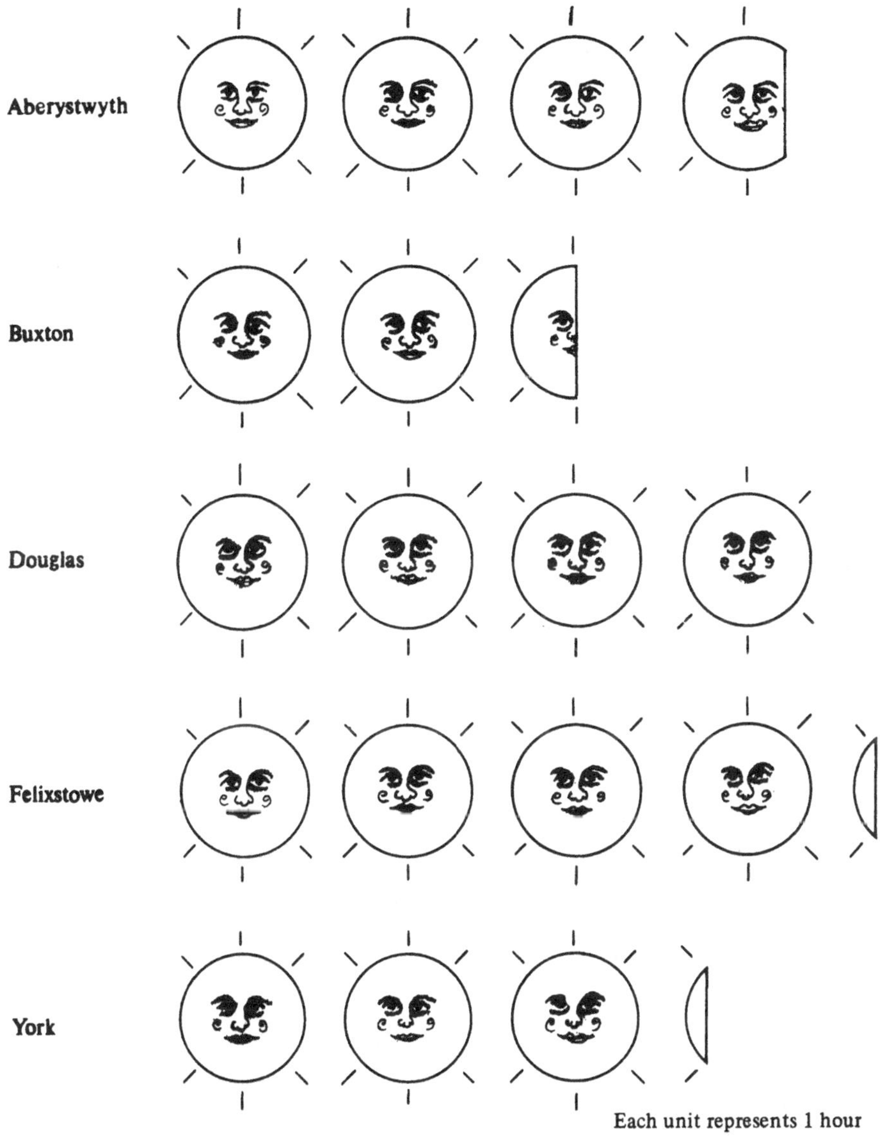

Fig. 1.3. Pictogram to show the average number of hours of Bright Sunshine per day for the year 1954 at the stated places

In a pictogram, each unit is a small picture in some way associated with the data. They have popular appeal and are used frequently, but they are open to abuse. For instance, if one wished to double the size of the unit with a view to expressing two units in one picture, the following difficulty would emerge. If the area of the picture represents the unit, and the length of the diameter (or lengths of the sides if the unit were rectangular) is doubled, then the area of the new figure would be four times that of the old unit. Thus the new figure would be four times the old unit and not two as required. This device is occasionally used when it is desired to present material in a way such that it can be claimed that it is correctly presented but in fact it is presented in a slightly distorted fashion. Thus any pictogram which contains elements of different sizes needs very careful examination.

1.4 Bar Graphs

Raw data: The strength of the Police Force in England and Wales, and Scotland for the years concerned are tabulated below:

Year	England and Wales	Scotland
1960	72396	8669
1961	76324	9015
1962	77860	9527
1963	79709	9738
1964	80614	9857
1965	83221	10175

Source: Whitaker's Almanack 1967

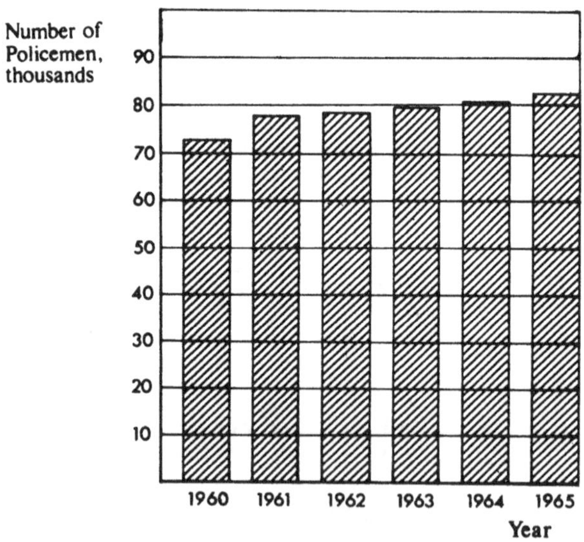

Fig. 1.4 (a). Bar graph to show the strength of the Police Force in England and Wales for the years shown

A bar graph consists of bars of equal width placed either vertically or horizontally and having a gap – usually half the width of a bar – between them. The scale is shown at the side or, if it is wished, the scale may be omitted and the actual figures placed at the ends of the bars. If a scale is used then the zero of the scale must always be shown, but if the figures are large and it is required to compress the graph, the following device can be used

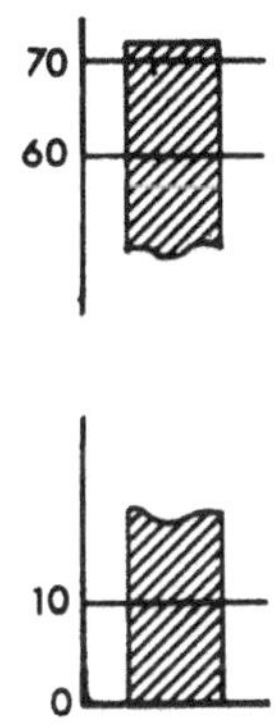

Fig. 1.4(b)

the break extending over the full width of the graph.

Although bar graphs are frequently used for showing data which changes with time, this is not the best way of presenting this sort of data. A better method will be shown later.

1.5 Adaptations of Bar Graphs

Various adaptations of bar graphs are frequently seen. Two are given below.

Fig. 1.5(a) shows how two sets of data relating to similar subjects may be shown in comparison with each other.

Fig. 1.5(b) shows two sets of similar data but this time they have been added. Here the totals are the most important feature although it is still possible to compare the two sets of data.

1.6 Review

We are now in a position to make remarks on points that have emerged so far from the work.

First of all, whatever form of graph is used certain details should always be present. They are title, source of data, key (where appropriat

Fig. 1.5(a). Bar graph to show the strength of the Police Forces of England and Wales, and Scotland, for the stated years.

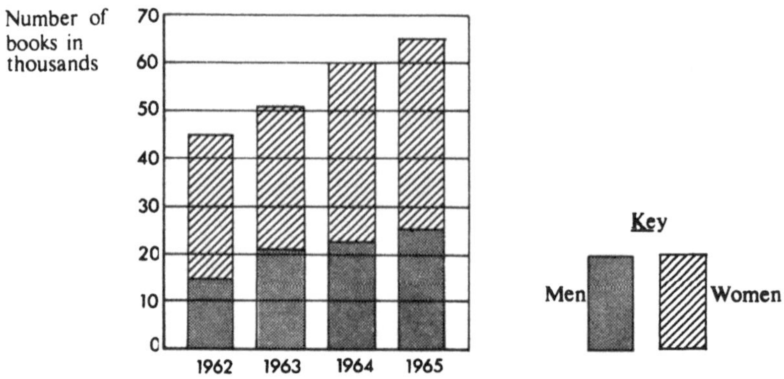

Fig. 1.5(b). Bar graph to show the number of books taken out of a library by men and women

and scales. It is worth recalling that one of the reasons for graphing data is for easy assimilation on the part of a reader and so the clarity of symbols and good layout should be born constantly in mind.

Secondly, it will no doubt have been seen by now that it is possible to express the same data in different graphical forms. The choice of graph is dependent upon which feature of the data it is wished to highlight. For example, if it is the relationship of the parts of the data to the whole of the data which is important, then a pie graph could be used with advantage. It sometimes happens that no particular graphical form is suggested by the raw data. In this case it sometimes happens that once the data is graphed, it becomes obvious which particular graph should have been used and this leads to regraphing. This point serves to bring out another feature of graphs, other than the easy assimilation one. That is that the graph of data can suggest further developments.

Next, it should be noted that other names are used for these graphs, e.g. *pictograms* are sometimes called *pictographs*. *Bar graphs* are sometimes called *bar charts* and so on. All the names used are so similar that the student should have no difficulty on this point.

Finally, colour and shading can be used to enhance the appearance or bring out a particular feature of a graph, and there are endless variations on the above graphs possible. The student should try his hand at taking some of the above data and graphing it in different forms aiming for originality. Graphs are used frequently in the press and government publications and these two sources should be watched with care.

1.7 Broken-line Graphs

If a subject is chosen which varies with time, then the bar graph is not the best method of representing it visually. This is because the bar graph does not indicate the way the subject may vary at times other than at those points which represent the readings. This drawback may be overcome by using a broken-line graph.

Raw data: Table to show the daily average hours of sunshine at Costa del Sol and London

	Oct	Nov	Dec	Jan	Feb	Mar	Apr
Costa del Sol	7·8	6·2	5·9	6·5	7·1	7·0	9·6
London	2·68	1·36	0·86	0·95	1·60	2·97	4·39

Source: a travel brochure, 1969

The graph of this data is shown in Fig. 1.7(a). It is clear that it is now possible to assess better what is happening at different times throughout the period in question. If we assume that the figures given in the table were taken at the mid-point of the month, then we can easily estimate the average number of hours of sunshine at other times in the month. If we take, for example, the point which represents the end of

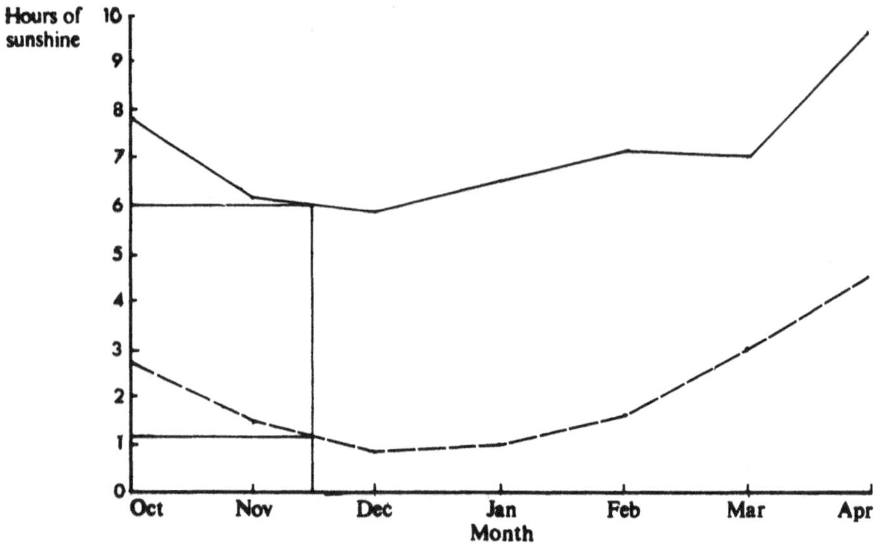

Fig. 1.7 (a). Graph to show the daily average hours of sunshine at
(a) Costa del Sol ————
(b) London — — — — —

November and the beginning of December we can, by following the heavy vertical line to the points where it crosses the two lines of the graph, take readings from the vertical scale. In the case of London we get approximately 1·1 hours of sunshine, and in the case of Costa del Sol we get approximately 6·0 hours of sunshine.

Estimating unknown figures by taking a figure which is indicated by the known figures in this way is called *interpolation*, provided that the estimated figure is within the range of the known figures.

The process whereby figures are estimated from given data but the estimated figures fall *outside* the range of the data is called *extrapolation*. If we were asked to estimate the daily average hours of sunshine at London for May then we would be going outside the given data. In this case we could estimate roughly six hours but it must be noted that we are not going entirely from the given figures but using our knowledge of the London climate. It should be remembered that in cases like this extrapolation can be justified but there are cases where not enough is known about the circumstances surrounding the data to make a legitimate extrapolation.

A word of caution must be added about interpolation. Consider the following graph:

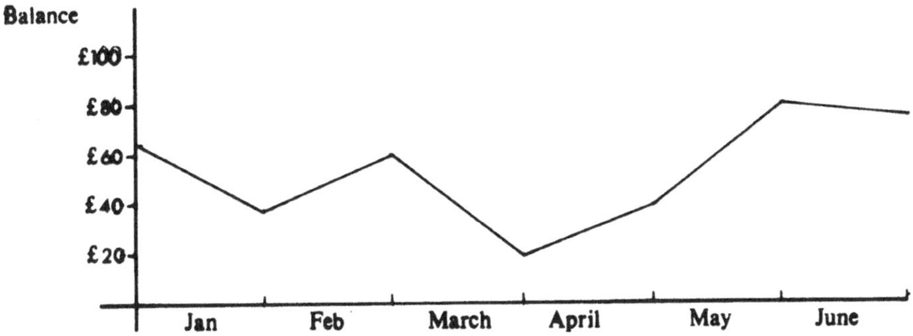

Fig. 1.7 (b). Graph to show the bank balance of Mr. W. over the given period

On the face of it this looks to be a healthy balance in the black. We note, however, that the readings are taken at the beginning of the month. It so happens that Mr. W. is paid monthly and his salary cheque is paid directly into the bank on the last day of the previous month.

If we were to take readings more often we might find something like the following.

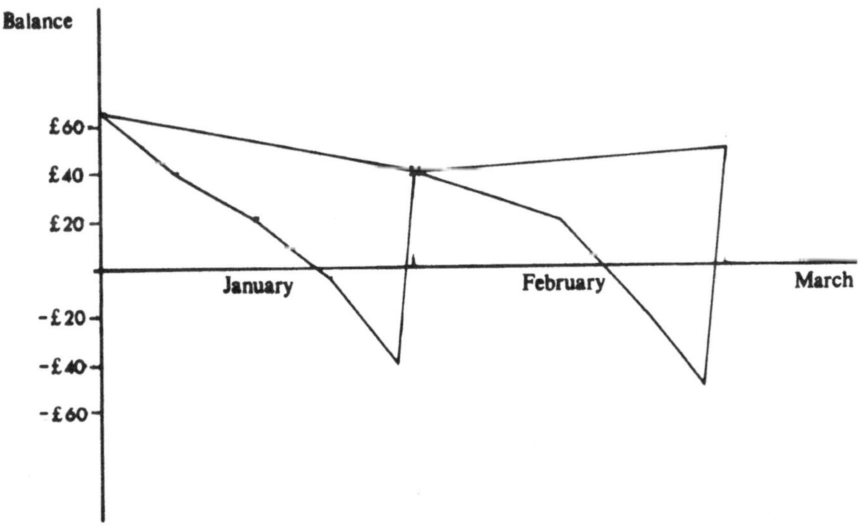

Graph to show the bank balance of Mr. W. over the given period

The original line is left in for comparison but now that readings have been taken more frequently a different picture is revealed. For some period in each month, Mr. W. has an overdraft.

The point of this example is to show that for interpolation to be accurate, the gaps between the original readings must not be too large. Sufficient readings should be taken to ensure that a true picture of the trend of the figures can be brought out.

Another example of the same lines would be that of unemployment figures graphed only once a year. If this were the case then the summer and winter seasonal alterations in employment would be missed.

1.8 Curve-line Graphs

The straight-line graph has one disadvantage and that is that a subject rarely varies in the way that the straight lines between the counts suggests. A more accurate estimation of the way a subject varies may be obtained by replacing the straight lines with curves. In this case it is called a curve-line graph.

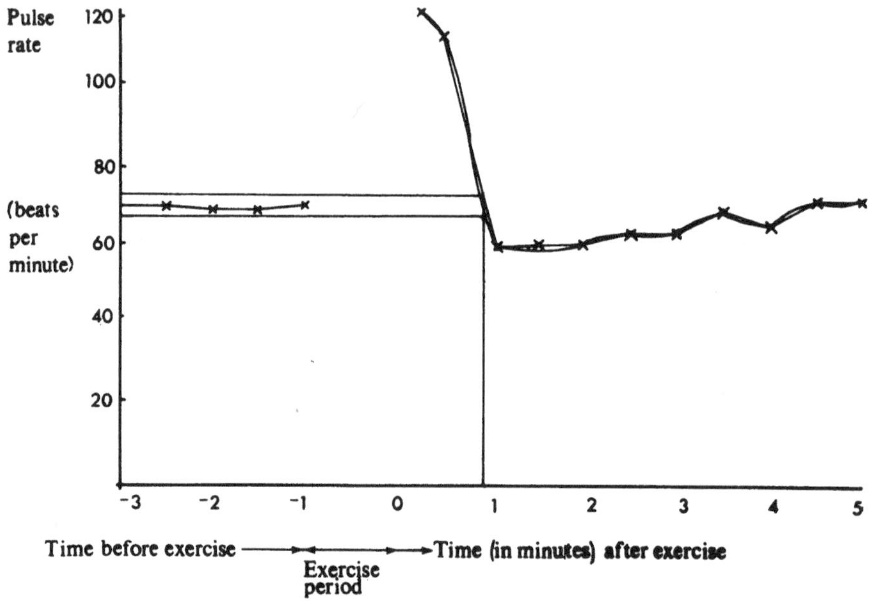

Fig. 1.8(a). Curve-line graph to show the pulse rate of a student before and after one minute of intensive exercise. The broken-line graph is shown for purposes of comparison.

Example 1: Estimate from the graph, the pulse rate of the student 51 seconds after the exercise period using:

(i) the curve-line graph

(ii) the broken-line graph

Answer

By following the vertical line which represents the 51-second point – shown in the graph – and reading the scale where this line cuts the two graphs we obtain

(i) 67 beats per minute
(ii) 74 beats per minute

Example 2: Estimate from the graph the pulse rate of the student 3 minutes 12 seconds after the exercise period using

(i) the curve-line graph
(ii) the broken-line graph

Answer

Using the same method as in Example 1 we obtain

(i) 63 beats per minute
(ii) 65 beats per minute

From these two examples two points emerge:

1. The difference in estimation by the straight-line graph and the curve-line graph is likely to be greatest at points midway between the known figures.

2. Where movement in the figures is small, a straight-line is as useful as a curve.

It should be remembered that both straight lines and curves as used here are only estimates for intermediate values and if any greater accuracy is required then readings should be taken at more frequent intervals.

1.9 The Histogram

Example 1

Raw data: 100 pupils took an Arithmetic Test and their scores were as follows:

0	1	1	1	1	2	2	2	2	3	3	3	3	3	3	4	4	4	4
4	4	4	4	4	4	5	5	5	5	5	5	5	5	5	5	5	5	5
5	5	5	6	6	6	6	6	6	6	6	6	6	6	6	6	6	6	7
7	7	7	7	7	7	7	7	7	7	7	7	7	7	7	7	7	7	8
8	8	8	8	8	8	8	8	9	9	9	9	9	9	9	9	10	10	10
10	10	10	10	10														

(For convenience the scores have been put in order)

Tabulated form:

Score	Number of pupils
0	1
1	4
2	4
3	6
4	10
5	16
6	15
7	19
8	9
9	8
10	8

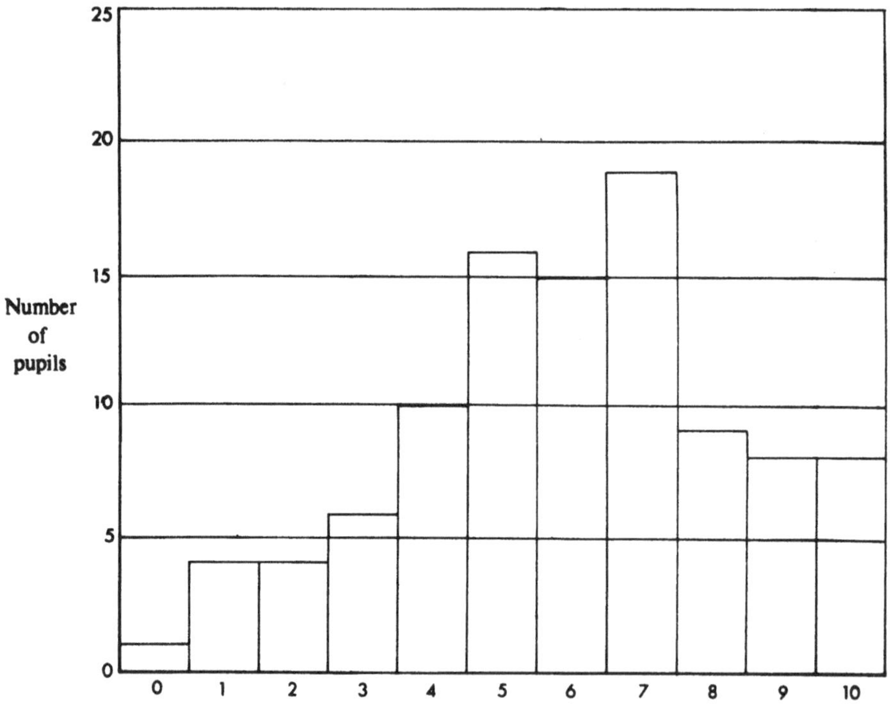

Fig. 1.9 (a). Histogram to show the scores of 100 pupils who took an Arithmetic test

The reader will note that the only difference between the above graph – labelled as a histogram – and a bar graph, is that the gaps between the bars have been omitted. However the difference between them is much more marked than this, and it is the aim of this section to develop fully the concept of a histogram.
We start this by considering *Example 2*:

Example 2
Raw data: 100 pupils took an end of term examination and their scores were as follows:

3	5	5	7	7	8	10	10	10	12	12	12	13	13	13	13
15	15	15	15	16	16	16	16	16	18	18	18	18	18	18	20
20	20	20	20	21	21	21	21	21	21	23	23	23	23	23	24
24	24	24	25	25	25	26	26	26	26	26	26	26	27	27	28
28	28	28	28	28	28	28	29	31	31	31	32	33	33	34	37
37	38	38	38	38	39	39	40	40	40	40	41	41	41	41	41
42	44	48	50												

Tabulated form:

Score	Number of pupils	Score	Number of pupils	Score	Number of pupils
0		21	6	41	5
1		22		42	1
2		23	5	43	
3	1	24	4	44	1
4		25	3	45	
5	2	26	7	46	
6		27	2	47	
7	2	28	8	48	1
8	1	29	1	49	
9		30		50	1
10	3				
11		31	3		
12	3	32	1		
13	4	33	2		
14		34	1		
15	4	35			
16	5	36			
17		37	2		
18	6	38	4		
19		39	2		
20	5	40	4		

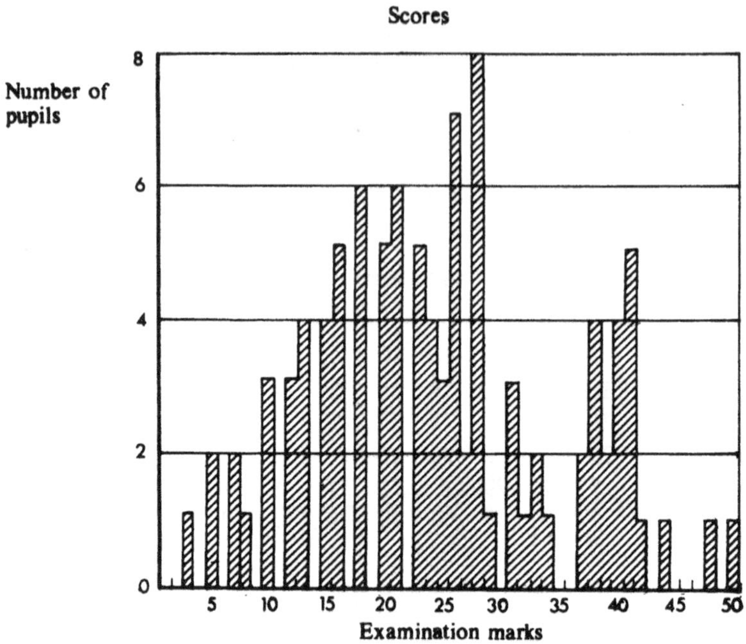

Fig. 1.9 (b). Histogram to show the examination marks of 100 pupils

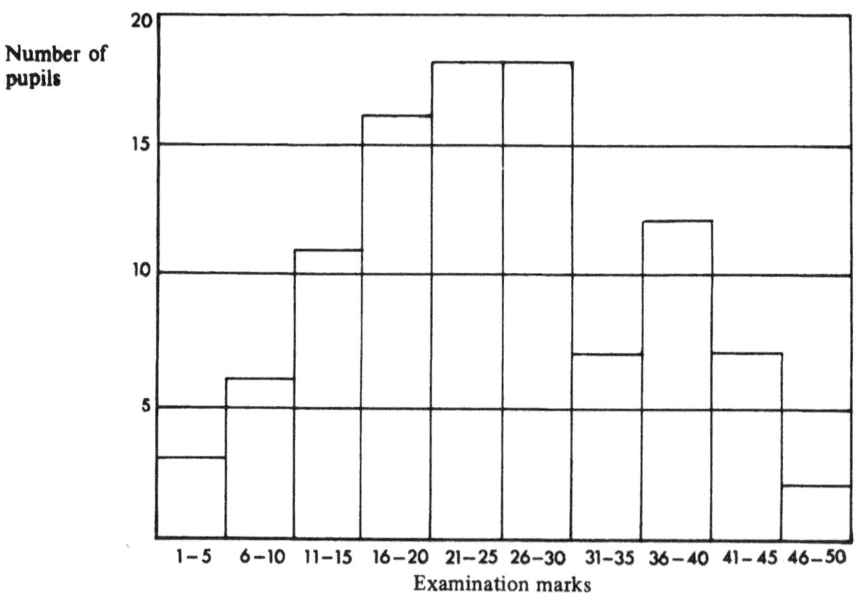

Fig. 1.9 (c). Histogram to show the examination marks of 100 pupils

The first point that is evident here is that there is a lot of labour involved in both the tabulated form and the graph [Fig. 1.9(b)]. This leads us to consider the possibility of reducing this labour and at the same time arranging things so that as little information as possible is lost.

This can be done by putting the individual scores into groups. All those people who scored between 1 and 5 (inclusive) are put into one group, and all those who scored between 6 and 10 (inclusive) into a second group, and so on until all the marks have been grouped. This is shown in the following table

Group	marks								total
1– 5	3	5	5						3
6–10	7	7	8	10	10	10			6
11–15	12	12	12	13	13	13	13	15	11
	15	15	15						
16–20	16	16	16	16	16	18	18	18	16
	18	18	18	20	20	20	20	20	
21–25	21	21	21	21	21	21	23	23	
	23	23	23	24	24	24	24	25	18
	25	25							
26–30	26	26	26	26	26	26	26	27	
	27	28	28	28	28	28	28	28	18
	28	29							
31–35	31	31	31	32	33	33	34		7
36–40	37	37	38	38	38	38	39	39	12
	40	40	40	40					
41–45	41	41	41	41	41	42	44		7
46–50	48	50							2

These figures can then be graphed as shown in Fig. 1.9(c).

A comparison shows that Fig. 1.9(c) still has the same general outline as Fig. 1.9(b) and yet the labour has been considerably reduced.

At once the following question arises. Could we reduce the number of groups? The scores were rearranged as follows and then graphed, Fig. 1.9(d).

Group	Total
1–10	9
11–20	27
21–30	36
31–40	19
41–50	7

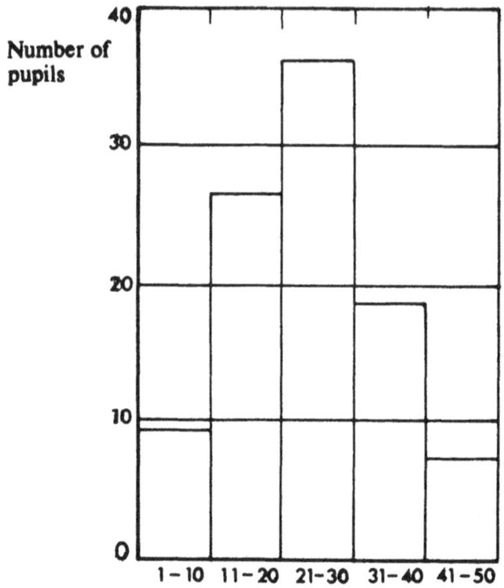

Fig. 1.9 (d). Histogram to show the scores of 100 pupils in their end of term examination

and it is now evident that the general outline of the graph has been changed. In particular it has lost the 'two humps' characteristic. It is left as an exercise for the student to put the scores into a smaller number of groups and see what further effect it has upon the graph. The process of putting scores into groups is called *grouping the data.*

The conclusion we can now draw is that there is a limit to the amount of reduction that can be done in this way if we wish to retain the main characteristics of the data. Experience has shown that the best number of groups to choose is between 5 and 20, depending upon such factors as the number of scores and the range of marks. It is now convenient to make the following points:

1. The groups into which the scores are put are called *classes*

2. The endpoints of these classes are called *class limits* or *class boundaries*

e.g. the class 21–25 has a lower class limit of 21 and an upper class limit of 25.

3. The size or width of a class is found by subtracting two consecutive lower class limits:

e.g. class 11–15
class 16–20
16 – 11 = 5, and the size of the class is 5,

or by subtracting two consecutive upper class limits

4. The size of the class is frequently called the *class interval*

5. Usually it is convenient to make all the classes of equal size, but there are exceptions to this rule

6. When putting scores into classes it is not actually necessary to put the score in, as we did.

e.g. 6–10 7 7 8 10 10 10 6

it saves time, and is much more common, to use what is called a gate check. In this case, the working would look as follows:

e.g. 6–10 ~~1111~~ 1 6

7. It will be noted that in the graph – Fig. 1.9(c) – it is not possible to pick out the individual scores within any particular class. It so happens that the three scores in the class 1–5 are 3 5 5 but this is not evident. They might just as easily have been 1 1 2 or 4 4 3, or any other set of three numbers between 1 and 5. It is one of the characteristics of statistics in cases like this that the individual scores are lost in the effort to obtain an overall picture.

8. To emphasise the point that the graph of data can often suggest further ideas to explore it is pointed out that a teacher examining the graph of these examination results might be inclined to split the pupils into groups commensurate with their attainment as suggested by their marks. The graph suggests that the large majority of the pupils are contained in the 'hump' round the scores 16–30 but that there is a group of pupils above the average centred round the scores 36–45 and these might well benefit by being taught as a group on their own. The teacher might also think that all those who scored less than 15 could also form a group that would benefit similarly. He would therefore divide the 100 pupils into three groups as below:

Scores	Number of pupils
1–15	20
16–30	52
31–50	28

It might have been thought that if the 100 pupils were to be split into 3 groups that it would be better to put them into 3 groups of roughly equal size, however the graph suggests that membership of a group should be on attainment and the above 3 groups are the best to choose.

9. A set of objects may have a common characteristic. This characteristic, though common to all members of the set, may be such that it is

quantitatively different from member to member of the set.

Example 3: The set of human beings: Characteristic – *weight*: People vary in weight so we say the characteristic of having a certain weight varies from individual to individual.

Example 4: A set of pupils: Characteristic – examination score: The examination score varies with the individual pupil.

A characteristic of a set which varies from member to member of the set is called a *variable*.

	Group	*Variable*
Example 5:	Horses	Number of hands high
Example 6:	Sailing ships	Square feet of sail
Example 7:	Aeroplanes	Number of engines

Individual examples of a variable are called *variates*.

	Group	*Variable*	*Individual*	*Variate*
Example 8:	Human beings	Height	Mr. W.	5′ 7″
Example 9:	Buildings	Number of storeys	Bungalow	1

It is not always known which particular individual element belongs to any given variate, and there also may be more than one individual element associated with a variate, i.e. Mr. W. and Mr. T. may both be 5′ 7″.

The set of numbers that a variable may assume is called the *domain* of the variable.

Example 10: The domain of *Example* 7 is 1 2 3 4 and so on, up to the maximum number of engines that aeroplanes have.

Example 11: The domain of *Example 3* is from a few pounds up to 77 stones
(The heaviest man yet recorded is Robert Earl Hughes of Monticello, Illinois, U.S.A. whose maximum weight was recorded at 76 stones 5lb)

Variables are of two kinds:

(a) *Discrete* – where the domain contains only whole numbers

(b) *Continuous* – where the variable can assume any value, whole number or decimal, within its domain.

Example 12: The number of children in a family is a discrete variable since it may only be 0 1 2 3 and so on.

Example 13: The height of an individual is a continuous variable since it may be 70″, 70·1″, 70·1258″ and so on, depending on the accuracy of the measuring instrument.

In general discrete variables are associated with counting, and continuous variables with measuring

10. The number of times that a score occurs in a set of data is called the *frequency* of that score.

In *Example 1*, the score 6 occurs 15 times, therefore the frequency of 6 is 15.

The number of scores that fall into a class is called the *class frequency*.

In *Example 2*, there are 12 scores that fall into the class 36–40, therefore the class frequency of the class 36–40 is 12.

The tabulated form of scores together with their frequencies is called a *frequency table* or *frequency distribution*

11. Later on calculations will be performed with data, and in particular with grouped data, and we therefore have to consider what variate from a class we can take as representative of that class. The variate that is taken is the mid point of the class and this is called the *class mark* or *class mid-point*.

In *Example 2*:

Class	Class mark
1– 5	3
6–10	8
11–15	13

The full point of doing this will be seen shortly.

12. If we take a set of raw data and subtract from the highest variate the lowest variate we get the *range*:

In *Example 1*:

Lowest variate		0
Highest variate		10
Range 10 – 0	=	10

In *Example 2*:

Lowest variate		3
Highest variate		50
Range 50 – 3	=	47

We now consider an example of a continuous variable and see how these remarks apply.

Example 14:

Task: Measure the height of 45 college students and draw a histogram of the data.

The first decision to be made is on the question of accuracy of measurement. How accurate shall we measure? Shall we measure to the nearest inch, half-inch, or tenth of an inch? In general terms the question of accuracy of measurement is conditioned by how accurate the measuring instruments are and the character of the objects to be measured. We elect to measure to the nearest half-inch. Anyone who on our apparatus measures 57·3″ we will record as 57·5″, and anyone who measures 57·2″ will be recorded as 57″.

The 45 recordings are, in inches:

50·0	51·5	52·5	53·0	54·0	56·0	56·0
56·5	57·0	57·5	58·5	58·5	59·0	60·0
60·5	61·0	61·0	61·0	61·5	62·0	62·5
63·0	63·5	63·5	64·0	64·0	64·0	66·0
66·0	66·5	67·0	67·0	67·0	67·0	67·5
68·0	69·0	69·5	70·0	72·0	72·5	73·0
73·0	73·0	75·0				

We come now to grouping the data.

The lowest variate is 50·0″ and the highest is 75·0″, therefore the range is 25″. We want, roughly, ten classes and if we take nine with a class interval of 3″ this will enable us to cover a range of 27″. We now have to decide on class marks and class boundaries.

As previously pointed out, calculations will be performed on the grouped data and the class mark will be used in these calculations. It is convenient to choose class marks that will make these future calculations as simple as possible, and therefore want whole numbers if possible. Under this consideration we chose

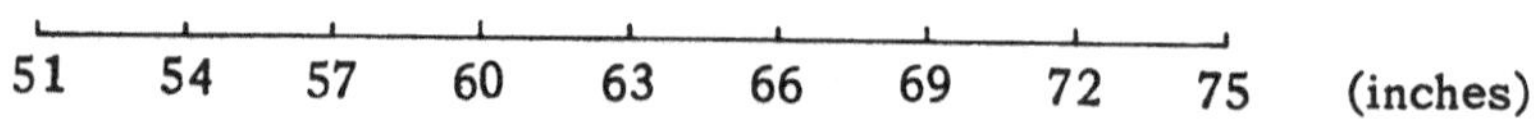

as class marks and this gives us class boundaries as follows:

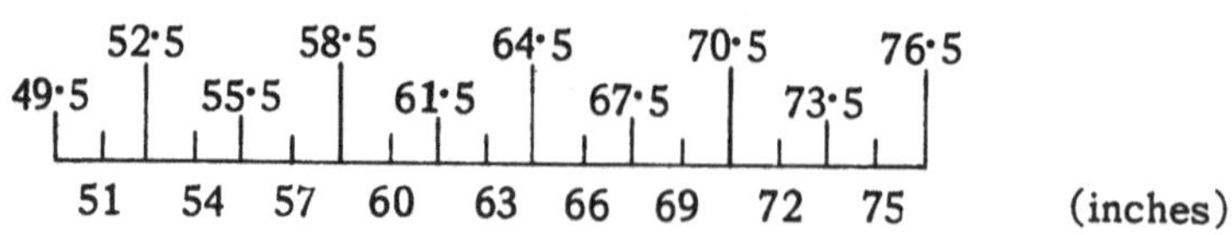

i.e. any height that falls between 49·5″ and 52·5″ will go into the class whose class mark is 51″, and any height that falls between 52·5″ and 55·5″ will go into the class whose class mark is 54″.

But what of a height that falls on a class boundary? For instance 52·5″ – does this go into the 51″ or the 54″ class? We elect for the moment to put it into the 54″ class and so our class intervals become:

49·5″ and less than 52·5″
52·5″ and less than 55·5″
55·5″ and less than 58·5″ and so on

We can now tabulate the data as follows (see Fig. 1.9 (e)):

Classes	Class mark	Gate check- tally sheet	Frequency
49·5 –	51	1 1	2
52·5 –	54	1 1 1	3
55·5 –	57	~~1111~~	5
58·5 –	60	~~1111~~ 1 1 1	8
61·5 –	63	~~1111~~ 1 1 1 1	9
64·5 –	66	~~1111~~ 1 1	7
67·5 –	69	~~1111~~	5
70·5 –	72	~~1111~~	5
73·5 –	75	1	1
		Total	45

Fig. 1.9 (e). Frequency table of the heights of 45 college students (in inches)

and graphing this, gives us the following histogram – Fig. 1.9 (f).

It was stated earlier that is is usual to have class intervals of an equal size. This is, generally speaking, true but there are occasions when class intervals of varying sizes can be used effectively.

It might well happen that in some particular topic we are much more interested in one or two sections rather than in the whole range. For instance, in *Example 2*, we might be more interested in those pupils who did badly and those who did very well and temporarily ignore the main bulk of the pupils who lie in the middle of the range. To this end we use *unequal class intervals* as follows:

Marks	*Size of class interval*	*Number of pupils*
1– 5	5	3
6–10	5	6
11–15	5	11
16–35	20	59
36–40	5	12
41–45	5	7
46–50	5	2

and graph this frequency table as the following histogram (Fig. 1.9(g)).

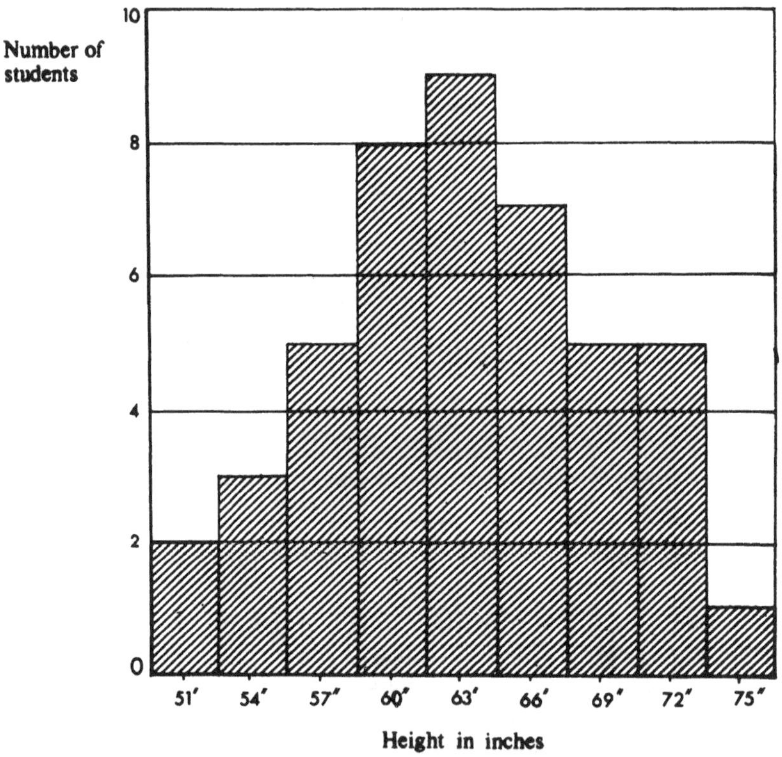

Fig. 1.9 (f). Histogram to show the height of 45 college students

Now obviously the height of the column representing the 16–35 class will not be 59 – the number of scores in that interval – because these 59 scores are spread over 4 class. The height is therefore found by

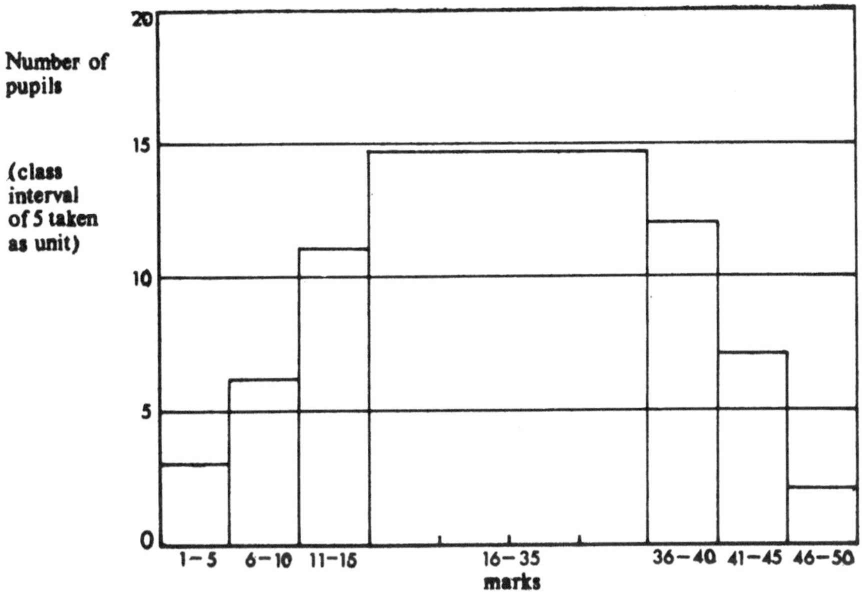

Fig. 1.9(g). Histogram with unequal class intervals to show the examination marks of 100 pupils

dividing the 59 by 4 (i.e. 14·75) and this method should be used in all problems of this type. See *Example 2* of Section 1.13, where a problem is worked out in more detail.

We are now in a position to give a definition of a histogram. A *histogram* is a graph of a frequency table consisting of vertical rectangles that are as wide as the class interval and centred on the class mark. The height of the rectangles are such that the areas are proportional to the class frequencies. It must be emphasised that the latter property is the fundamental property of histograms. If the class intervals are equal then the heights of the columns will be proportional to the class frequencies as well as the areas. If the class intervals are not equal the heights of the rectangles have to be adjusted as just explained.

There are other 'solutions' to the problem of variates that fall on class boundaries as follows (using *Example 14*):

(a) Have class boundaries 49·5–52·5
52·5–55·5
55·5–58·5

and so on, as before, and when the variates fall on a particular boundary, put half into the lower class and half into the upper class around this boundary. We have two scores of 58·5 so one goes into the class 55·5–58·5 and the other goes into the class 58·5–61·5. The advantage of this method is that it tends to reduce errors brought about by grouping.

(b) Vary the class boundaries so that no variate falls on a boundary. This may or may not be possible.

(c) Express the class boundaries to one half unit beyond the accuracy of the original measurement. Here the data is accurate to half an inch, we would therefore express the boundaries in quarter-inches. Frequently this means the loss of the convenient integral class mark.

We elect in the remainder of this book to 'solve' this problem by using the method first indicated in the text, i.e. by putting boundary variates into the class above. Strictly speaking this method tends to introduce a grouping error – the error being a slight tendency to shift the data to the right, i.e. slightly increase it. However the error introduced is generally very slight.

1.10 The Frequency Polygon

A *frequency polygon* is a broken-line graph obtained by joining the centres of the top of the rectangles of a histogram. The frequency polygon for *Example 14* of Section 1.9 is shown in Fig. 1.10 (a).

It will be noticed that the two outer classes are joined to points outside the original graph. If the triangles that are 'cut off' from the histogram by the lines of the frequency polygon are compared to the triangles that are 'brought into' the graph it will be seen that they pair off – one pair is shaded in the figure. If the extreme classes are joined to points outside the original graph then two more pairs of similar triangles will be formed. Thus the area under the frequency polygon will be the same as the area of the histogram and will be proportional to the number of readings.

It would be a mistake to use a frequency polygon in preference to a histogram for most situations. To begin with there is a difficulty over area. It will be seen that in the histogram the area of the class with class mark 63″ is proportional to the reading of that class, i.e. proportional to the readings that fall between 61·5″ and 64·5″. In the case of the frequency polygon although the area under the graph *as a whole* is proportional to the whole set of data it is not the case that the area under the graph and between class boundaries is proportional to the number of readings between those class boundaries. In the case of the area between 61·5″ and 64·5″ the area is less than that of the histogram because the two triangles have been 'cut out'.

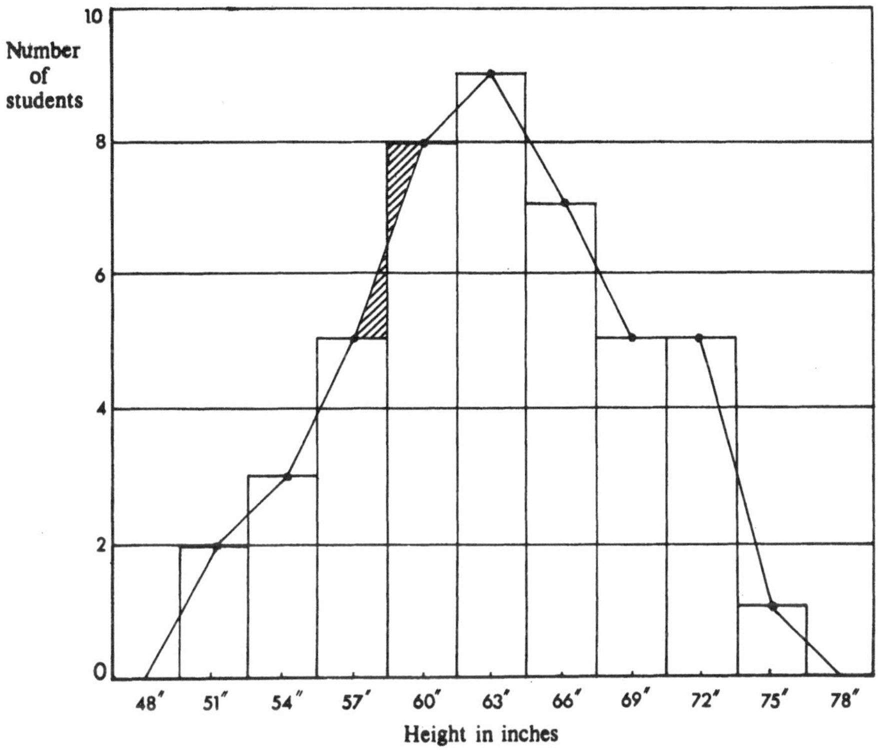

Fig. 1.10 (a). Frequency polygon to show the height of 45 college students

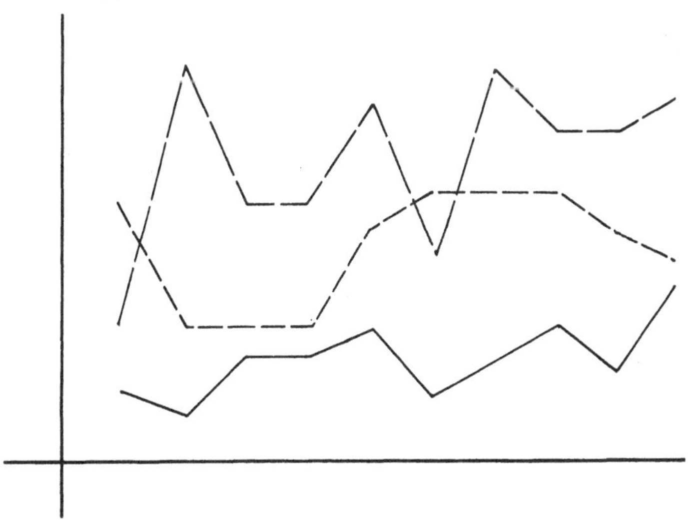

Fig. 1.10 (b).

Where the frequency polygon is preferable to the histogram is in the case of comparison of different sets of data. In Fig. 1.10 (b), three sets of data have been put on the same graph and differences and similarities are clearly seen. If histograms had been superimposed on the same graph in a like manner the result would have been a confused jumble.

A point in favour of the frequency polygon is that it points the way to the replacement of the blocks of the histogram with a smooth curve. It is important in statistics to find, if possible, mathematical expressions that mirror the distributions most commonly found. These expressions have been found in a number of cases and are important in more advanced statistics.

1.11 Relative frequency

It is often required to know not just the frequency of a variate but its frequency in relation to the data as a whole. The *relative frequency* of a class is found by expressing the frequency of that class as a percentage of the whole data. For example:

What is the relative frequency of the class 58·5–61·5 (not inclusive) of *Example 14* of Section 1.9.
Frequency of this class = 8
Total data = 45
Relative frequency is $\frac{8}{45} \times 100 = 17{\cdot}77\%$

The *relative frequency table is as follows and the relative frequency graph is shown in Fig. 1.11(a)*

Classes	Class mark	Frequency	Relation frequency %
49·5 –	51	2	4·44
52·5 –	54	3	6·66
55·5 –	57	5	11·11
58·5 –	60	8	17·77
61·5 –	63	9	20·00
64·5 –	66	7	15·55
67·5 –	69	5	11·11
70·5 –	72	5	11·11
73·5 –	75	1	2·22

1.12 Cumulative Frequency

The frequency tables and graphs so far seen indicate clearly the frequencies or relative frequencies of the different classes, but they

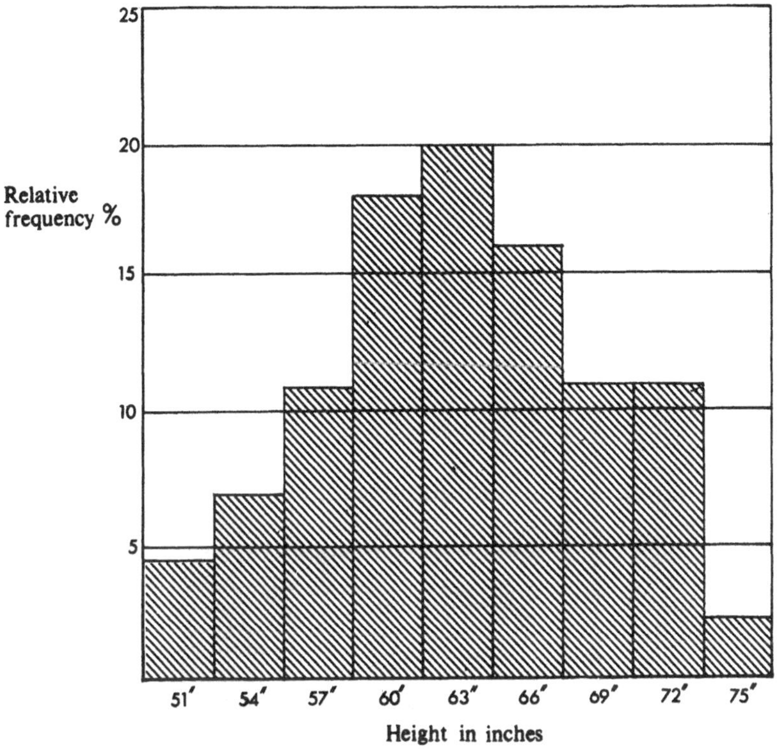

Fig. 1.11(a). Relative frequency graph of the heights of 45 college students

are not very convenient for answering questions such as, 'How many variates fall below a particular score?' They can be used to answer this question but a much more convenient method has been developed in *cumulative frequency tables* and *cumulative frequency graphs.*

Example 1: Tabulate the cumulative frequency of *Example 1* of Section 1.9, and draw the graph

Scores	Cumulation frequency (Number of pupils)
Less than 0	0
Less than 1	1
Less than 2	5
Less than 3	9
Less than 4	15
Less than 5	25
Less than 6	41
Less than 7	56
Less than 8	75
Less than 9	84
Less than 10	92
Less than 11	100

The cumulative frequency is found merely by adding the variates of succeeding classes.

i.e.
$$5 = 1 + 4$$
$$9 = 1 + 4 + 4$$
$$15 = 1 + 4 + 4 + 6 \quad \text{and so on}$$

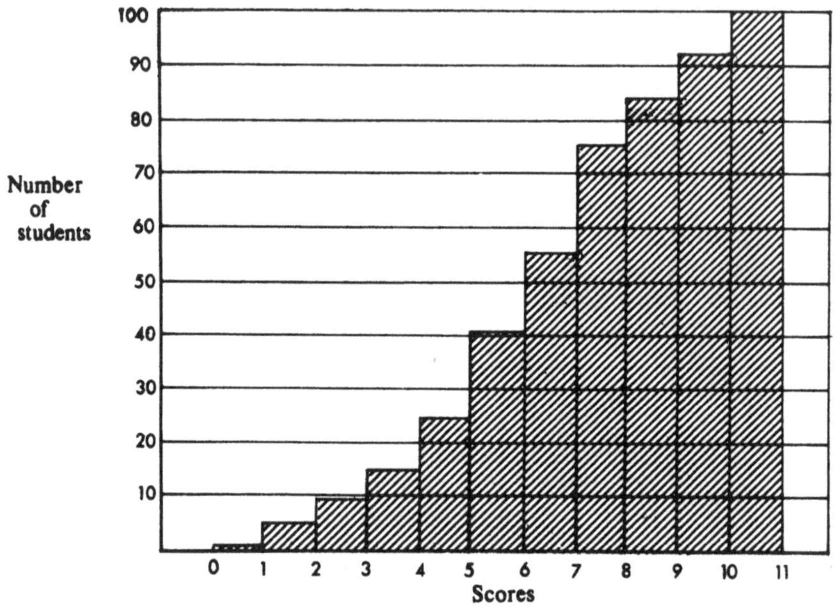

Fig. 1.12(a). Graph of the cumulative frequency table

From either the table or the graph, the number of pupils who score less than a given score may be found with ease.

The block form of the graph as shown above is the most natural form in which to represent discrete data; continuous data is more naturally represented in a broken-line or a curve-line fashion as will be seen in the next example.

Example 2: Tabulate the data of *Example 14* of Section 1.9, in a cumulative frequency table and show also the *relative* cumulative frequency. Graph both the cumulative frequency and the relative cumulative frequency tables.

Notice that the cumulative frequency and the relative cumulative frequency may be shown on the same graph by using opposite sides for the two scales.

Heights (inches)	Cumulative frequency (Number of students)	Relative cumulative frequency (percentage of students)
Less than 49·5	0	0
52·5	2	4·44
55·5	5	11·11
58·5	10	22·22
61·5	18	39·97
64·5	27	59·95
67·5	34	75·53
70·5	39	86·65
73·5	44	97·78
76·5	45	100·00

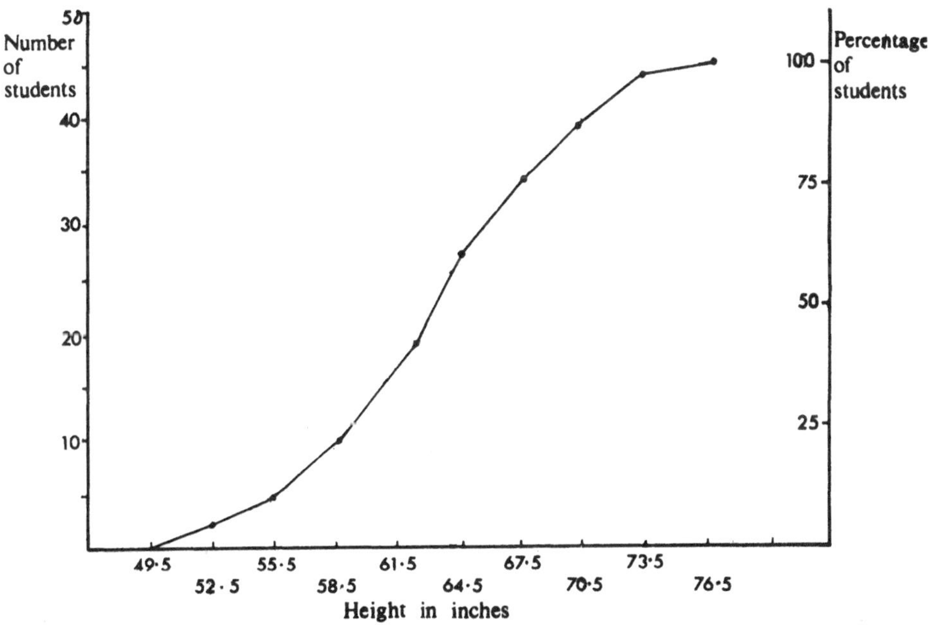

Fig. 1.12(b). Graph to show the cumulative frequency and the relative cumulative frequency of the heights of 45 college students

The relative cumulative frequency can be found in two ways:

(1) by finding the relative frequencies first and then adding in the same way as the relative frequency is found from the frequencies, or

(2) directly from the cumulative frequency and expressing it as a percentage of the total.

For example, there are 10 scores less than 58·5, therefore

$$\frac{10}{45} \times 100 = \frac{200}{9} = 22{\cdot}22\%$$

In the first column of the cumulative frequency tables it should be noted that the phrase 'less than 2' or 'less than 70·5' does not include the values 2 or 70·5. It is possible to use the phrases '2 and under' and '70·5 and under' if it is so wished.

Often after the points of the cumulative frequency table have been plotted a curve-line graph is used so that more accurate interpolation will be possible.

All the previous parts of this section can be repeated but instead of paying attention to the idea of 'less than' the idea of 'more than' can be used and a very similar result will be obtained. The difference will be that instead of getting a curve whose general shape is that of Fig. 1.12(c), a curve of the shape of Fig. 1.12(d) will be obtained

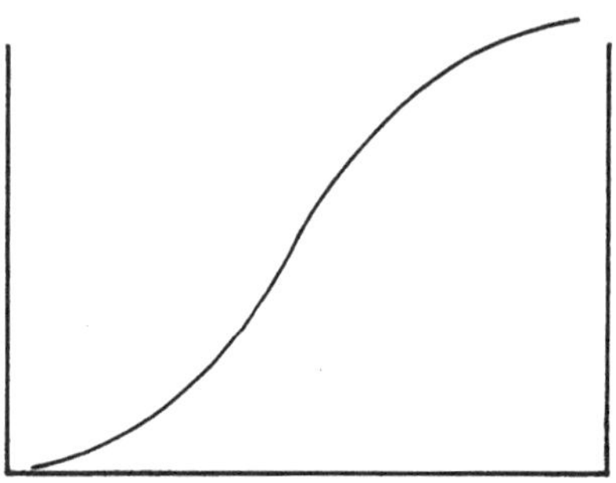

Fig. 1.12(c)

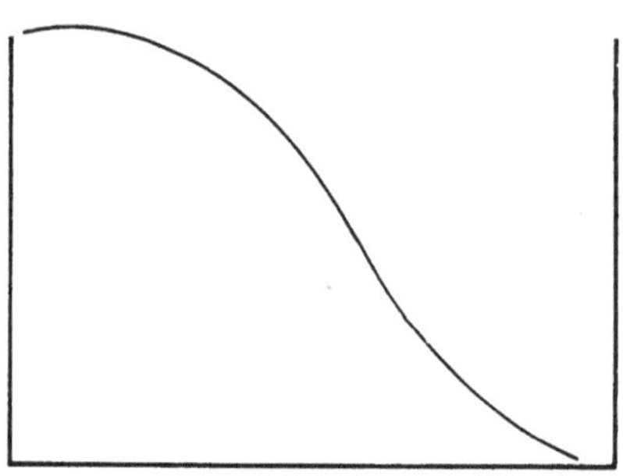

Fig. 1.12(d)

For obvious reasons these curves are frequently referred to as 'more than' and 'less than' curves. They are sometimes also called 'ogives' but this terminology seems to be going out of fashion.

1.13 Supplementary Examples

Example 1: The following graph shows another method of graphing the data of Section 1.4.

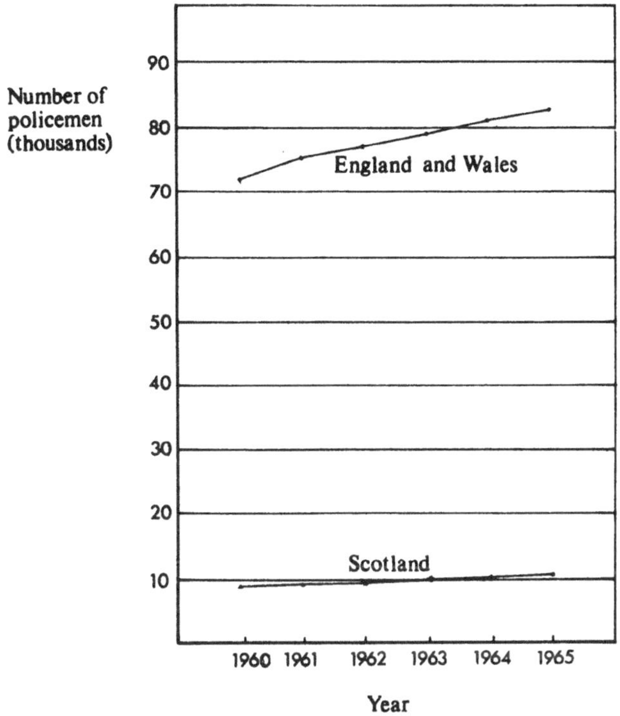

Fig. 1.13(a). Graph to show the strength of the Police Force in (a) England and Wales and (b) Scotland for the year shown

Example 2: For the given figures draw the histogram and the 'more than' cumulative frequency polygon.

Class intervals	*Size of class interval*	*Frequency*	*Cumulative frequency*	
0″– 3·99″	4″	10	More than 0″	70
4″– 9·99″	6″	6	4″	60
10″–19·99″	10″	5	10″	54
20″–29·99″	10″	15	20″	49
30″–39·99″	10″	14	30″	34
40″–42·99″	3″	10	40″	20
43″–50·00″	7″	10	43″	10
			50″	0

Answer:

The class boundaries indicate a continuous variable with classes of

0 up to, but less than, 4
4 up to, but less than, 10

The histogram is constructed as follows. There are class intervals of different widths and we pick the most common class interval to act as a unit in which to express the other classes. There are 3 classes of width 10 and these are put in the diagram first. We now look at the first class. This is $\frac{4}{10}$ as wide as the class interval we have chosen as the unit. Therefore we multiply the given frequency of the first class by $\frac{10}{4}$

i.e.
$$f_1 \times \frac{10}{4} = \frac{10 \times 10}{4} = 25$$

and this gives the height of the column in the histogram. The second class is $\frac{6}{10}$ as wide as the class interval chosen as the unit and so the height of the column in the histogram will be given by

$$f_2 \times \frac{10}{6} = \frac{6 \times 10}{6} = 10$$

The last two classes were calculated similarly and it is left to the reader to check this for himself.

The actual dimension of the graph can help us further clarify the notion that the area of the histogram represents the frequencies of the data. If we look at the class 20″–29·99″ we see that it measures on the graph 1 unit by $1\frac{1}{2}$ units. There are 15 readings in this class so each square unit represents 10 readings. Looking now at the class 0″–3·99″ we see that its dimensions on the graph are 0·4 by 2·5 units; therefore it has area $0{\cdot}4 \times 2{\cdot}5 = 1$ square unit. And this square unit represents the 10 readings of the class.

N.B. To read a graph with unequal class intervals the reverse process must take place. The class interval which is the unit must be found, then the width of the other classes must be expressed as a fraction of this unit, then the height of the column of any class must be multiplied by this fraction. In the case of the first class in this example the width is $\frac{4}{10}$ of the width of the unit class, therefore, the actual reading i.e. 25 must be multiplied by $\frac{4}{10}$ to give us $25 \times \frac{4}{10} = 10$, as given in the frequency table.

The cumulative frequency polygon is drawn from the figures in the frequency table.

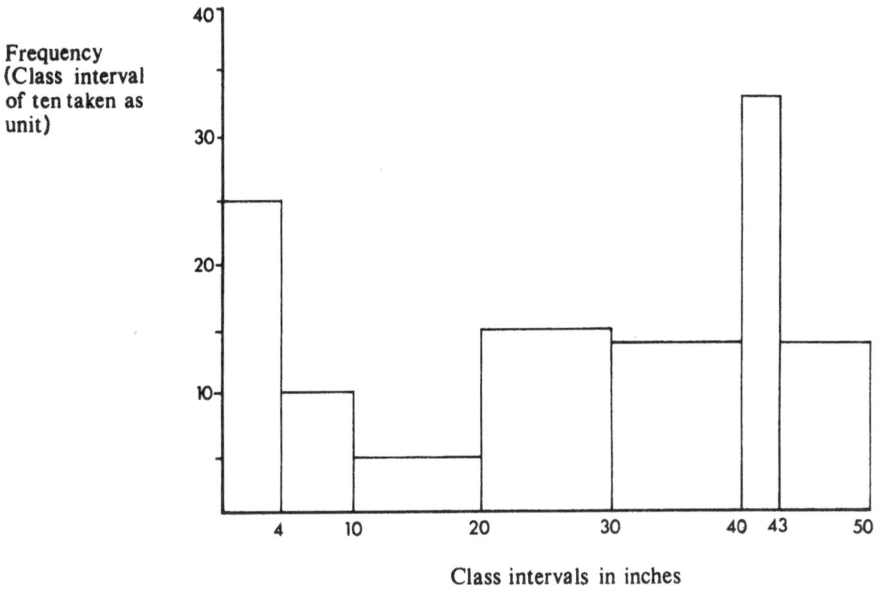

Fig. 1.13(b)

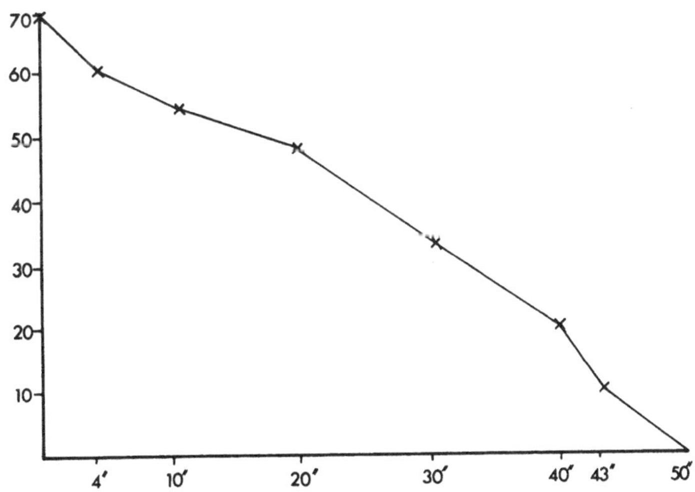

Fig. 1.13(c)

Note: If the cumulative frequency is spoken of without qualification, then it is usual to assume that the reference is to the 'less than' type.

Example 3: Twenty-eight houses were selected at random from a housing estate and the number of children at school in each house were counted. The data is shown next.

Number of children	0	1	2	3	4	5
Number of houses with the stated number of children	5	9	6	6	1	1

Graph the data

Answer:

The data can be graphed in either of the two ways shown below but it seems more natural to graph it as in Fig. 1.13 (d) since the number of children will always be a whole number. Graphs of this sort are called line graphs (Not to be confused with broken-line graphs).

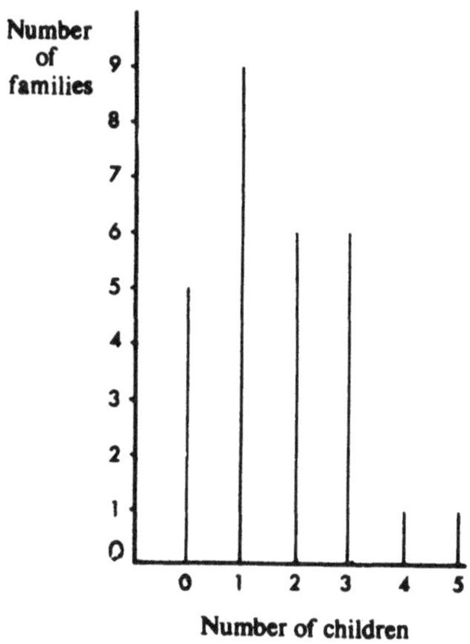

Fig. 1.13(d)

Note 1: The total length of all the 'rods' in Fig. 1.13 (d) comes to 28 – the number of houses. In graphs of this sort the total length of the rods will always represent the total number of reading.

Note 2: Fig. 1.13 (e) is the histogram of the data. The histogram is more appropriate for continuous, rather than discrete, data, but when it is used for discrete data, it treats the data as if it were

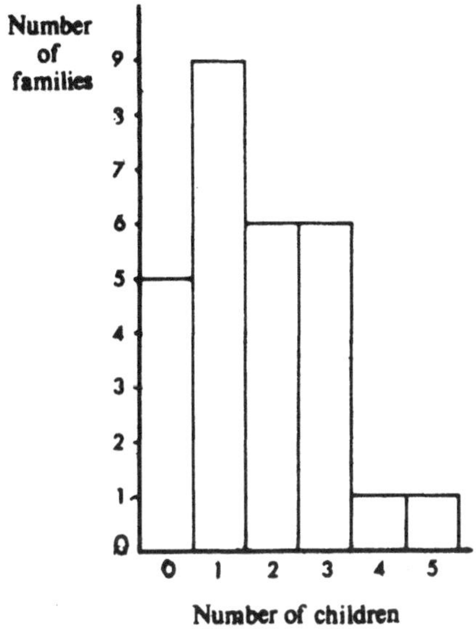

Fig. 1.13 (e)

continuous. It will be found later that continuous approximation to discrete data can be very useful.

Example 4: The following table shows the data showing the earnings of the 86 employees of a factory. Discuss:

Earnings	Less than £10	£10–£15	£15–£20	£20–£30	Over £30
Number of Employees	5	21	41	15	4

Answer:

One difficulty is the unequal class intervals – this point has already been dealt with. Another difficulty is the question of the size of the upper and lower classes. As they stand they are 'open ended'. Over £30 could mean anything from £31 to £100 or even more. Less than £10 could mean anything down to £0. In practice these cases are dealt with in 'common sense' terms. It is realised that few people will earn over £30 at this factory but that it will not be vastly bigger than £30 so an interval of £30–£40 is taken. At the lower end of the scale it is realised that no one at the factory would work for nothing and if a class interval of £0–£10 was taken for the first class interval this would give a class mid point of £5. If a class interval of £4–£10 was taken it would give a class mid point of £7. As subsequent calculations will be based on the class mid point a class mid point of £5 would tend to 'pull down' the figures. A class mid-point of £7 is therefore to be preferred.

The frequency of the 'over £30' class is only 4. It is better if it can be done to arrange data so that each class contains a frequency bigger than 5.

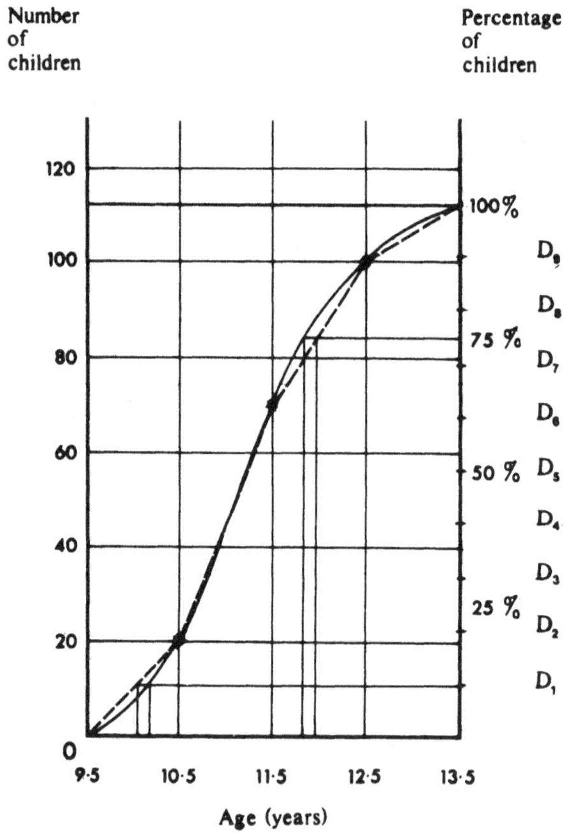

Fig. 1. 13 (f)

Example 5: The following data shows the ages of children in a Sunday school.

Age in years	9·5–10·5	10·5–11·5	11·5–12·5	12·5–13·5
Number of Children	20	45	35	12

(a) Draw the cumulative frequency polygon
(b) Draw the smoothed cumulative frequency curve
(c) Draw the frequency polygon
(d) Draw the relative frequency polygon
(e) Draw the smoothed relative frequency curve
(f) Below what age are 75% of the children
(g) Below what age are 10% of the children
(h) What percentage of children are between 11 and 12 years

Answer:

(a) Shown by the dotted line in Fig. 1.13 (f).

(b) Shown by the unbroken line in Fig. 1.13 (f).

(c) Shown by the dotted line in Fig. 1.13 (g). The left hand vertical axis is the appropriate axis for this graph.

(d) Shown by the dotted line in Fig. 1.13 (g). The right hand vertical axis is the appropriate axis for this graph.

(e) Shown by the unbroken line in Fig. 1.13 (g). Again the right hand vertical axis is the appropriate one.

(f) Looking at the right hand vertical axis in Fig. 1.13 (f) for the 75% figure we see where the horizontal line cuts the two graphs. If we use the cumulative frequency polygon then the age is seen to be 11·96 years, but if we use the smoothed cumulative frequency curve we see that the age is 11·84 years.

(g) Looking at the right hand vertical axis in Fig. 1.13 (f) for the 10% figure we again see that there are two readings; one of 10·09 years for the cumulative frequency polygon and one of 10·24 years for the smoothed cumulative frequency curve. The 10% figure has been labelled D_1. One the same axis the 20% figure has been labelled D_2, the 30% figure has been labelled D_3, and so on up to D_9. These nine points split the distribution into ten equal sections – hence the name deciles is given to them – and if we wish to know for example the ages for the 10% of the distribution between D_4 and D_5 we can easily read them from the graph.

(h) Using the smoothed cumulative frequency curve in Fig. 1.13 (f) we look where the vertical lines through 11 and 12 cut the curve and read off the figures on the right hand vertical axis. We get for 11 the figure of 40%. This means that 40% of the children are below 11 years. We get for 12 the figure 80%. This means that 80% of the children are below 12 years. We therefore find the percentage of children between 11 and 12 years by subtracting 40% from 80% and get 40%.

We could also use the relative frequency polygon in Fig. 1.13 (g) to answer this question since the area under this graph represents the percentage of pupils between any two ages. It is also theoretically possible to use the smoothed relative frequency curve to answer the same question but the difficulty of finding an area when one 'side' is a curve suggests that it is better to use the smoothed cumulative frequency curve.

We recall that the curve-line graph is a method of replacing a broken-line graph in order to get more accurate readings at intermediate points. The smoothed cumulative frequency curve is a similar device in relation to the cumulative frequency polygon and a similar remark holds for the smoothed relative frequency curve.

There are several methods of obtaining the smoothed curves from the broken-line graph but they involve either tedious arithmetic labour or very complex mathematics. A simpler, and in most cases as effective a method is to draw a freehand curve and this method was used in the above example (See Fig. 1.13(g)).

Example 6: The nine diagrams of Fig. 1.13 (h) show the outline of graphs commonly met in statistics:

(i) is a symmetrical curve about the mid point of the distribution. This form is called the 'normal curve' and many measurements such as heights, weights, and so on approximate to it.

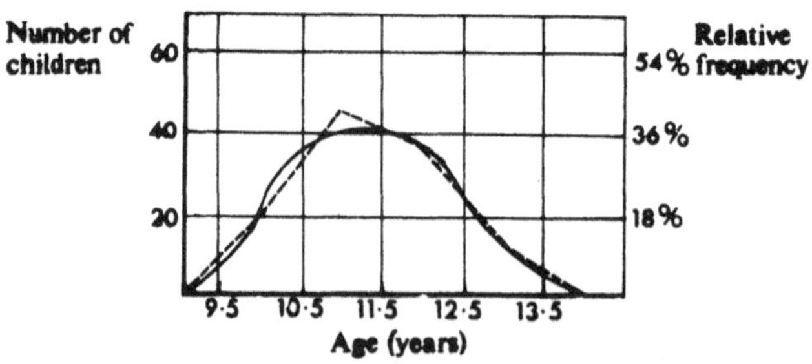

Fig. 1.13 (g)

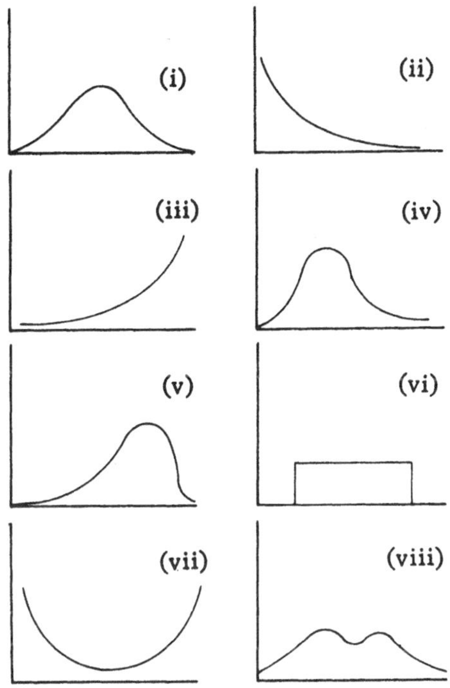
(i)
(ii)
(iii)
(iv)
(v)
(vi)
(vii)
(viii)

(j)

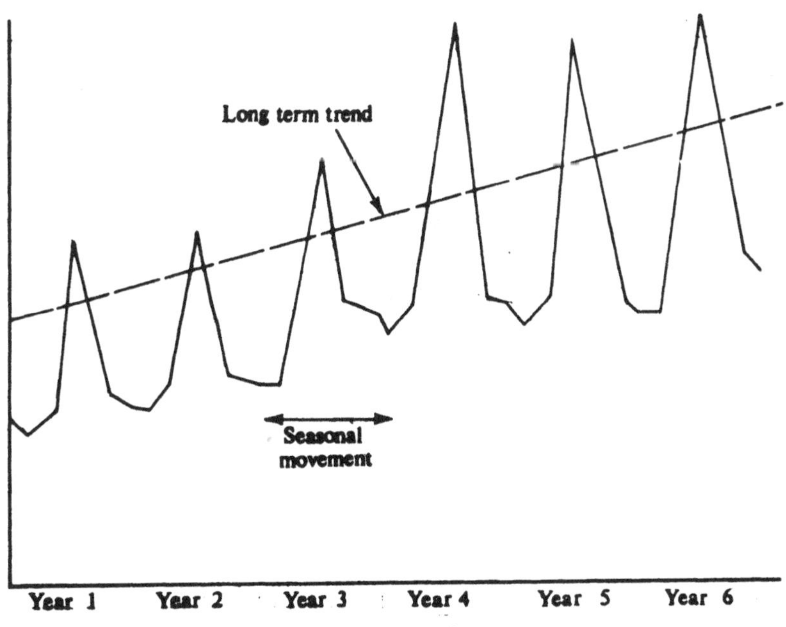
Long term trend
Seasonal movement
Year 1
Year 2
Year 3
Year 4
Year 5
Year 6

Fig. 1.13(h)

(ii) is called a 'reverse-*J* shape' curve. It has its peak at the extreme left of the graph and occurs in cases concerned with 'waiting time' for various services, as well as other places.

(iii) is called a '*J*-shape' curve. It is less commonly met but occurs in such things as population growth, production increase, and so on.

(iv) is a distribution with a tendency for the majority of the readings to be on the left of the graph but a few of the readings fall well to the right and produce a 'tail'. This is known as a *skewed* distribution, in this case the skew being to the right. Examples occur in income measurement.

(v) is similar to (iv) but this time the skew is in the opposite direction, i.e. to the left. This is not commonly met but can occur in such cases as examination results.

(vi) is called a 'uniform' distribution because the items are distributed evenly over the range of their values. This curve is rarely met in practice but is commonly used in statistical theory because of its simplicity.

(vii) is called a '*U*-shaped curve' because the large frequencies appear at the upper and lower ends of the graph. Commonly met in geographical statistics.

(viii) is a 'two humped' -- later to be called a 'bimodal' – distribution, because the data falls into two separate regions. Again not commonly met in practice but can occur in examination results.

(ix) is a graph of a 'time series'. Many examples of this type of graph occur in business and economics. The readings are taken over a period of time and then patterns are sought. In this case, two features of time graphs have been shown – first the 'trend line' for long term trends, in this case the trend is upwards, and second, regular fluctuations brought about by seasonal demands. There are other features of time graphs but there is not space here to develop them. The graph shown here is typical of such things as electricity production, coal consumption, milk yield, employment and so on.

1.14 Review

Now that we have looked at some further examples of graphs we can add more detail to the remarks made in Section 1.6.

It is worth repeating that one of the main points about organising and graphing data is to enable anyone who reads it to assimilate the information with the minimum of effort – all the following remarks are made in amplification of this primary aim.

There are four stages that can be traced in the organisation of data. First, there is the array consisting of the data as it came to hand and devoid of any order. Second there is the array consisting of the raw data but placed in some sort of order – either numerical or in alphabetical or some other order that the data suggests. Third, the data can be condensed into grouped data as in a frequency table, and finally a graph can be drawn.

It will be noted that each stage makes the assimilation of the data an easier task.

In both arrays and graphs positions of prominence should be reserved for the most important information. The top of the array or graph makes an ideal place for the title as this can be seen and read first. The title itself should be as concise as possible consistent with clarity. It should be clear and informative and not too long. If further information is necessary it can be incorporated in the text just prior to the graph.

Bold faced type or italic type can be used to emphasise or contrast certain parts of arrays and frequency diagrams. This method picks out certain parts to highlight while at the same time providing the other information as a background.

The size and shape of the table are important. Individual columns and rows should be wide enough to take their information while leaving a margin of space round them so as to set them off more clearly. The more densely packed a diagram becomes the more difficult it is to extract the information from it. Completeness consistent with the requirements of condensation is to be aimed for – but with the warning that too much detail defeats the primary aim of easy assimilation.

Using alphabetical order – when the data allows it – can be useful in helping the reader locate individual items. Data can be grouped in a variety of ways – again depending on its nature. It can be grouped in geographical areas, in terms of magnitude, by commodity (exports are a good example of this), historically, or by subject. These are just a few that can be used independently or in combination with one another.

Graphs should aim at accuracy and simplicity. It is surprising that the number of different ways of presenting graphical information seems endless. Magazines and newspapers are constantly finding fresh ways of presenting their readers with information and they should be studied to see how they measure up to the principles so far expounded.

Graphing brings out patterns that exist in the data that may be missed by an observation of the figures only. Take as an example of this Fig. 1.8(a). The figures for the period after the exercise may have been looked at without complete care but once the data has been graphed the pattern comes out. It is, perhaps, surprising to see in this graph that the pulse rate – after going to a high figure as a consequence of the exercise – falls not just to the rate it was before the exercise but dips down to a slower rate than normal, before returning to its normal rate. One can see easily that when this was first noticed several lines of enquiry could have been suggested. Were the figures correct? (Always a good point to check). Does this happen with all people – it so happened that the student chosen was a Physical Education student and fairly fit – would the same curve appear for a less fit person? Would the shape of the curve vary with age? Would the time taken for a return to the normal rate indicate fitness – or lack of it? This sort of analysis amply bears out the remark in Section 1.6 that the graph of data can be instrumental in suggesting further lines of enquiry.

Finally we remark that the audience for whom the graph is intended is another point to be considered. Both bar graphs and pictograms convey the same information but the pictograms seem to get the information over to the less technically minded more readily. The more technically minded can absorb the information by means of a bar graph and the latter are less expensive to produce than pictograms.

Exercise 1

1. Draw graphs of different sorts for each of the following sets of data. Which do you consider to be the most appropriate graph in each case:

(a) divide a typical day of your own into (i) work (ii) leisure (iii) sleep (and so on) and graph the result.

(b) Count the number of words in sentences of the first two or three pages of a book. Choose more than one book and pick them from different categories, i.e. fiction, technical, etc. Graph the results and see if there is any differences in them. Explain any differences.

(c) Repeat (b) but count letters in words.

(d) Sit at the roadside and count the traffic in different groups, e.g. lorries, cars, cycles, etc.

(e) Consult prices quoted on the Stock Exchange and plot day to day prices for three or four companies. Put them on the same graph. What conclusions can you draw from these graphs?

(f) Look in your local paper for prices of cars. Graph a large number. Then confine your attention to a particular make of car. Then confine your attention to a particular year of a particular make of car.

The reader is urged to 'go out' and collect data for himself. Many text books 'iron out' some of the difficulties found when raw data is considered so that the student will not meet any difficulty that is beyond him. If the reader collects data he will see for himself what difficulties these are and he will have to make decisions that make the data manageable. Three of the very many sources that may be consulted with profit are

(a) government publications
(b) industrial publications
(c) statistical digests

2. Of the following which are discrete and which are continuous variables?

(a) Heights of human beings
(b) Peas in a pod
(c) Accidents on a certain stretch of road during a particular period
(d) Appendix operations in a hospital for one day
(e) Apples on a tree
(f) Age of animals
(g) Bullets fired by a gun on one day
(h) The deviation of a watch from G.M.T.
(i) Area of a square
(j) The diagonal of a rectangle
(k) The volume of a cube
(l) The duration of a symphony
(m) Players in a football club

Answers (a), (f), (h), (i), (j), (k), (l) continuous – the remainder discrete

3. Write a summary of the method for taking raw data, grouping it, and drawing the histogram.

4. Eighty pupils took an exam and scored the following marks

3	5	6	6	11	15	16	20
3	5	6	7	12	15	16	20
4	5	6	7	13	15	16	21
4	6	6	8	13	16	16	21
4	6	6	8	14	16	17	22
5	6	6	9	14	16	18	23
5	6	6	10	14	16	18	23
5	6	6	10	15	16	19	25

(a) draw a frequency table – including a tally sheet – for class intervals of width (i) 3 (ii) 5 (iii) 8. Comment on any differences

(b) graph the data using the intervals in (a)

(c) draw frequency tables using unequal class intervals

(d) graph (c)

(e) draw the cumulative frequency table

(f) graph the cumulative frequency table

5. 75 males were weighed to the nearest quarter of a kilogram

54·25	65·75	70·25	78·75	81·50	86·25	90·00
55·75	66·50	70·25	79·00	82·25	86·50	91·00
56·25	66·50	75·75	79·00	82·75	86·75	92·25
61·50	67·25	76·25	79·25	82·75	87·00	93·75
62·50	67·50	76·50	80·00	83·50	87·00	94·25
62·75	67·75	77·25	80·00	84·00	88·25	
63·50	68·00	77·75	80·50	84·00	88·75	
64·25	68·25	78·25	80·50	85·25	89·25	
64·50	69·00	78·75	81·25	85·75	89·50	
65·50	69·75	78·75	81·50	86·00	89·75	

(a) draw a frequency table with suitable class intervals
(b) draw the histogram of the data
(c) draw the relative frequency table
(d) draw the frequency polygon
(e) draw the relative frequency polygon
(f) draw the cumulative frequency table
(g) draw the relative cumulative frequency table
(h) draw the cumulative frequency polygon
(i) draw the relative cumulative frequency polygon
(j) draw the smoothed cumulative frequency curve
(k) using the cumulative frequency polygon find
  (i) the weight below which 75% of the men lie
  (ii) the weight below which 25% of the men lie
  (iii) find the 'middle' weight

6. The following figures show the purchasing power of the £ in the years 1946–56, based on the year 1946

Year	1946	1947	1948	1949	1950	1951	1952	1953	1954	1955	1956
Purchasing power of the £	£1	93·8p	85·8p	84·2p	82·5p	75p	71·3p	70p	68·8p	67·5p	65p

Graph the data

7. The following table shows the number of articles handed in as lost to a Police Station over a period of twenty weeks.

Number of articles lost in one day	0	1	2	3	4	5	6
Number of days with the stated number of articles lost	42	51	33	8	4	1	1

Graph the data. Comment on the shape of the graph

8. One hundred watches were tested over a 24-hour period and the following figures obtained:

Lost more than 4 seconds	19	Gained more than 4 seconds	18
Lost 4 seconds	15	Gained 4 seconds	15
Lost 3 seconds	11	Gained 3 seconds	3
Lost 2 seconds	6	Gained 2 seconds	9
Lost 1 second	5	Gained 1 second	4
Two watches kept perfect time			

Graph the data and comment on the shape of the graph

9. Comment on the following statement. 'If class intervals are chosen so that class mid-points coincide with the observed data as much as possible, then errors brought about by grouping will be reduced'

10. A garage supplying new cars carried out pre-delivery checks and recorded the number of defects in each car. They obtained the following figures:

Number of defects	0	1	2	3	4	5	6	More than 6
Number of cars with the stated number of defects	1	3	8	17	31	25	16	8

Graph these figures and comment on them

11. A car-hire firm recorded the following figures for the hire of their cars.

Months	Jan	Feb	Mar	Apr	May	Jun	Jul	Aug	Sep	Oct	Nov	Dec
Number of cars hired	4	5	6	18	11	22	25	25	18	10	8	16

Graph these figures. What conclusions can you draw from them?

12. A caravan site has the following fleet of caravans:

Number of berths	2	3	4	5	6
Number of caravans	8	11	24	20	12

Graph these figures

13. The following figures show the ages of boys in a certain school:

Age in years Class mark	Number of pupils
11·5	200
12·5	150
14·0	240
15·5	60
17·0	19
Over 18	6

Draw the histogram of the data. What do the figures suggest?

14. Before doing the following experiments try and guess the outcome.

(a) Toss a single dice a large number of times and record the number of one's, two's, . . . , six's. Then graph the results.

(b) Toss more than one dice and again record the number of one's, two's, . . . , six's. Graph the results.

(c) Toss two dice, add the figures shown for each throw, and record the results. Graph the results.

(d) Toss a penny and record the number of heads and number of tails. Graph the results.

(e) Toss a penny and graph the fraction $\frac{\text{number of heads}}{\text{number of throws}}$

(f) Toss two pennies and for each throw record the number of heads. Graph the results.

(g) Toss three pennies and for each throw record the number of heads. Graph the results.

(h) Put 8 white and 2 red marbles in a bag. Draw out 3 marbles and record the number of red ones drawn. Repeat a large number of times and graph the results.

(i) Repeat (h) but this time count the number of white marbles drawn.

15. The marital condition of United Kingdom males for the year 1961 for given age groups is given in the following table:

Age		0–14	15–19	20–24	25–34	35–44	45–54	55–64	65–74	75 and over
Number in Thousands	single	6333	1883	1177	805	442	342	249	128	67
	married	–	21	516	2556	3052	3098	2427	1234	415
	widowed	–	–	1	20	55	103	168	242	298

Divorced men who have not remarried are included under widowed. Data taken from the Annual Abstract of Statistics 1967.
Graph the data and comment

16. The following table shows deaths from natural causes in Scotland for the stated years:

Year	1957	1958	1959	1960	1961	1962	1963	1964	1965	1966
Number of Deaths	58342	59215	60201	58897	61017	60133	62506	57973	59922	60721

Data taken from the *Annual Abstract of Statistics* (1967).
Graph the data

17. The population of the United Kingdom for the stated years is shown in the following table:

Year	1960	1961	1962	1963	1964	1965	1966
Population in thousands	52559	52941	53458	53797	54213	54595	54895

Graph the data. (You will find it necessary to 'round off' these figures – what effect does this have?)

18. Get hold of the following two publications and browse through them

(a) *The Annual Abstract of Statistics* (any year)

(b) *Government Statistical Services* – a pamphlet published by

H.M.S.O. (1962).

19. A certain regiment will only accept recruits who are over 5 ft 11 inches tall. What will a graph of the heights of the regiment look like?

20. The minimum height for the Police Force is 5 ft 8 inches. How will the graph of the Police Force differ from the graph of question 19?

21. If the girths of fir trees 'growing wild' were measured and the results plotted what would the graph look like? How would the graph of fir trees growing on plantations compare?

2 Measures of Central Tendency

2.1 Introduction

We saw in Chapter 1 how data, after collection, is organised and graphed; the graph, being a visual demonstration, readily revealed the main characteristics of the data. It is possible, by comparing their graphs, to make a rough comparison between two or more sets of data. A comparison of this sort is called a *qualitative* comparison and may be of use on many occasions. However qualitative comparisons are of little use to the statistician as they are not capable of mathematical manipulation and can on occasions be subject to personal likes and dislikes. For these reasons it is necessary to characterise data in numerical, i.e. *quantitative*, terms. Once this has been done two advantages emerge. One is that the data has been summarised even further in terms of two or three numbers, and the other is that different sets of data may be more exactly and dispassionately compared. In order to carry out this characterisation it is necessary to decide which are the most important features of a set of data and then to decide on a uniform method of measuring them.

Experience has shown that a set of data has two main features. One is its 'centre', and the other is the way it is 'arranged' around this centre.

Example 1: The following diagrams show three different sets of data all of which have their 'centres' at the point 20, but which are arranged around this centre in different ways, Fig. 2.1 (a), (b) and (c).

Example 2: Figures 2.1 (d)–(e) show how different sets of data may be 'arranged' in the same way, but about different centres.

The study of the ways in which the centre of a set of data is characterised is called the study of *measures of central tendency*.

The study of the ways in which a set of data is arranged around its centre is called the study of *measures of dispersion*, i.e. the way the data is dispersed around its centre.

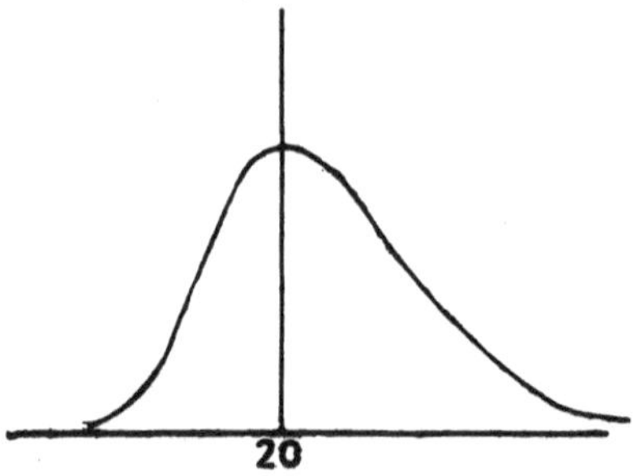

Fig 2.1(a)

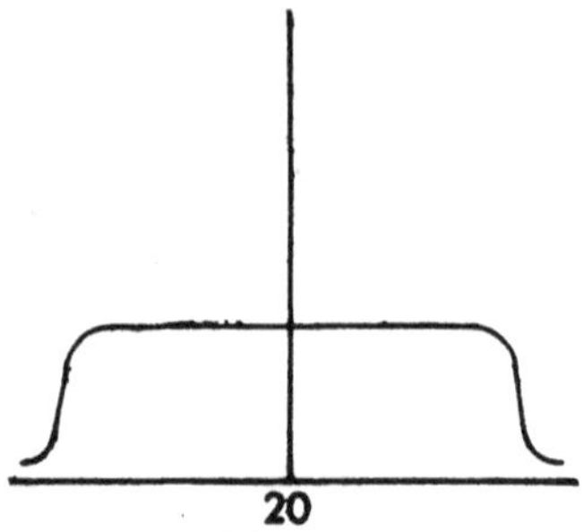

Fig 2.1(b)

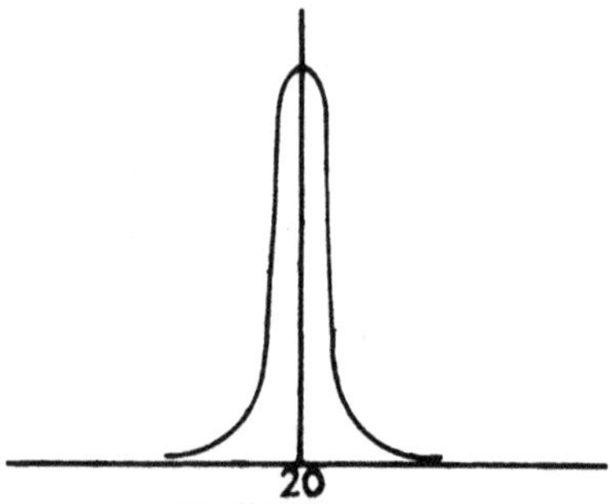

Fig 2.1(c)

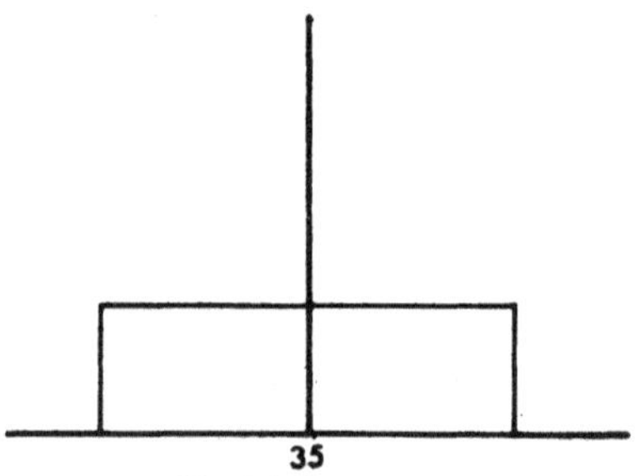

Fig 2.1(d)

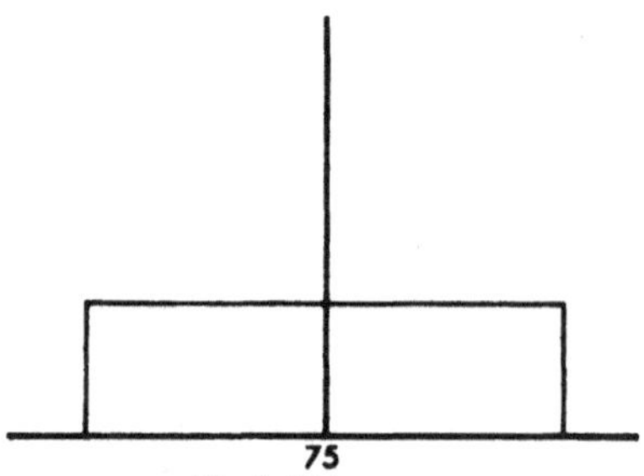

Fig 2.1(e)

In this chapter we will look at measures of central tendency and defer dispersion until the next chapter.

2.2 Measures of Central Tendency

The various measures of central tendency are also called *averages*, but this use of the word 'average' is used in a wider sense than that used by the man in the street. To most people *the* average is the arithmetic mean arrived at by adding up all the numbers of a given set, and then dividing by the number of numbers in this set. To a statistician *an* average is a number which is extracted from a set of data as being, in some way, typical of all the numbers in the set. Using this sense of the word, several averages can be defined and we now look at the most common in turn.

2.3 The Mode

The mode is defined to be that number which occurs the greatest number of times in a set of data.

Example 1: Which is the mode in the following set of data:

2, 5, 7, 8, 8, 9, 11, 24, 45

Answer

Since the number 8 occurs twice and all the other numbers only once, the mode is 8

Example 2: Which is the mode in *Example 1* of Section 1.9 (page 11)?

Answer

We look for the mark that was awarded to the greatest number of pupils, and therefore, the mode is 7.

Example 3: Which is the mode in *Example 2* of Section 1.9 (page 13)?

Answer

By looking at the first tabulated form of the data we can see that more pupils scored 28 than any other score, therefore the mode is 28.

Note: We looked at the first tabulated form of the data since the second tabulated form was not so convenient. Also when we wrote out the second tabulated form the idea of tally sheets and a gate check had not been introduced. When these latter ideas are used it is not possible to pick out the mode from the frequency table but if it is essential to find the mode in terms of strictest accuracy it can be done by going back to the original raw data.

Finding the mode in the case of ungrouped data is usually possible even though, in the case of a large number of readings, it may be tedious. But when data is arranged into groups certain difficulties arise. In the first place when items are placed into a class interval they lose their individual identities and become, in effect, the class mark of that class interval.

Now it is possible to use the class mark of the class interval having the highest frequency – this is sometimes called the *crude mode* – but this is not always accurate enough. Therefore consideration has to be given to whereabouts in the class interval the mode is located. We will look at this in a moment.

Another difficulty may arise – in the actual readings there may be a mode, but when the data is grouped two class intervals may appear with equal frequencies. These may be adjacent, in which case things are a little simpler, or they may not be adjacent. Which to choose as the mode then becomes a matter of choice in the light of the data and which average is going to be the most useful. Distributions with two equal modes are called *bimodal*.

A final difficulty is that the alteration of class boundaries in grouped data may alter the position of the class interval with the highest frequency.

These remarks go to reveal that the mode is the least 'stable' of the commonly used averages, and this makes it the least used.

We now turn to methods of finding the mode in the case of grouped data where one class interval has a greater frequency than any other.

Method 1

Construct the two diagonals shown dotted in the following diagram. Then drop a perpendicular from their point of intersection onto the horizontal axis – this point is the mode.

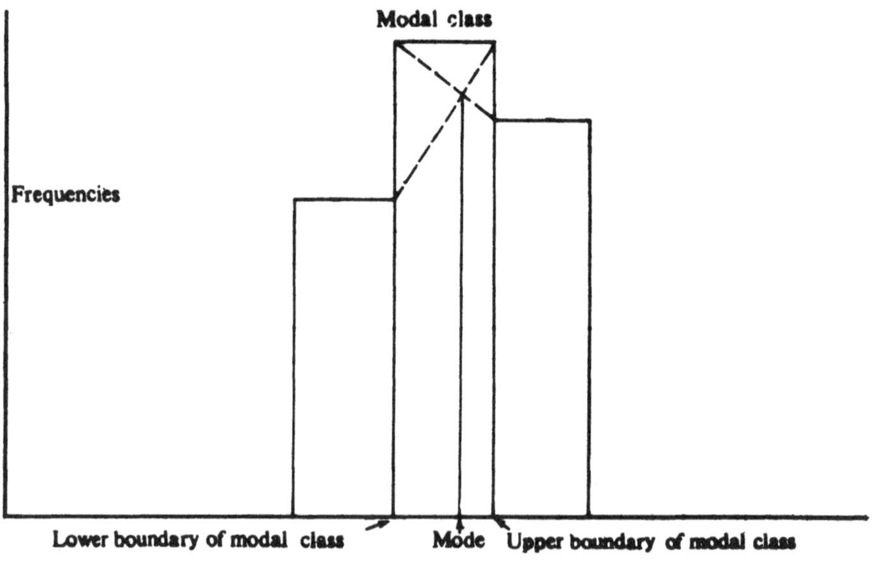

Fig. 2.3 (a)

Note that this construction is only possible when the modal class is not an end class.

Example 4: Use Fig. 1.9(f) (page 22) to estimate the mode of the heights of 45 college students.

Answer

Constructing as above we get the mode to be 62·6″.

Method 2

By using the formula

$$\text{Mode} = L_{\text{mode}} + \left[\frac{f_{\text{mode}} - f_{\text{mode}-1}}{(f_{\text{mode}} - f_{\text{mode}-1}) + (f_{\text{mode}} - f_{\text{mode}+1})}\right] c$$

where

L_{mode} = the lower boundary of the modal class

f_{mode} = the frequency of the modal class

$f_{\text{mode}-1}$ = the frequency of the class immediately preceeding the modal class

$f_{\text{mode}+1}$ = the frequency of the class immediately above the modal class

c = the class interval of the modal class.

Example 5: Find the mode of the data of *Example 14* of Section 1.9.

Answer

Looking at Fig. 1.9(e) (page 21) we see that the modal class is the one with a class mark of 63″ as it contains 9 items. We therefore get

$$L_{\text{mode}} = 61{\cdot}5''$$

$$f_{\text{mode}} = 9$$

$$f_{\text{mode}-1} = 8$$

$$f_{\text{mode}+1} = 7$$

$$c = 3''$$

and

$$\begin{aligned}\text{Mode} &= 61{\cdot}5'' + \left[\frac{(9-8)}{(9-8)+(9-7)}\right]3'' \\ &= 61{\cdot}5'' + \tfrac{1}{3}(3'') \\ &= 62{\cdot}5''\end{aligned}$$

Again it must be noted that this method can only be used if the modal class is not an end class. It can also be shown, by using the ratio properties of similar triangles, that the above formula is equivalent to the geometrical construction. This accounts for the close agreement of the answers obtained by the two different methods.

Method 3

There is an empirical relationship between the mean, median and the mode given by the formula

$$\text{mean} - \text{mode} = 3(\text{mean} - \text{median})$$

which is true for unimodal distributions which are only moderately skewed. This means that the mean and median must be known before the mode can be found.

The advantages of the mode are its common use and its ease of understanding. An election winner has received the largest number of votes and this is the mode of the distribution of votes. Shops stock items such as shoes, clothes, etc. so that they have more of 'average sizes' in stock than any other – this again is the mode of the various distributions.

The mode is relatively easy to find and it is not disturbed by extreme items which sometimes appear in a set of data but which are nevertheless uncharacteristic of that set.

The disadvantages of the mode are its unstable nature, making it difficult to determine the *true mode*, and its inability to lend itself to algebraic manipulation in anything other than advanced work. Although it may be the most common reading in a set of data, there may be several others that are only slightly less common and in these circumstances its claim to be representative of the data is not clear cut.

The name and meaning of the mode is easily remembered by associating it with the French expression 'à la mode', i.e. in the fashion.

2.4 The Arithmetic Mean

The *arithmetic mean* of a set of numbers is found by first adding together all the numbers in the set, and then dividing this total by the number of numbers in the set.

Example 1: Find the arithmetic mean of

$$3 \quad 4 \quad 5 \quad 2 \quad 8 \quad 5$$

Answer $3 + 4 + 5 + 2 + 8 + 5 = 27.$

There are six numbers here, so $\frac{27}{6} = 4\frac{1}{2}$. $4\frac{1}{2}$ is the arithmetic mean

Note: We started with whole numbers but the arithmetic mean is not a whole number.

Before we can go further we must develop a little symbolism. Let the symbol **X** refer to a variable, and let the symbols $X_1, X_2, X_3, X_4, \ldots$

refer to variates of this variable. Similarly let **Y**, and Y_1, Y_2, Y_3, Y_4,... refer to a different variable and its variates.

Example 2: Let **X** refer to the variable 'heights of human beings' and let

$$X_1 = 70'' \quad X_2 = 36''$$
$$X_3 = 59{\cdot}2'' \quad X_4 = 72{\cdot}34''$$

Example 3: Let **Y** refer to the variable 'ages of insects', and let

$$Y_1 = 2 \text{ hours} \quad Y_2 = 5 \text{ minutes}$$
$$Y_3 = 1 \text{ day} \quad Y_4 = 3 \text{ weeks}$$

In order to shorten X_1, X_2, X_3, X_4, ... we use the notation X_i where i takes the numbers 1, 2, 3, 4, 5, and so on. Any letter other than i could have been used here; commonly used letters are i, j, k, l.

Example 4: Put the numbers in *Example 1* into the above notation.

Answer

$$X_1 = 3, \quad X_2 = 4, \quad X_3 = 5$$
$$X_4 = 2, \quad X_5 = 8, \quad X_6 = 5$$

If there are N numbers in a set then the last number than i can take is N.

Example 5: In *Example 1* there are 6 numbers, therefore $N = 6$. The letters i, j, k, l, in the above notation are called *subscripts* and the notation itself is called *subscript notation*.

We must now look at *sigma notation*. In the simple exercise $4 + 3 - 2 = 5$, the signs '+' and '–' order the reader to perform certain operations, namely the operations of addition and subtraction. Without this particular sort of sign the exercise would have to be written 'add 3 to 4 and then subtract 2' and it can be seen immediately how much more convenient the '+' and the '–' are to use. Since a lot of addition is performed in statistical calculations, it is very convenient to have a sign which orders the reader to 'add together all the numbers like...'

The sign commonly used in mathematics to order such an operation is the Greek letter capital sigma, Σ.

In the context of

$$\sum_{i=1}^{i=N} X_i$$

the order would be 'add together all the numbers like X_i, letting the subscript i start at the number 1, and take the numbers 2, 3, 4, etc. up to N, in turn'.

For example:

$$\sum_{i=1}^{i=5} X_i = X_1 + X_2 + X_3 + X_4 + X_5$$

Example 6: Exemplify *Example 1* of this section

Answer

$$\sum_{i=1}^{i=6} X_i = X_1 + X_2 + X_3 + X_4 + X_5 + X_6$$

$$= 3 + 4 + 5 + 2 + 8 + 5 = 27$$

We can now give a slightly different approach to the definition of the arithmetic mean. The arithmetic mean of a set of numbers $X_1, X_2, X_3, \ldots X_N$, is defined as

$$\frac{X_1 + X_2 + X_3 + \ldots + X_N}{N} = \frac{\sum_{i=1}^{i=N} X_i}{N} = \bar{X}$$

It is common practice to denote the *arithmetic mean as* $\bar{X}$. When there is no possibility of confusion the notation

$$\sum_{i=1}^{i=N} X_i$$

is shortened to $\sum_i X_i$ or $\sum X_i$.

We now look at some further examples in Σ notation.

Example 7: $\sum_{i=1}^{i=3} 3X_i$ means 'multiply each X_i by three and then add the results'. i.e.

$$\sum_{i=1}^{i=3} 3X_i = 3X_1 + 3X_2 + 3X_3$$

Example 8: $\sum_{i=1}^{i=3} (X_i - 5)$ means 'subtract 5 from each X_i and then add the result'. i.e.

$$\sum_{i=1}^{i=3} (X_i - 5) = (X_1 - 5) + (X_2 - 5) + (X_3 - 5)$$

If we now put $X_1 = 7$, $X_2 = 3$, $X_3 = 5$ the above two examples become:

$$\sum_{i=1}^{i=3} 3X_i = (3 \times 7) + (3 \times 3) + (3 \times 5) = 21 + 9 + 15 = 45$$

$$\sum_{i=1}^{i=3} (X_i - 5) = (7 - 5) + (3 - 5) + (5 - 5) = 2 + (-2) + 0 = 0.$$

The student is advised to get as much practice as possible in Σ notation, ensuring that the translation of the symbols into words is clearly understood.

Exercises: Write out in full:

(1) $$\sum_{i=1}^{6} 4X_i =$$

(2) $$\sum_{i=1}^{7} (X_i + 3) =$$

(3) $$\sum_{i=1}^{4} (3X_i + 2) =$$

Note: the upper limit of the Σ sign is often written as N, rather than $i = N$. This is done in these three exercises.

We now proceed to a further point by considering the following example:

Example 9: Find the arithmetic mean of

2, 2, 2, 4, 4, 5, 5, 5, 7, 0

Answer

We proceed as before,

$$\frac{2+2+2+4+4+5+5+5+7+0}{10} = \frac{36}{10} = 3{\cdot}6$$

We now ask ourselves, 'could we have simplified this working?' We note that there are three 2's, two 4's, and three 5's and therefore we could have written the above as

$$\frac{(3\times 2)+(2\times 4)+(3\times 5)+(1\times 7)+(1\times 0)}{10} = \frac{36}{10} = 3{\cdot}6$$

Note: $10 = 3 + 2 + 3 + 1 + 1$

Now in each case the variate is multiplied by its own frequency. Thus we can say that to find the arithmetic mean we 'multiplied each variate by the frequency with which it occured, added the results, and then divided by the total number of numbers'. This operation can be expressed in mathematical symbols as follows:

$$\bar{X} = \frac{\sum_{i=1}^{M} f_i X_i}{\sum_{i=1}^{M} f_i} \qquad \text{where } \sum_{i=1}^{M} f_i = N,$$

and f_i means the frequency of the variate X_i.

In the above example $N = 10$, and $M = 5$. This means that the above 10 numbers are broken down into 5 classes. f_iX_i means f_i multiplied by X_i.

Note in $\sum_{i=1}^{M} f_iX_i$ the subscripts 'i' in f_iX_i always match, i.e. f_1X_1, or f_4X_4, never f_4X_5.

X_i	f_i	f_iX_i
0	1	0
2	3	6
4	2	8
5	3	15
7	1	7
	10	36

The work may be conveniently arranged in a table as shown.

$$\sum_{i=1}^{5} f_i = 10 \qquad \sum_{i=1}^{5} f_iX_i = 36$$

Note:

$$X_1 = 0 \quad X_2 = 2 \quad X_3 = 4 \quad X_4 = 5 \quad X_5 = 7$$

$$f_1 = 1 \quad f_2 = 3 \quad f_3 = 2 \quad f_4 = 3 \quad f_5 = 1$$

We now work the *Example 14* of Section 1.9

Classes	class mark X_i	frequency f_i	f_iX_i
49·5 –	51	2	102
52·5 –	54	3	162
55·5 –	57	5	285
58·5 –	60	8	480
61·5 –	63	9	567
64·5 –	66	7	462
67·5 –	69	5	345
70·5 –	72	5	360
73·5 –	75	1	75
Totals		$\sum_{i=1}^{9} f_i = 45$	$2838 = \sum_{i=1}^{9} f_iX_i$

$$\bar{X} = \frac{\sum_{i=1}^{9} f_iX_i}{\sum_{i=1}^{9} f_i} = \frac{2838}{45} = 63{\cdot}06$$

Therefore, the arithmatice mean of the heights of 45 students is 63·06″. The remark made previously that computation would be done using the class marks will no doubt have been noted in this last example.

We now proceed to find a method of reducing the amount of computation we had to do in this last example.

Consider the following: Find the arithmetic mean of

106, 105, 101

We could proceed as before and get

$$\frac{106 + 105 + 101}{3} = \frac{312}{3} = 104$$

or we could use the following device. Subtract 100 from each of the numbers and get 6, 5, and 1. Add these together and divide by 3, giving $\frac{12}{3} = 4$, and then add this 4 to the 100 that we subtracted in the first place, giving 104, the same as the first method. This method is called 'finding the arithmetic mean by the assumed mean method' because we assume a mean and then calculate the true mean. We now have to put this method into symbolic form and it will help if we repeat what we did above but put it into a more general case.

We look for a number near what we estimate the mean will be, we then subtract this number from each X_i, add the results of this and divide this total by the number of numbers, finally we add back on again the number we subtracted in the first place.

In symbols this becomes

$$\bar{X} = \frac{\sum_{i=1}^{N} (X_i - A)}{N} + A$$

where A is the assumed mean.

This formula is applicable to numbers of a set that have a frequency of 1. If numbers occur with frequencies greater than one, then the above formula has to be modified in the way that

$$\bar{X} = \frac{\Sigma X_i}{N}$$

had to be modified into

$$\bar{X} = \frac{\Sigma f_i X_i}{\Sigma f_i}$$

and it becomes

$$\bar{X} = \frac{\sum_{i=1}^{M} f_i (X_i - A)}{\sum_{i=1}^{M} f_i} + A$$

In words this would read 'subtract the assumed mean from each class mark, X_i, multiply this result by the class frequency, add these results together, divide by the total number of frequencies, and finally add on the assumed mean'. *Example 14* of Section 1.9 is now reworked using this method.

A look at the data suggests that the mean will be somewhere near 63, we therefore elect to take our assumed mean to be 63. Note that we don't have to select an assumed mean to be a class mark, but by so doing we reduce the labour involved.

Classes	class mark X_i	frequency f_i	$(X_i - 63)$	$f_i(X_i - 63)$
49·5 –	51	2	– 12	– 24
52·5 –	54	3	– 9	– 27
55·5 –	57	5	– 6	– 30
58·5 –	60	8	– 3	– 24
61·5 –	63	9	0	0
64·5 –	66	7	3	21
67·5 –	69	5	6	30
70·5 –	72	5	9	45
73·5 –	75	1	12	12
Totals		$\Sigma f_i = 45$		$\Sigma f_i(X_i - 63) = 3$

To get the total for the last column, the negative quantities are first added, then the positive quantities are added, and then the subtraction is performed i.e.

Sum of negative quantities = –105
Sum of positive quantities = 108

$$108 - 105 = 3$$

Substituting in the formula now gives,

$$\bar{X} = \frac{\Sigma f_i(X_i - A)}{\Sigma f_i} + A$$

$$= \frac{3}{45} + 63$$

$$= 63\tfrac{1}{15}$$

which shows that our original guess was close to the actual mean. A comparison with this frequency table and the previous one (page 58) will immediately show how the arithmetical labour has been reduced.

If the class intervals are of equal size and there are a lot of them, a convenient method to use to find the mean is the method known as the *coding method.* The motivation behind this method will become apparent if the column head $(X_i - 63)$ in the last table is examined. All the numbers in this column are multiples of 3 – the size of the class interval, and if they were all divided by 3 the column would then read, −4, −3, −2, −1, 0, 1, 2, 3, 4. This new column would be headed

$$\frac{X_i - 63}{3}$$

and we would now be working in 'class intervals'. If this column is now multiplied by the frequency column the next column would be headed

$$f_i\left(\frac{X_i - 63}{3}\right)$$

We could now add this column as before to get

$$\Sigma\, f_i\left(\frac{X_i - 63}{3}\right)$$

and we must then convert back from class intervals by multiplying by 3, and so we get

$$3\left\{\Sigma\, f_i\left(\frac{X_i - 63}{3}\right)\right\}$$

We now proceed as before, dividing by $\Sigma\, f_i$ and adding 63, to get

$$\bar{X} = \frac{3\left\{\Sigma\, f_i\left(\frac{X_i - 63}{3}\right)\right\}}{\Sigma\, f_i} + 63$$

The new table would read

Classes	class mark X_i	frequency f_i	$\frac{(X_i - 63)}{3}$	$f_i\left(\frac{X_i - 63}{3}\right)$
49·5	51	2	− 4	− 8
52·5	54	3	− 3	− 9
55·5	57	5	− 2	− 10
58·5	60	8	− 1	− 8
61·5	63	9	0	0
64·5	66	7	1	7
67·5	69	5	2	10
70·5	72	5	3	15
73·5	75	1	4	4
		$\Sigma\, f_i = 45$	$\Sigma\, f_i\left(\frac{X_i - 63}{3}\right)$	$= 1$

The total for the last column is found as before, by adding the positive and negative quantities separately, and then subtracting, i.e..

Sum of negative quantities = −35

Sum of positive quantities = 36

$$36 - 35 = 1$$

Substituting

$$\bar{X} = \frac{3 \times 1}{45} + 63$$

$$= 63\tfrac{1}{15} \text{ as before}$$

Putting this into general terms, we note that if c is the width of a class interval, and all the class intervals are equal then

$$\bar{X} = \frac{c\left\{\Sigma f_i\left(\frac{X_i - A}{c}\right)\right\}}{\Sigma f_i} + A$$

where A is an assumed mean, is the coding method for finding the arithmetic mean. The student is advised to use this method whenever possible though he should be warned that a common mistake is to omit the multiplication stage in converting back from class intervals.

A word must now be said about the use of the arithmetic mean. As a statistic it is well known and understood, consequently it is commonly used. It is fairly easy to calculate and every item in the set of data makes a contribution to the result. It is capable of algebraic manipulation and hence leads to further developments. It is the centre of the data in the sense that the values of the readings on either side of the mean are equal. In the language of physics it is the centre of gravity of the distribution.

It is typical of the set of data in another way – if the mean were allocated to each item in the set then the total of the data would remain unchanged. Because of this the use of the form $n\bar{X} = \Sigma X_i$ is common. What this says is that if the mean is known then simply multiplying it by any given n will give the total. If, for example, the average weight of each person's luggage is 50 lb, then 100 passengers will have luggaging weighing 5000 lb.

Although it requires more computation than, for example, the mode, it has to be calculated if the data is to be analysed further. It is of fundamental importance in further work in both practical and theoretical statistics – the truth of this statement will emerge as the student gets further into his study of statistics.

Apart from considerations shortly to be mentioned the mean locates the centre of distribution with a high degree of precision and it is more stable than the mode.

It is because every item in the set of data makes a contribution in the calculation of the arithmetic mean that its chief disadvantage lies. It can be adversly affected by extreme values in the set. A set of data may settle conveniently round one area but at the same time, contain one or two readings some distance from the bulk of the data. These *outriders*, as they are called, then tend to pull the arithmetic mean away from the position where it would be more typical of the data. One solution to this problem is to ignore the outriders and regard them as untypical of the data.

An example will make the point clear. Consider the set

$$3,\ 4,\ 4,\ 5,\ 6,\ 4,\ 3$$

then this will have an arithmetic mean of 4·14 and clearly is typical of the data. Now consider the set

$$3,\ 4,\ 4,\ 5,\ 6,\ 4,\ 121$$

this has a mean of 21 and can hardly be considered as representative of the set.

Because of this, an arithmetic mean, if given without qualification, may give misleading information. It disguises abnormal values and it is often these abnormal values that are of greater interest than the others.

2.5 The Median

Example 1: Find the middle number in the following set, when they have been ordered.

$$2,\ 4,\ 6,\ 3,\ 1$$

Answer

We must first arrange them in order, and get

$$1,\ 2,\ 3,\ 4,\ 6$$

Immediately we see that 3 is the middle number.

Example 2: Find the middle number in the following set, when they have been ordered.

$$2,\ 4,\ 6,\ 3,\ 1,\ 5,\ 9,\ 21$$

Answer

Arranging in order gives,

$$1,\ 2,\ 3,\ 4,\ 5,\ 6,\ 9,\ 21$$

Immediately we see that because there are 8 numbers – an even number – there is no middle number, but there are two middle numbers. We might then be inclined to say that we can consider the middle number of the set to be the number mid-way between these two middle numbers. This number is in fact the arithmetic mean of the two middle numbers and is found in this case as follows:

$$\frac{4+5}{2} = 4\tfrac{1}{2}$$

We then consider $4\frac{1}{2}$ to be the middle number of this set.

These two examples lead us to the definition:
The *median* of a set of N numbers, arranged in order, is the middle number if N is odd, and the arithmetic mean of the two middle ones if N is even.

This is a very simple average to find if the set of numbers in question is small, but if, as is usually the case, we have a large set of numbers, and these numbers have been put into classes, then we are not able to find it with such ease. In fact, as has been previously remarked, once the data is put into classes then we lose individual scores in the process of obtaining a general picture. However, we can approximate to the real median by considering the class into which the median falls. This class is called the *median class* and is found as follows:
Using *Example 14*, Section 1.9, Fig. 1.9(e).
There are 45 numbers to consider, therefore the median height will be the twenty-third since there are twenty-two heights before this one, and twenty-two heights after it. Referring to the table we see that there are

2 scores below 52·5″
5 scores below 55·5″
10 scores below 58·5″
18 scores below 61·5″

and since there are 9 scores in class 61·5–64·5 the median score will fall in this class. Hence this is the median class for this distribution.

We come now to locating the median within this median class. For this we assume that all the scores falling in this class are evenly distributed over the class interval and we argue as follows:
We want the twenty-third score and have used 18 scores in getting up to the median class, we therefore, need to count 5 into the median class to reach the median. This will take us five ninths of the distance into the median class. As the class intervals are 3″ we find five ninths of 3″

$$\text{i.e.} \quad \tfrac{5}{9} \times 3'' = 1\tfrac{2}{3}''$$

we now see that the median score will be found by adding $1\frac{2}{3}''$ to the lower class boundary – 61·5″ – giving 63·17″. If we look now at the original data we can see that the true median is 63·5″, so our estimate is quite accurate.

The following diagram may also help,

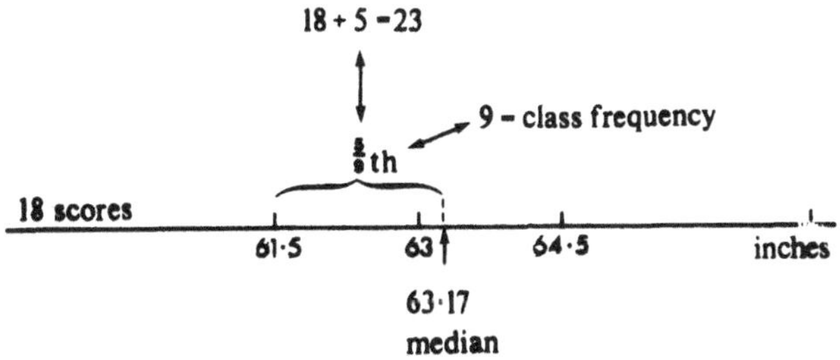

Fig. 2.5(a)

To sum up this method generally:

(i) Find the median class by finding the class into which the median score falls

(ii) Count how many scores fall below the median class

(iii) Count how many more scores are required to get to the median score, say d

(iv) Put d over the frequency of the median class to find the fraction of the way along the class interval the median score will fall

(v) Multiply this fraction by the size of the class interval to convert the fraction to the units of the variable

(vi) Add this number to the lower class boundary of the median class

The median, unlike the arithmetic mean, is defined because of its *position* in the data. Thus the values of the individual items in the data will have no bearing on the median other than in this positional manner. The median therefore, will not be affected, as the mean is, by abnormally small or large items in the data.

If the number of items in the data is odd then the mode will coincide with one of the readings – if, however, there are an even number of items in the data then, as the median in this case is the arithmetic mean of the two middle ones, it may, or may not, coincide with one of the readings.

Because of its definition the median is especially useful in characterising data that naturally falls into rank order – such as grades, examination marks, earnings. It is less effective when used with data that is counted or measured, and in the case of purely qualitative data it cannot be applied.

In the case of data with open ended class intervals the arithmetic mean, as we have seen, has to be calculated after assumptions about the mid point of the open ended class which may, or may not, be justified. But in the case of the median the opened ended class does not affect it at all. This together with the fact that the median is easier to calculate than the arithmetic mean are two main points where the median has advantages over the arithmetic mean.

When it comes to algebraic manipulation then the arithmetic mean is much superior to the median. Take the simple case where two groups of data are combined. It is impossible to find the median of the combined group solely from the knowledge of the medians of the two individual groups. In cases such as this the two groups have to be combined and the median recalculated. The mean, as we will see in *Example 1* of Section 2.7 can easily be found in this situation.

The median given by raw data may not be the same as that found when the data has been grouped into class intervals.

We can now slightly extend the idea of the median. If a set of data is arranged in order then those variates which divide the data into four equal parts are called *quartiles*. The middle quartile is, of course, the median and the other two are sometimes called the lower and upper quartiles. In calculations they are best manipulated by using Q_1, Q_2 and Q_3, going from the lowest to the highest.

Carrying on in this manner we can consider those variates which divide a set of data into ten equal parts. These are called *deciles* and are denoted by $D_1, D_2, \ldots, D_9$.

Finally we can define *percentiles*, $P_1, P_2, \ldots, P_{99}$, as dividing data into 100 equal parts.

If the way in which we found the number of scores below the median class is studied it will be seen that much the same process was used as was used in the compiling of the cumulative frequency tables. This suggests that cumulative frequency may be a help in finding medians. This is in fact the case and if the graph of the cumulative frequency of *Example 14* of Section 1.9, shown in Section 1.12, is examined it will be seen that if we look up the left-hand scale until we come to the twenty-third student, and then look along the graph until we meet the cumulative frequency curve, and then drop down to the horizontal scale we will find the median. This method is not quite as accurate as the first one but in many cases is accurate enough. The reader may note that by using the cumulative frequency graph not only the middle score may be found but also such scores as

(i) the score below which $\frac{1}{4}$ of the scores lie and above which $\frac{3}{4}$ of the scores lie

(ii) the score below which $\frac{3}{4}$ of the scores lie and above which $\frac{1}{4}$ of the scores lie

(iii) the scores below which 10% of the scores fall

(iv) the scores below which 20%, 30%, ... 80%, 90% lie

2.6 Relative Merits of the Arithmetic Mean, the Median and the Mode

We have now looked at three different averages and we now have to consider them in the light of the various information they give about a distribution. The main criterion in the selection of one measure from a set to serve as a representative of that set is what meaning it has in relation to the data as a whole and its suitability for the problem in hand.

The arithmetic mean is derived by calculation and is called a *computed* average, but the median and the mode are not derived by calculation – except insofar as simple formulae are used to locate them in grouped data – and are averages defined in terms of their position in the data – hence they are called *positional* averages.

Because of this we can regard them as doing different jobs. Unfortunately many people believe that by simply following the definitions they must be obtaining useful and worthwhile results. This is not the case. There are times when an arithmetic mean, although properly computed, may give a very wrong impression. To combat this and similar errors it is necessary to return to the questions – What do you expect to find out? What do you expect the average will tell you?

The answer to these and similar questions is that each of the three averages mentioned tells a different story. There are cases when, for a set of data, they are all the same, but, usually, the different averages will be numerically different for the same set of data.

We refer the reader now to the sections in the text that discussed the advantages and disadvantages of the individual averages. It is by knowing the strengths and weaknesses of the different averages that we may know what information they give.

The question is often asked: Which is the best average to use? It will now be evident that there is no overall best. In some situations the arithmetic mean is the best, in others the mode, and so on.

A couple of examples will be useful here. If the frequency distribution is of a symmetrical nature then the three averages coincide and it does not matter which one is used purely for the purpose of locating the centre. If however, further analysis of the data is planned then the arithmetic mean would be the most useful one to know.

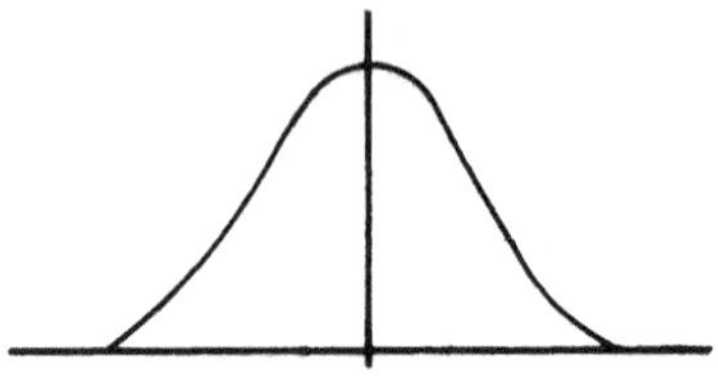

Fig. 2.6 (a)

If a frequency distribution is skewed

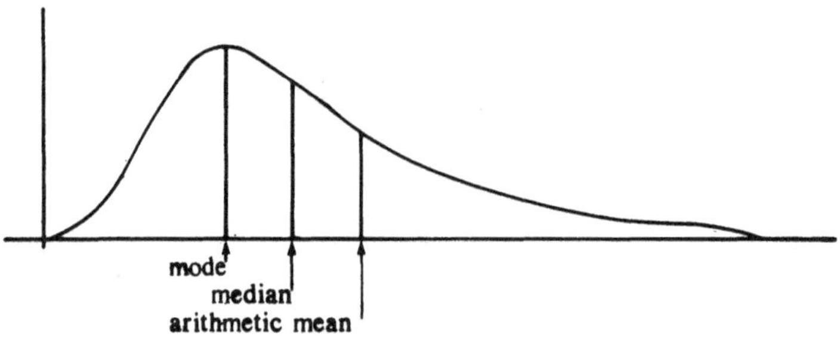

Fig. 2.6 (b)

then greater care is needed. For instance, a typical distribution which is skewed to the right, or positively skewed, is the distribution of incomes. If one uses the arithmetic mean a slightly false impression is given since the higher values in the distribution make this the highest of the three averages. It is of little comfort to a man whose average wage is the modal wage to be told that his average wage is £x if this latter average is the arithmetic mean. The press is a frequent offender in this respect in that they rarely do specify which average they are using, and it does make a difference.

If you happen to be a manufacturer then you might be more interested in the mode than in any other average since this will give you a better idea of which particular size product to manufacture in excess of the others. It will, for example, be of little use to you to find out that the arithmetic mean c.c. of car engines bought by the public is 1234·5 c.c., but you would welcome the news that more cars of 1100 c.c. were bought than any other size.

It is impossible to give more examples than this and we leave this with the remark that each case should be treated on its merits.

There are many, some would say most, situations where one average is anadequate to describe the data. Two, or even three, will be necessary. Asking for a single figure to summerise what could be a vast set of data is asking rather a lot. It would not be unreasonable to ask for two or three figures so that a greater degree of comprehension could be obtained.

This leads to the point that there are situations where the use of *any* average will be misleading. Take the case of a markedly *U*-shaped distribution. In this case the arithmetic mean and the median coincide at the central value but obviously cannot be taken as representative of the data. Similarly how would the choice of a mode by any less inconvenient? In this case by presenting any statistic the wrong impression will be given.

Because of this, before any average is used at all it must be under the assumption that the situation is such that the use of averages is meaningful. Thus, having the assurance that the use is meaningful, the average to use is determined by what purpose it must serve. The average which has the characteristics that will best serve this purpose is the one to choose.

2.7 Supplementary Examples

Example 1: The arithmetic mean of n_1 numbers is m_1, and the arithmetic mean of n_2 numbers is m_2. Find the mean of the set formed by combining the two sets of numbers.

Answer

$$m_1 = \frac{\sum_{i=1}^{n_1} X_i}{n_1} \quad \text{and} \quad m_2 = \frac{\sum_{k=1}^{n_2} Y_k}{n_2}$$

therefore

$$n_1 m_1 = \Sigma X_i \quad \text{and} \quad n_2 m_2 = \Sigma Y_k$$

The mean of the combined set is given by

$$m = \frac{\Sigma X_i + \Sigma Y_k}{n_1 + n_2}$$

$$= \frac{n_1 m_1 + n_2 m_2}{n_1 + n_2}$$

Example 2: Develop a formula for locating the lower quartile, Q_1, in grouped data.

Answer

By arguing as in section 2.5 for the median, we locate the lower quartile by finding its position in the class interval in which it is contained. We do this by finding the class containing Q_1 and then working out how far from the lower boundary of this class it will be. This gives

$$Q_1 = L_{Q_1} + \left(\frac{\frac{n}{4} - \sum_{i=1}^{Q_1 - 1} f_i}{f_{Q_1}} \right) \times c$$

where L_{Q_1} = the lower boundary of the class containing the quartile

n = the total frequencies

$\sum_{i=1}^{Q_1-1} f_i$ = those frequencies in the classes *below* the class containing the lower quartile

f_{Q_1} = the frequency of the class containing the lower quartile

c = the width of the class containing the lower quartile

Note that the part in the bracket represents the fraction of the way along the class interval Q_1 lies.

Example 3: Using the formula in *Example 2* find Q_1 for the 45 students of *Example 14* of Section 1.9.

Answer

$$n = 45, \text{ therefore } n/4 = 11{\cdot}25$$

There are ten items in the first three classes, and so Q_1 will lie in the fourth class. This gives

$$\sum_{i=1}^{Q_1-1} f_i = 10, \quad L_{Q_1} = 58{\cdot}5'', \quad f_{Q_1} = 8, \quad c = 3''$$

and

$$Q_1 = 58{\cdot}5'' + \frac{(11{\cdot}25 - 10)}{8} \times 3''$$

$$= 58{\cdot}97''$$

Exercise 2

1. Find the mean of the following sets:

(a) 1, 2
(b) 1, 2, 3
(c) 1, 2, 3, 4
(d) 1 to 5
(e) 1 to 6
(f) 1 to 7
(g) 1 to 8
(h) 1 to 9
(i) 1 to 10

What pattern emerges?
Compare the median of these sets with their means

2. Find the mean of the first n natural numbers

Answer

$$\frac{n+1}{2}$$

3. The mean of two numbers is 7·5. One is twice as big as the other. Find them

Answer
5 and 10

4. Four whole numbers in arithmetic progression have a mean of 15·5. Find them

Answer
14, 15, 16 and 17

5. Find the mean of the set of numbers

$$2, \; 5, \; 9, \; 11, \; 3$$

Add 4 to each number and again compute the mean
Add 5 to each number and again compute the mean
Add 6 to each number and again compute the mean
Add n to each number and again compute the mean
What pattern emerges?
Multiply each number by 2, 3, 4, etc. and again compute the means. Look for any pattern emerging

6. Prove that if 3 sets of numbers have n_1, n_2, n_3 elements respectively, and all have mean $\bar{x}$, then if the 3 sets are combined the mean of the resulting sets will be $\bar{x}$.

7. If the mean of 50 scores is 15, and the mean of another 100 scores is 16, what is the mean of the 150 scores. Does the answer suggest anything?

Answer
$15\frac{2}{3}$

8. The mean of a set of n_1 numbers is m_1, the mean of a set of n_2 numbers is m_2, the mean of a set of n_3 numbers is m_3. Show that the mean of the set formed by adding all three sets together is

$$\frac{n_1 m_1 + n_2 m_2 + n_3 m_3}{n_1 + n_2 + n_3}$$

9. Extend the previous question to 4, 5 and 6 different sets. Then extend the result to the general case.

10. The mean of 21 numbers is 13, the mean of 15 numbers is 9. What is the mean of the 36 numbers?

Answer

$$\frac{408}{36} = 11\tfrac{1}{3}$$

11. The mean of 13 numbers is 21, the mean of 9 numbers is 15. What is the mean of the 22 numbers?

Answer
18·54

12. In a mechanical aptitude test, the mean of 300 people tested was 65. Of this 300, 100 were ladies. If the mean score of these ladies was 55, what is the mean score of the men.

Answer
70

13. 250 pupils took an end of year exam and the mean score was 60. This group of 250 pupils was then divided into two groups having means of 63 and 57. How many pupils were put into each group.

Answer
125 in each group

14. Repeat the previous question if the mean of the two groups are 63 and 56.

Answer
107 and 143

15. A football team scores in successive matches 3, 1, 0, 4, 4, 2, 6, 7, 2 goals. What is the least number of goals the team must score in their next game to average more than 6 goals per match.

Answer
11 goals

16. Given the following distribution:

Class boundaries	Frequencies
0– 4	15
5– 9	12
10–14	12
15–19	10
20–24	2
25–29	1

Find the mean (a) without using an assumed mean
(b) using an assumed mean
(c) using a coding method
Find the median and the mode

Answer
mean = 9·6

17. Show (a) by induction
(b) by a dot pattern
that the sum of the first n odd numbers is n^2. Find the mean of the first n odd numbers. Relate your answer to the dot patterns.

Answer
$\bar{x} = n$

18. Given the following distribution

Class boundaries	Frequencies
0–	15
5–	12
10–	12
15–	10
20–	2
25–30	1

Find the arithmetic mean (a) without using an assumed mean
(b) using an assumed mean
(c) using a coding method
Compare the results with Question 16 and account for any differences or similarities. Find the median and the mode

19. Four pennies were tossed 100 times and the number of heads counted. The results were tabulated as:

Number of heads	0	1	2	3	4
Number of times the stated number of heads appeared	7	24	41	20	8

Find the mean, median and mode

20. Three sets of figures with 25, 40 and 75 scores had means of 10, 12, and 9 respectively. Find the mean of the three sets combined.

Answer
10·04

21. If $x_i = y_i + z_i$ for $i = 1, 2, 3, \ldots, n$, prove that $\bar{x} = \bar{y} + \bar{z}$

22. Extend the previous problem to $x_i = y_i + z_i + w_i$, and then to $x_i = a_i + b_i + \ldots + m_i$

23. Five people have annual incomes of £220, £350, £750, £750 and £35000. Find the mean, median and mode and discuss their relative merits as an average for this set.

Answer
mean = £7414, median = £750, mode = £750

24. Find the arithmetic mean, the median and the mode of the data in *Example 1* of Section 1.9.

Answer
arithmetic mean = 5·97, median = 6, mode = 7

25. Find the arithmetic mean, the median and the mode of the data in *Example 2* of Section 1.9.

Answer
arithmetic mean = 24·9, median = 24 from raw data, 25 from grouped data, mode = 28 from raw data

26. Find data concerned with the following and discuss the most suitable average to use

(i) Incomes/pocket money

(ii) Road accident figures

(iii) Toss 100 coins a large number of times and count the number of heads on each throw

(iv) Election votes

(v) The average number of letters per word in varying books – technical, literary, newspapers

27. Give examples to show when

(i) the mode would be a better average to use than the arithmetic mean

(ii) the mean, median and mode would all be equally satisfactory

(iii) the mode does not exist

(iv) the arithmetic mean would be a poor average to use

Invent similar questions to these and try to answer them

28. Which average is intended in the following situations:

(i) a cigarette kiosk sells, on average, 500 packets of 'Smoko' cigarettes a day

(ii) the average rain fall for March is 2·5 inches

(iii) the average number of children in a family is 2·4

(iv) the average number of children in a family is 2

(v) the average number of rooms in houses being built at the present time is 6

(vi) the average earnings of car workers

(vii) the average number of miles per gallon of petrol is 31

29. Can you think of situations whereby interested parties can take the same set of figures and by taking different averages draw different inferences?

30. Show that $\Sigma \mid x_i - k \mid$ is a minimum when k is the median. Can you think of a practical application of this property?

31. The number of persons per house in a street of ten houses were as follows:

9, 5, 4, 2, 2, 4, 5, 4, 3, 5

Find the arithmetic mean, the median and the mode. Which of these averages do you think is most representative of the data?

Answer

arithmetic mean = 4·3, median = 3, mode = 4

32. Write out in full

(i) $\sum_{i=1}^{5} X_i$ (ii) $\sum_{j=1}^{5} X_j^2$ (iii) $\sum_{t=1}^{7} W_t^3$

(iv) $\sum_{i=1}^{3} (X_i - A)$ (v) $\sum_{k=1}^{2} (X_k - Z)$ (vi) $\sum_{i=1}^{N} (X_i - B)$

Answer

(i) $X_1 + X_2 + X_3 + X_4 + X_5$

(ii) $X_1^2 + X_2^2 + X_3^2 + X_4^2 + X_5^2$

(iii) $W_1^3 + W_2^3 + W_3^3 + W_4^3 + W_5^3 + W_6^3 + W_7^3$

(iv) $(X_1 - A) + (X_2 - A) + (X_3 - A) = X_1 + X_2 + X_3 - 3A$

(v) $(X_1 - Z)^2 + (X_2 - Z)^2 = X_1^2 + X_2^2 - 2Z(X_1 + X_2) + 2Z^2$

(vi) $(X_1 - B) + (X_2 - B) + \ldots + (X_N - B) = X_1 + X_2 + \ldots + X_N - NB$

33. Condense by using sigma notation

(i) $Y_1 + Y_2 + Y_3 + Y_4 + Y_5$

(ii) $Y_1^2 + Y_2^2 + Y_3^2 + Y_4^2$

(iii) $Z_1^3 + Z_2^3 + \ldots + Z_N^3$

(iv) $X_1 + X_2 + X_3 + X_4 - 4A$

(v) $X_1^2 + X_2^2 + X_3^2 - 2A(X_1 + X_2 + X_3) + 3A^2$

(vi) $X_1(X_1 - 2A) + X_2(X_2 - 2A) + X_3(X_3 - 2A) + X_4(X_4 - 2A)$

Answer

(i) $\sum_{i=1}^{5} Y_i$ (ii) $\sum_{k=1}^{4} Y_k^2$ (iii) $\sum_{i=1}^{N} Z_i^3$

(iv) $\sum_{i=1}^{4} (X_i - A)$ (v) $\sum_{k=1}^{3} (X_k - A)^2$ (vi) $\sum_{L=1}^{4} X_L(X_L - 2A)$

34. Prove that

(i) $\sum_{i=1}^{N} (aX_i + b) = a \sum_{i=1}^{N} X_i + Nb$

(ii) $\sum_{i=1}^{N} (aX_i + b)^2 = a^2 \sum_{i=1}^{N} X_i^2 + 2ab \sum_{i=1}^{N} X_i + Nb^2$

(iii) $\sum_{i=1}^{N} (aX_i + b)^3 = a^3 \sum_{i=1}^{N} X_i^3 + 3a^2b \sum_{i=1}^{N} X_i^2 + 3ab^2 \sum_{i=1}^{N} X_i + Nb^3$

35. Given $\bar{X} = \dfrac{\sum_{i=1}^{N} X_i}{N}$ prove that

(i) $\sum_{i=1}^{N} (X_i - \bar{X})^2 = \sum_{i=1}^{N} X_i^2 - \bar{X}^2$

(ii) $\sum_{i=1}^{N} (X_i - \bar{X}) = 0$

(iii) $\sum_{i=1}^{N} (aX_i^2 - b\bar{X})^2 = a^2 \sum_{i=1}^{N} X_i^4 - 2ab\bar{X} \sum_{i=1}^{N} (X_i - \bar{X}) + 2ab\bar{X}^3 + Nb^2\bar{X}^2$

36. Show that

(i) $\sum_{i=1}^{N} (X_i + a)(X_i + b) = \sum_{i=1}^{N} X_iY_i + a \sum_{i=1}^{N} Y_i + b \sum_{i=1}^{N} X_i + Nab$

(ii) $\sum_{k=1}^{17} X_k(X_k + a) = \sum_{k=1}^{17} X_k^2 + a \sum_{k=1}^{17} X_k$

(iii) $\sum_{j=1}^{100} X_j(X_j - b)^2 = \sum_{j=1}^{100} X_j^3 - 2b \sum_{j=1}^{100} X_j^2 + b^2 \sum_{j=1}^{100} X_j$

37. Produce formulae similar to that of *Example 2* of Section 2.7 for locating (a) the median (b) the upper quartile (c) the tenth decile (d) the ninetieth decile, in grouped data.

38. Find Q_3 for the 45 students of *Example 3* of Section 1.9.

Answer

67·39″

3 Measures of Dispersion

3.1 Introduction

In the last chapter we considered ways of summarising in averages the centre of a distribution. It may have been evident to the reader that, although the location of the centre of a distribution is important, there is another characteristic of a distribution which is also significant, namely the way the distribution is arranged around its centre.

In the diagram we see the outline of two distributions that have the same centre – and would have equivalent arithmetic means, medians and modes – but are obviously quite different in character.

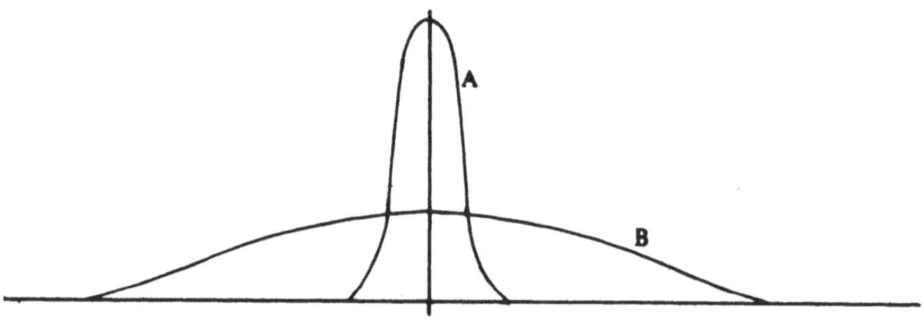

Fig. 3.1 (a)

The majority of distribution A is packed close to the centre while that of distribution B is spaced much further out. Thus it is clear that averages alone will tell us little, or nothing, about the way a distribution is dispersed.

What we wish to find then is some way of indicating how a distribution is arranged around its centre. As in all statistics it has to be a quantitative rather than qualitative, and, in the case of distributions A and B above, we would want a number, or numbers, that would show distribution A to be less dispersed than distribution B. What we want then is a number such that the larger it is the greater the degree of dispersion.

At this point the reader is invited to leave this text and see if he might make an educated guess as to how this might be done – thus placing himself in the position of the early statisticians.

Other words that are used to describe dispersion are *scatter* and *variation*.

The way a distribution is dispersed can have important consequences in several ways. For example, obviously a car manufacturer must know the average leg length of people, but he must also know what variation to expect in this measure so that he can provide the necessary facilities for adjustment so that as many people as possible are catered for adequately. It is important too in statistical theory to know how distributions are dispersed as a knowledge of this is a prerequisite for such facets of statistics as decision making, confidence limits, and so on, and these in turn have practical applications.

Another important feature about the dispersion of a distribution is whether or not it is symmetrical. Clearly distributions which are symmetrical are distinctly different from those which are asymmetrical or *skewed*.

Again a quantitative measure of skewness is required and – to anticipate a little – it must indicate not only the degree of skewness but also whether it is skewed to the right or to the left.

It will be seen that when we have not only its averages but also some measure of its dispersion and skewness we can more accurately describe any given distribution.

Finally it can be pointed out that not only can individual distributions be better described but comparisons with other distributions can be made with greater facility.

3.2 The Range

One of the first ways that dispersion might be measured is in terms of the range – this has already been defined in Section 1.9 as the difference between the highest variate and the lowest variate. For certain situations – such as the comparison of similar distributions – this can be very useful since it is very easy to find and understand. However if distributions are differently dispersed they may well have the same range as in the figures below, and thus it can be seen that the range alone is very much a blunt instrument and will fail to discriminate various differences as suggested by the figure. This is because the range is in no way connected to the centre of the distribution and therefore can tell us nothing about the dispersion of the distribution with respect to its centre.

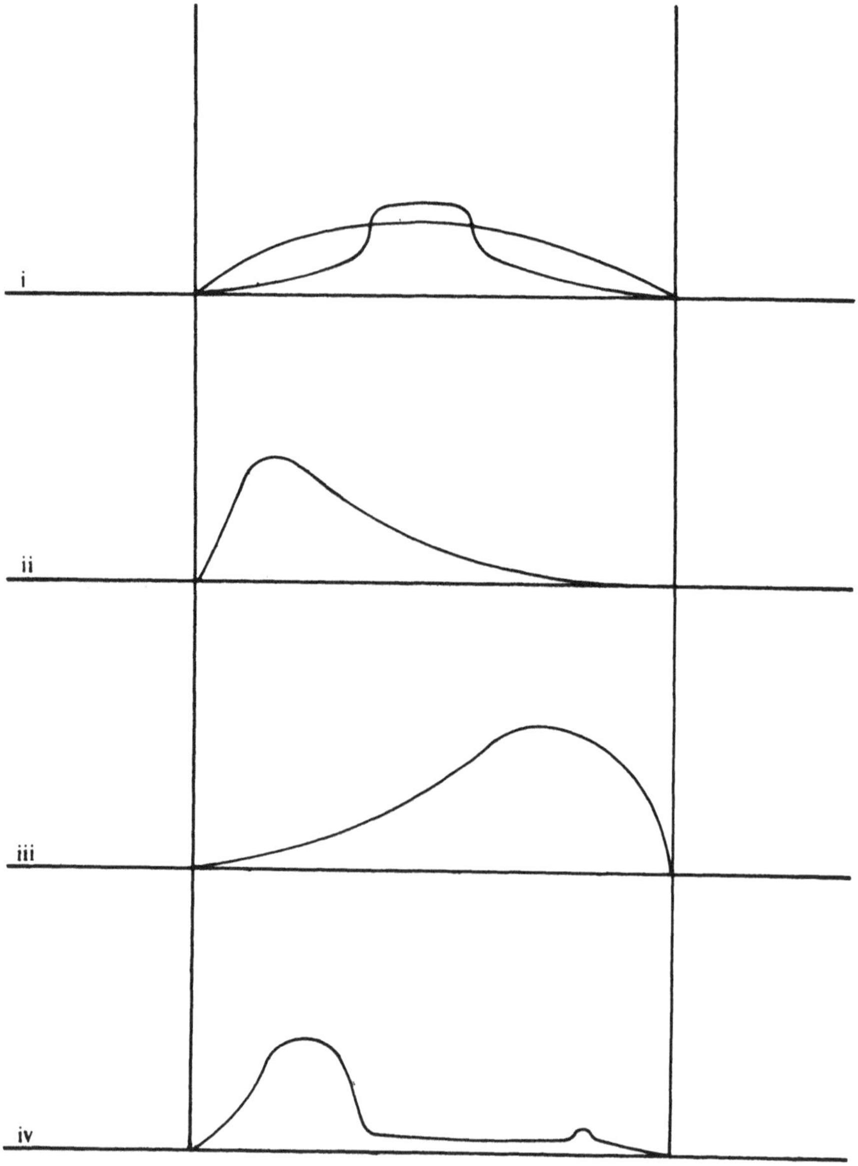

Fig. 3.2 (a)

Since the range depends solely upon the extreme values in the set the presence of an outrider can considerably affect it. In this case we can only know the full range but, if the outrider were removed, then the new range might be quite useful – the graph of Fig. 3.2(a) (iv) indicates this point clearly.

The range is capable of quite a degree of variation in itself depending on the size of the set of data, particularly if this set of data is a sample from a population. If the sample is small then the range will tend to be small. If the sample is large then it will tend to be more representative of the population and contain the full range of the population. This point is important when the question of the relationship of a sample to a population is considered.

Finally it can be said that the range is a frequently used statistic. Two examples of its use will suffice. The financial papers in their reports of the Stock Exchange dealings usually include a high and a low figure for the price of individual shares over a given period – the difference between these two being the range. Medical reports too commonly use the idea of the range.

3.3 The Mean Deviation

In the previous section it was suggested that a measure of dispersion in some way connected with the centre of a distribution may be of more use than any other and so we follow this line of thought. There are several possibilities. We could take the mean as the particular measure of central tendency and subtract it from the highest value of the distribution. This would tell us how far above the centre the highest value lies. We could then subtract the mean from the lowest value of the distribution and this should give us some indication of how far below the mean the lowest value lies. e.g.

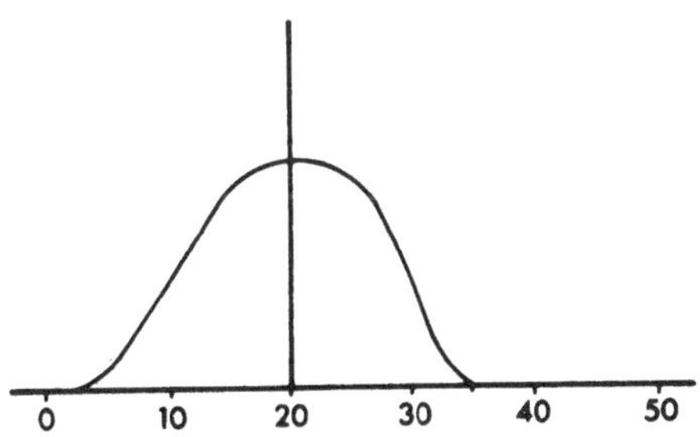

Fig. 3.3(a)

the mean = 20 highest value = 35 lowest value = 3

35 – 20 = 15, therefore the highest value is 15 units from the mean.
3 – 20 = –17. What does this tell us? We can see that the lowest value

is 17 units below the mean but if we carry out the same operation for this second part as we did for the first we get a negative answer, and it only requires a little thought to realise that if this process is carried out for any distribution then there will be a positive and a negative number each time. We can refine this idea if we make use of the notion of absolute value. The *absolute value* of a number is defined to be that positive number with which it may be associated:

e.g. the absolute value of $+16 = 16$
the absolute value of $-12 = 12$

thus all that happens when absolute values are taken is to take the number normally if it is positive and reverse the sign if it is negative. It is sometimes called the *modulus* of the number and is denoted by two vertical lines on either side of the number, i.e. $|-12| = 12$. It is in effect a measure of how far from the origin a number lies. $+13$ is the same distance from the origin as -13. It follows that $|0| = 0$. Going back to our example now will enable us to take the two numbers 15 and 17 as measures of the extremes from the mean. They might be put in brackets, (17, 15) as an ordered pair such that the first number always refers to the lower extreme and the second to the upper extreme.

Let us reverse the process now and see what can be deduced from numbers taken at random.

Example 1: Given a distribution has mean 55, and a bracket value (10, 45). We plot these figures below:

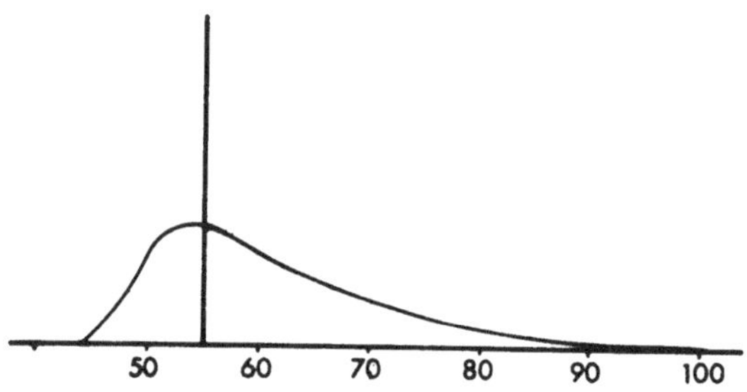

Fig. 3.3 (b)

and it can be seen that these figures suggest the distribution drawn. This looks promising then, but let us take another example.

Example 2: Given a distribution has a mean of 40, and a bracket value (10, 9). We plot these figures below:

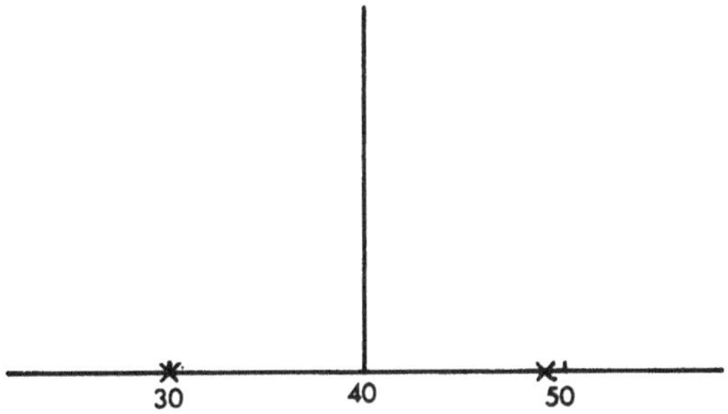

Fig. 3.3(c)

but we can draw more than one distribution through them as follows:

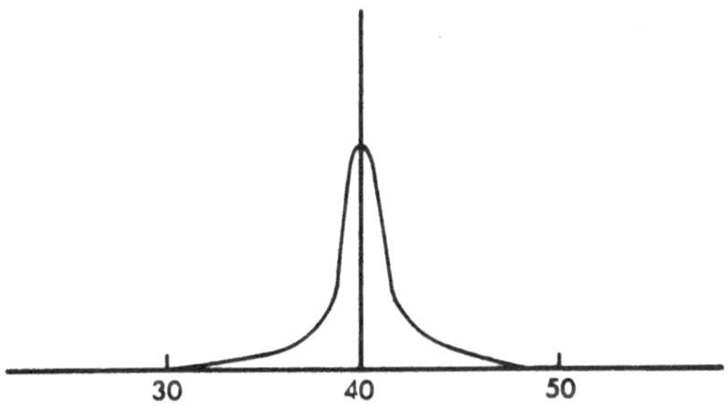

Fig. 3.3(d)

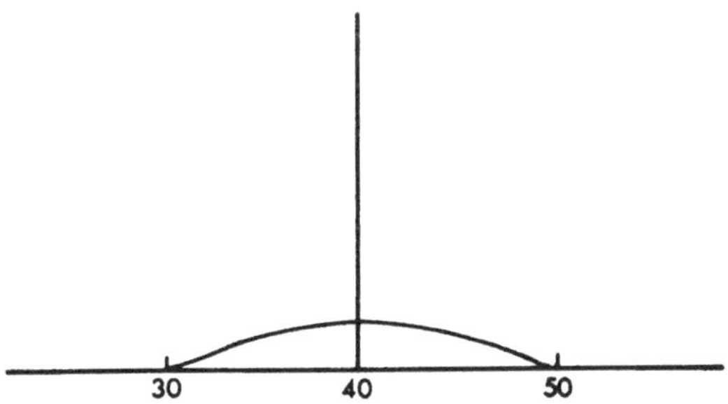

Fig. 3.3(e)

and both of these would be reasonable curves to draw. In the first case the values are closely packed round the mean and in the second they are dispersed more widely. From the figures alone then we are not able to deduce the exact shape of the distribution. The reason for this is that only two of the variates in the distribution – and the extreme ones at that – make any contribution in the computation. The question therefore arises, 'Can we make it so that all the variates make a contribution?' The answer to this is that we can. We therefore take from each variate the mean, take the modulus of the result and add them together. In symbols this is:

$$\sum_{i=1}^{N} |X_i - \bar{X}|$$

and this gives us the sum of the deviation of the variates from the mean. What we want is an idea of the average spread of the deviation and so we divide by the number of variates in the distribution to finally get the *mean deviation* denoted by

$$\text{M.D.} = \frac{\sum_{i=1}^{N} |X_i - \bar{X}|}{N}$$

A better phrase to use would be the *absolute mean deviation* but common usage has settled on the first version.

Example 3: Find the mean deviation of the set

1, 2, 5, 7, 7, 8, 10, 16

Answer

The mean is $\frac{56}{8} = 7$

$$\begin{aligned} &|1-7|+|2-7|+|5-7|+|7-7|+|7-7|+|8-7|+|10-7|+|16-7| \\ &= |-6|+|-5|+|-2|+|0|+|0|+|1|+|3|+|9| \\ &= 6+5+2+0+0+1+3+9 \\ &= 26 \end{aligned}$$

therefore, *mean deviation* $= \dfrac{26}{8} = 3{\cdot}25$

For sets which contain numbers with frequencies higher than one we make the following modification:

$$\text{M.D.} = \frac{\sum_{i=1}^{M} f_i |X_i - \bar{X}|}{\sum_{i=1}^{M} f_i}$$

where $\sum_{i=1}^{M} f_i = N$ and this will also apply to data in class intervals, the X_i are taken as the class mid-points and the f_i as the frequency of the class.

An example showing the best method of setting out the table is given below.

Example 3: Find the mean deviation of the distribution given in the first two columns of the table below

X_i	f_i	f_iX_i	$\lvert X_i - \bar{X} \rvert$	$f_i \lvert X_i - \bar{X} \rvert$
0	2	0	2·4	4·8
1	3	3	1·4	4·2
2	5	10	0·4	2·0
3	4	12	0·6	2·4
4	5	20	1·6	8·0
	$\sum_{i=1}^{5} f_i = 19$	$\sum_{i=1}^{5} f_iX_i = 45$		21·4

$$\bar{X} = \frac{\Sigma f_iX_i}{\Sigma f_i} = \frac{45}{19} = 2{\cdot}4 \text{ approximately}$$

$$\text{M.D.} = \frac{\Sigma f_i \lvert X_i - \bar{X} \rvert}{\Sigma f_i} = \frac{21{\cdot}4}{19} = 1{\cdot}1$$

We now have a measure of dispersion which takes account of all the variates in a distribution, is fairly easy to compute and understand. It must be noted that we took the mean as our measure of central tendency at the beginning of this section, and it would have been possible to carry out exactly the same sort of discussion by starting with the mode, or the median. In these latter cases we would have arrived at the *absolute mode deviation* and the *absolute median deviation* respectively. It is pointed out that this latter choice of the median is in one respect a better choice than the mean. It was set in Exercise 2 (question 30) to thow that the quantity $\Sigma \lvert x_i - k \rvert$ is a minimum when k equals the median and this makes the median a more natural choice. However the difference between use of the mean and the median is quite small.

Because of its simplicity it can be understood by people with little knowledge of statistical methods.

Usually the mean deviation is used with small samples and when further investigation is likely to be limited – it is rarely used with large samples and grouped data.

If the distribution is normal or only slightly skewed then 57·5% of the items are within the range $\bar{X} \pm$ the mean deviation, Fig. 3.3(f).

Perhaps the biggest drawback of the mean deviation is the fact that given several groups of data and their respective mean deviations, it is not possible algebraically to find the mean deviation of the group formed

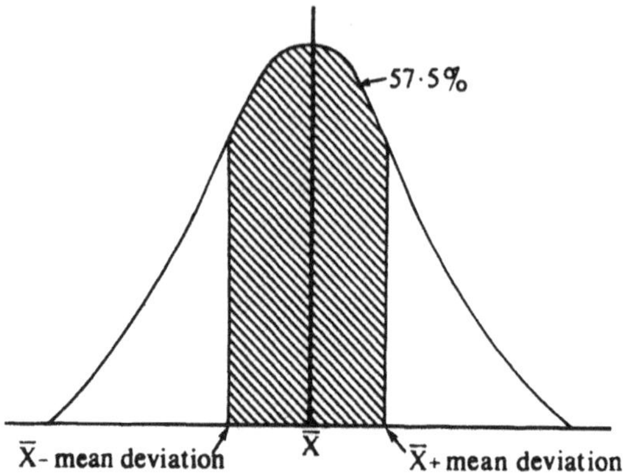

Fig. 3.3(f)

by combining these groups. In order to find the combined mean deviation the groups have to be combined and the computation carried out from the beginning. Because of this deficiency in its capacity for algebraic manipulation it is not used a great deal. Preference is given to a measure called the standard deviation which does not have this defect. We now turn to consider this.

3.4 The Variance – The Standard Deviation

A simple device that can be used to convert negative numbers into positive ones – apart from taking their moduli – is the process of squaring.

Example 1:

$$(+4)^2 = 16 \qquad (-4)^2 = 16 \qquad (-9)^2 = 81$$

and so instead of using moduli we can now use squares. The mean is subtracted from each X_i to give

$$(X_i - \bar{X}) \quad \text{[the deviation of } X_i \text{ from } \bar{X}\text{]}$$

this is then squared

$$(X_i - \bar{X})^2$$

and we get the square of the deviation of X_i from the mean. All these can then be added to give

$$\sum_{i=1}^{N} (X_i - \bar{X})^2$$

which is the sum of the squares of the deviation from the mean. And, as before, we want an average value of this, so we divide by N to get

$$s^2 = \frac{\sum_{i=1}^{N} (X_i - \bar{X})^2}{N}$$

and this quantity, denoted by s^2, is called the variance, i.e. the *variance* of a distribution is the mean of the squares of the deviations from the mean. N.B. The word 'mean' is used here in two senses. There is the mean of the squares, obtained by dividing the sum of the squares by N, and then there is the mean, $\bar{X}$, of the distribution.

The disadvantage of this is that by virtue of squaring we have moved away from the dimensions of the original data, i.e. if our original data had been in inches, then the variance is in square inches.

It is much more convenient to talk about the spread of a distribution in terms of the original units, and we can do this if we make use of the reverse process of squaring, i.e. taking square roots.

Example 2:

(i) the square root of 25, written $\sqrt{25} = +5$, or -5 since $(+5)^2 = 25$, and $(-5)^2 = 25$

(ii) the square root of 2, written $\sqrt{2} = +1{\cdot}414$, or $-1{\cdot}414$ (to three decimal places)

thus we can see that every time we take a square root we will get two answers, one positive, and the other negative, but whose moduli are equal.

Since we want this result as a measure, and it is more convenient to measure in postive units, the positive sign is always taken and the negative result discarded.

This finally gives us

$$s = \sqrt{\frac{\Sigma (X_i - \bar{X})^2}{N}}$$

and is called the standard deviation of the distribution. The *standard deviation* of a distribution is the positive square root of the mean of the squares of the deviation from the mean. The phrase *root mean square* is frequently used as an abbreviation.

Example 3: Find the variance and the standard deviation of the set

1, 2, 5, 7, 7, 8, 10, 16

Answer

The mean is $\frac{56}{8} = 7$, therefore

$$(1-7)^2+(2-7)^2+(5-7)^2+(7-7)^2+(7-7)^2+(8-7)^2+(10-7)^2+(16-7)^2$$
$$= (-6)^2+(-5)^2+(-2)^2+(0)^2+(0)^2+(1)^2+(3)^2+(9)^2$$
$$= 36+25+4+0+0+1+9+81$$
$$= 156$$

$$\text{Variance} = \frac{156}{8} = 19{\cdot}5$$

$$\text{Standard deviation} = \sqrt{19{\cdot}5} = 4{\cdot}42$$

The above formula applies to sets of numbers where the frequency of each element in the set is unity. Where the frequencies are greater than unity the following modification is made:

$$s^2 = \frac{\sum_{i=1}^{M} f_i (X_i - \bar{X})^2}{\sum_{i=1}^{M} f_i} \qquad \text{where } \sum_{i=1}^{M} f_i = N$$

In words this says, subtract the mean from each variate, square the result, multiply by the frequency of the variate, add, and then divide by the total number of frequencies. This latter form can also be used for dealing with data grouped into class intervals. The X_i are taken as the class mid-points and f_i as the frequency of the class. *Example 4* shows the best way of setting down a table.

Example 4: Find the variance and standard deviation of the frequency table of *Example 3* of Section 3.3.

X_i	f_i	f_iX_i	$X_i - \bar{X}$	$(X_i - \bar{X})^2$	$f_i(X_i - \bar{X})^2$
0	2	0	−2·4	5·76	11·52
1	3	3	−1·4	1·96	5·88
2	5	10	−0·4	0·16	0·80
3	4	12	0·6	0·36	1·44
4	5	20	1·6	2·56	12·80
Total	19	45			32·44

$$\bar{X} = 2{\cdot}4 \text{ approximately}$$

$$s^2 = \frac{32{\cdot}44}{19} = 1{\cdot}7 \text{ approximately}$$

$$s = \sqrt{1{\cdot}7} = 1{\cdot}3 \text{ approximately}$$

It will be seen that the computation of the standard deviation involves a fair amount of arithmetical labour – even in the example above which is much smaller than one meets in practice – and the student may wonder why such a measure is used if it is so labourious to calculate. The answer to this is that there is an easier method of computation. The labour is reduced by taking an assumed mean and working from that, in much the same way as we shortened the labour involved in the calculation of the mean by taking an assumed mean. Unfortunately the idea is not as intuitive as in the case of the mean and we have to rely upon algebraic manipulation to arrive at the method.

Before we begin, the following results are recalled:

(1) $$\bar{X} = A + \frac{\Sigma (X_i - A)}{N}$$

(2) $$(\bar{X} - A) = \frac{\Sigma (X_i - A)}{N}$$

(3) $$\sum_{i=1}^{N} K = NK \quad \text{(where } K \text{ is a constant)}$$

(4) $$\sum_{i=1}^{N} a(X_i + b) = a \sum_{i=1}^{N} (X_i + b)$$

We now begin with $(X_i - \bar{X})$. This is the same as $(X_i - A) - (X - A)$. We can say therefore that

$$[X_i - \bar{X}]^2 = [(X_i - A) - (\bar{X} - A)]^2$$

and so

$$s^2 = \frac{\Sigma [X_i - \bar{X}]^2}{N} = \frac{\Sigma [(X_i - A) - (\bar{X} - A)]^2}{N}$$

$$= \frac{\Sigma [(X_i - A)^2 - 2(X_i - A)(\bar{X} - A) + (\bar{X} - A)^2]}{N}$$

$$= \frac{\Sigma (X_i - A)^2 - 2(\bar{X} - A)\, \Sigma (X_i - A) + \Sigma (\bar{X} - A)^2}{N}$$

$$= \frac{\Sigma (X_i - A)^2}{N} - \frac{2(\bar{X} - A)\, \Sigma (X_i - A)}{N} + \frac{N(\bar{X} - A)^2}{N}$$

but using (2) this becomes

$$= \frac{\Sigma (X_i - A)^2}{N} - 2(\bar{X} - A)^2 + (\bar{X} - A)^2$$

$$= \frac{\Sigma (X_i - A)^2}{N} - (\bar{X} - A)^2$$

In words, this says subtract an assumed mean from each X_i, square, add, and divide by N, then subtract the square of the difference between the assumed mean and the real mean, and this will give the variance. To get the standard deviation, as before, just take the square root. This last formula can be adapted for variates with frequencies greater than unity as follows:

$$s^2 = \frac{\sum^{M} f_i (X_i - A)^2}{\sum_{i=1}^{M} f_i} - (\bar{X} - A)^2$$

the student should work through the process for himself to get this result.

We now give a complete example of finding the mean, variance and standard deviation by the assumed mean method.

Example 5:

Class Interval	Class mark X_i	Frequency f_i	$(X_i - A)$ $X_i - 23$	$f_i (X_i - A)$ $f_i (X_i - 23)$	$(X_i - A)^2$ $(X_i - 23)^2$	$f_i (X_i - A)^2$ $f_i (X_i - 23)^2$
1– 5	3	3	−20	− 60	400	1200
6–10	8	6	−15	− 90	225	1350
11–15	13	11	−10	−110	100	1100
16–20	18	16	− 5	− 80	25	400
21–25	23	18	0	−340		
26–30	28	18	5	90	25	450
31–35	33	7	10	70	100	490
36–40	38	12	15	180	225	2700
41–45	43	7	20	140	400	2800
46–50	48	2	25	50	625	1250
Total		100		190		11740

$$\bar{X} = A + \frac{\sum f_i (X_i - A)}{\sum f_i} = 23 + \frac{190}{100} = 23 + 1{\cdot}9$$

$$\therefore \quad \bar{X} = 24{\cdot}9$$

Also

$$\bar{X} - A = \frac{\sum f_i (X_i - A)}{\sum f_i}$$

$$\therefore \quad \bar{X} - 23 = \frac{190}{100} = 1{\cdot}9$$

and

$$(\bar{X} - 23)^2 = (1{\cdot}9)^2 = 3{\cdot}61$$

$$s^2 = \frac{\Sigma f_i (X_i - A)^2}{\Sigma f_i} - (\bar{X} - A)^2$$

$$= \frac{11740}{100} - 3{\cdot}61 = 117{\cdot}4 - 3{\cdot}61$$

$$\therefore \quad s^2 = 113{\cdot}79$$

and $$s = 10{\cdot}7 \text{ approximately}$$

Drawing attention to the $(X_i - 23)$ column of this distribution we note that all the numbers in it are multiples of 5. We noted a similar feature when we calculated the mean of grouped data and used it to obtain the coding method for finding the mean. It is possible to perform an analogous analysis for the standard deviation and variance and the following result will be obtained

$$s^2 = \frac{c^2 \left\{ \Sigma f_i \left(\frac{X_i - A}{c} \right)^2 \right\}}{\Sigma f_i} - (\bar{X} - A)^2$$

and this can be used when data is grouped into equal class intervals. This method is by far the quickest when dealing with large sets of data and should be used whenever possible.

From

$$s^2 = \frac{\Sigma f_i (X_i - \bar{X})^2}{N}$$

can be deduced

$$s^2 = \frac{\Sigma f_i X_i^2}{N} - \bar{X}^2$$

in just the same way as before, i.e. expanding the square bracket, taking the summation sign through the bracket, substituting $\bar{X}$ for its equivalent and simplifying. This form is useful if the distribution has few variates with low frequencies, and the X_i's are small.

To summarise now all the various alternative methods of finding the standard deviation and variance are collected below. It should be noted that all the shorter methods are derived from the definition in identical fashions and if the reader works through several the point made earlier about algebraic properties will be meaningful. The similarities of their form should also be noted.

(1) Frequencies of unity

Definition

$$s^2 = \frac{\Sigma (X_i - \bar{X})^2}{N}$$

Short method

$$s^2 = \frac{\Sigma X^2}{N} - \bar{X}^2$$

(2) Frequencies greater than unity.
Definition

$$s^2 = \frac{\Sigma f_i (X_i - \bar{X})^2}{\Sigma f_i}$$

Short method

$$s^2 = \frac{\Sigma f_i X_i^2}{N} - \bar{X}^2$$

(3) Grouped data

As in (2) with X_i as the class mark, and f_i as the class frequency.

(4) Assumed mean method
Definition

$$s^2 = \frac{\Sigma f_i (X_i - \bar{X})^2}{\Sigma f_i}$$

Short method

$$s^2 = \frac{\Sigma f_i (X_i - A)^2}{\Sigma f_i} - (\bar{X} - A)^2$$

(5) Assumed mean method plus coding
Short method

$$s^2 = \frac{c^2 \left\{ \Sigma f_i \left(\frac{X_i - A}{c} \right)^2 \right\}}{\Sigma f_i} - (\bar{X} - A)^2$$

where A is the assumed mean and c is the class interval.

In all the algebraic manipulations performed with the standard deviation and variance, it is far better to work with the variance, as the square root sign required for the standard deviation can inhibit manipulation.

When this section was started the measure of central tendency that was taken was the mean. There was no necessity to take the mean. Any other centre would have done and exactly similar lines followed, but the mean was used so as not to draw in too many tricky points at one time. In fact it is possible to define a very general variance as follows

$$s^2 = \frac{\sum_{i=1}^{M} f_i (X_i - K)^2}{\sum_{1}^{M} f_i}$$

where K refers to any number whatsoever. This would then be the mean of the squares of the deviations about the point K. One of the reasons for taking the deviations about $\bar{X}$ is that of all the possible values of K, $K = \bar{X}$ produces a minimum value.

An important property of the standard deviation is that if the distribution is normal then about two thirds of the variates lie within one standard deviation from the mean i.e.

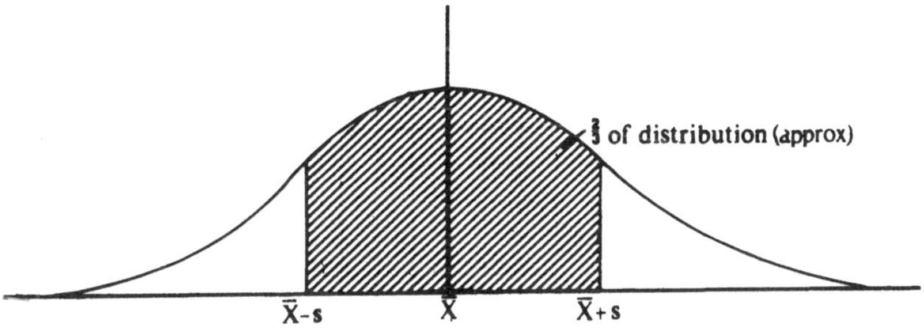

Fig. 3.4 (a)

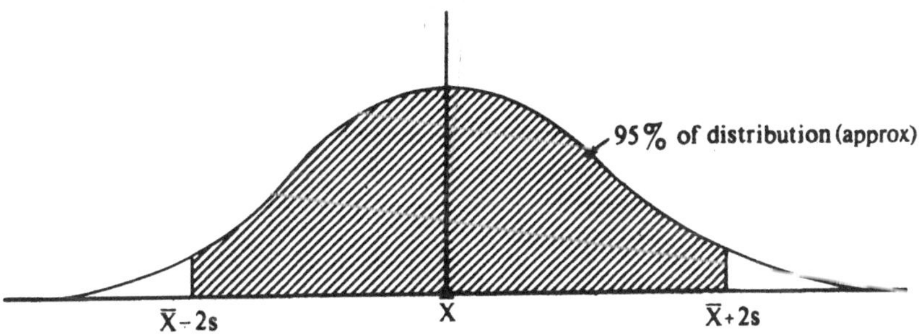

Fig. 3.4 (b)

About 95% of the variates of a distribution lie within two standard deviations from the mean, and about the whole of the distribution will lie within three standard deviations from the mean.

The standard deviation is the most important and widely used measure of dispersion. It is, however, more difficult to compute and understand than either the range of the mean deviation and can only be employed when the audience for which the information is intended has some understanding of its nature. Later on it will be seen that it plays an important part in statistical inference.

It will be noted that the standard deviation satisfies the condition expressed as being required at the beginning of Section 3.1 namely, that if the distribution is widely dispersed, then it will have a large value, but if the distribution is more narrowly concentrated it will have a smaller value. Thus because the standard deviation gives a measure of variability in respect of the mean – because the mean is used in its computation – a low standard deviation will tell us immediately that the distribution to which it belongs is concentrated round the mean.

The standard deviation is useful in comparing two sets of data. Suppose certain identical articles are produced by two different manufacturers A and B and that they both claim a mean life of $\bar{X}$ hours for their products.

Suppose now we have a purchaser who fits these articles in such a way that he must have at least a certain time a before any of them burn out. Let us now suppose that $\bar{X}$ is bigger than a. This purchaser must now examine the variability of these products before he can make a decision whether to purchase or not. Let us finally suppose that the variability of A's articles are less than the variability of B's. We could easily have the situation as shown in the following diagram.

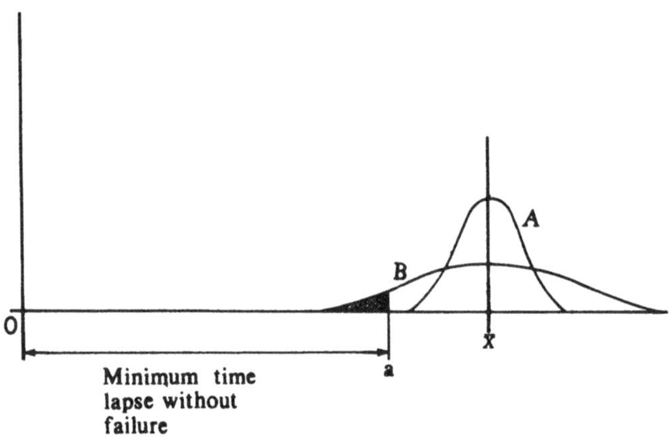

Fig. 3.4(c)

It will be seen that the greater dispersion of B's articles would make it impossible for this purchaser to buy them because a few of those bought would burn out before the minimum time lapse. The proportion of those articles that would burn out is shown shaded.

Because A's dispersion is less, those of his articles that burn out first – the left hand part of the graph – do so *after* the minimum time lapse. This would make A's products a possible purchase in this instance.

In order to make this decision it is obvious that the purchaser had to have knowledge of the variability of the articles and this variability is expressed in the standard deviation.

Other considerations are, of course, also possible in situations like this – the reader should try to think of examples for himself – but it always is necessary to know the standard deviation in order to make a decision correctly.

3.5 The Coefficient of Variation

If two – or more – distributions have the same mean then their variability may be compared by looking at their standard deviations; the one with the highest standard deviation being more variable than the other(s). If however two distributions do not have the same mean how can we compare their variability? First of all we note that if we are to compare variability we want relative and not absolute variability. *Absolute variability* or *absolute dispersion* is the measure of dispersion itself, e.g. a distribution has mean 90″ and standard deviation 13·5″. The absolute dispersion is 13·5″ and is in the same units of measurement as the variable. *Relative dispersion* is absolute dispersion divided by a measure of central tendency, i.e.

$$\text{Relative dispersion} = \frac{\text{Absolute dispersion}}{\text{Measure of central tendency}}$$

and because the absolute dispersion and the measure of central tendency are in the same units the relative dispersion is dimensionless i.e. just a number. If we restricted ourselves to the mean, median and mode as measures of central tendency, and to range, mean deviation and standard deviation as measures of dispersion then we could form nine fractions that would comply with the above definition of relative dispersion. The most commonly used one is

$$V = \frac{s}{\bar{X}}$$

and is called the *coefficient of variation* or the *coefficient of dispersion*, and is usually expressed as a percentage by multiplying by 100.

Example 1: Distribution A has mean 90″ and standard deviation 13·5″, the corresponding figures for distribution B are 83″ and 12·4″. Find their coefficients of variation.

Answer

For distribution *A*,

$$\frac{13 \cdot 5}{90} = 0 \cdot 1535$$

therefore, $V = 15 \cdot 35\%$

For distribution *B*,

$$\frac{12 \cdot 4}{84} = 0 \cdot 1494$$

therefore $V = 14 \cdot 94\%$

We conclude therefore that distribution *A* is more widely dispersed than distribution *B* in the sense of relative dispersion.

There are two limitation to the use of this coefficient of variation. If the mean of a distribution is close to zero then its coefficient of variation will be large – too large to be of any use. In comparing distributions it is not possible to compare them in this way if their means differ significantly – for instance two distributions may be identically distributed but about means of 10 and 80 and in this case the coefficient of variation of the distribution with mean 10 will be much larger than the other one. This again points to the fact that statistical techniques must not be used blindly but with due regard to the circumstances of each case.

3.6 Skewness

To describe adequately and summarise adequately a distribution we need, apart from some idea of its points of greatest density and its measure of variability, some idea as to its symmetry or asymmetry. If we look at Fig. 3.6(a) we can see that the two distributions have the same arithmetic mean and the same standard deviation but they are obviously very different.

What we want therefore is some quantitative measure that will indicate what degree and type of skewness is possessed by a distribution. The higher the degree of skewness the larger this number must be and at the same time the type of skewness must be indicated. This is done by associating a *negative* number with *negative* skewness (curve *A* in the following diagram) and a *positive* number with positive skewness. If there is no skewness, i.e. the distribution is symmetrical, then this is indicated by zero. These ideas are indicated in Fig. 3.6 (b).

The problem now arises in the finding of such a number. To motivate this let us consider the positions of the two measures of central tendency

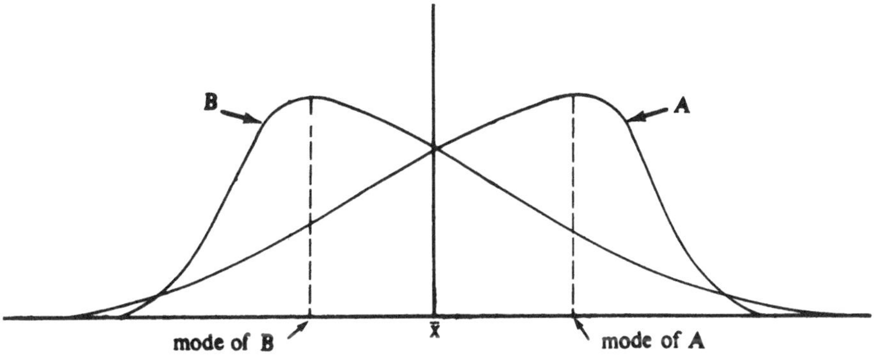

Fig. 3.6 (a)

the arithmatice mean and the mode in relation to the skewed distribution. In Fig. 3.6 (a) we see that curve A is negatively skewed. The arithmetic mean – influenced by all the smaller numbers – is pulled to the left of the mode. The opposite case is noted for curve B – the arithmetic mean is pulled to the right of the mode because of the higher values in the tail.

If we now consider the quantity

$$\text{mean} - \text{mode}$$

we see that for curve B, it is positive and for curve A, it is negative. It can also be seen that the more the skewness the more this quantity will increase. This, then, would seem to be a suitable measure of skewness but it is open to the objection that it would, as it stands, be a number still in the units of the variable, i.e. inches, miles, hours and so on.

To convert this from an absolute measure to a relative measure in a dimensionless form we divide by the standard deviation to finally get what is known as *Pearson's first coefficient of skewness*:

$$Sk_1 = \frac{\text{mean} - \text{mode}}{\text{standard deviation}} = \frac{\bar{X} - \text{mode}}{s} \qquad (1)$$

In theory there is no limit to the value this can take but in practice it is rarely very large and for moderately skewed unimodal distributions usually lies between $+1$ and -1.

We recall now the difficulties in the location of the mode and because of these there can be some inconvenience in the calculation of the skewness of a distribution by the above formula. One way – there are several – of circumventing this difficulty in the case of moderately skewed

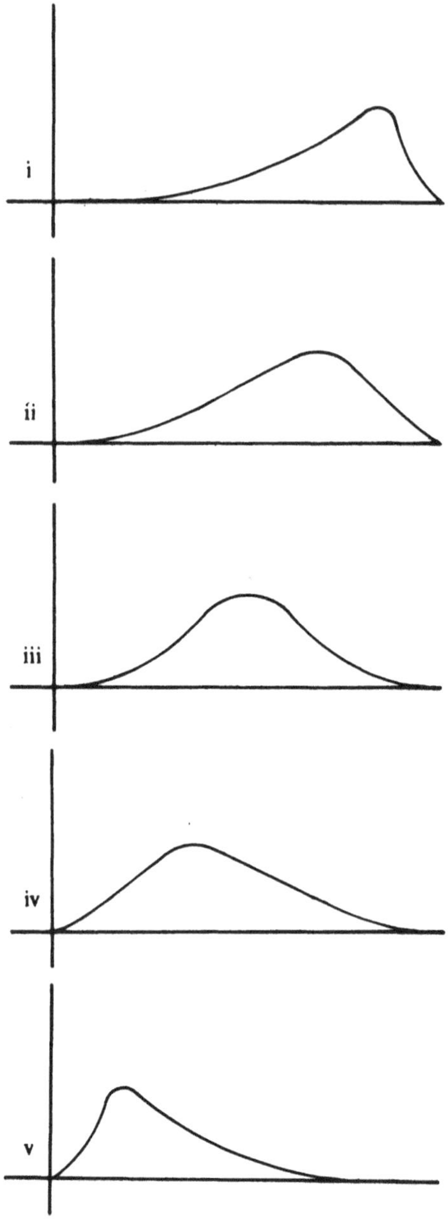

	type of skewness	number will be
i	high degree of negative skewness	large negative
ii	small degree of negative skewness	small negative
iii	no skewness	zero
iv	small degree of positive skewness	small positive
v	high degree of positive skewness	large positive

Fig. 3.6 (b)

distributions is to recall the empirical relation

$$\text{mean} - \text{mode} = 3(\text{mean} - \text{median})$$

and substitute this. This gives *Pearson's second coefficient of skewness*

$$Sk_2 = \frac{3(\text{mean} - \text{median})}{\text{standard deviation}} \qquad (2)$$

In practice this rarely approaches the limits +3 and −3 which are derived from the remarks about (1).

Example 1: The following figures show the birth weight in pounds, to the nearest pound, of single births for 1000 babies born at the SU hospital.

Weight (lb)	2	3	4	5	6	7	8	9	10	11
Number of babies	5	4	10	16	50	180	400	260	60	15

Calculate Pearson's first coefficient of skewness

Answer

By computing in the normal manner we get the results

$$\bar{X} = 8{\cdot}007$$

$$\text{mode} = 8{\cdot}111$$

$$s = 1{\cdot}265$$

Thus $$Sk_1 = \frac{8{\cdot}007 - 8{\cdot}111}{1{\cdot}265} = -0{\cdot}082$$

This confirms what can be seen by inspection of the frequency table, that the distribution is slightly negatively skewed.

3.7 Supplementary Examples

Example 1: The variance of a set of n_1 numbers is s_1^2, the variance of a set of n_2 numbers is s_2^2. Find the variance of the set of $n_1 + n_2$ numbers.

Answer

Let m_1 and m_2 be the means of the sets of numbers.

Then

$$s_1^2 = \frac{\sum_{i=1}^{n_1} (X_i - m_1)^2}{n_1} = \frac{\sum_{i=1}^{n_1} X_i^2}{n_1} - m_1^2 \qquad (1)$$

and

$$s_2^2 = \frac{\sum_{l=1}^{n_2} (Y_l - m_2)^2}{n_2} = \frac{\sum_{l=1}^{n_2} Y_l^2}{n_2} - m_2^2 \tag{2}$$

Let s^2 and m be the variance and mean of the combined set. Then

$$s^2 = \frac{\sum_{j=1}^{n_1+n_2} (Z_j - m)^2}{n_1 + n_2} = \frac{\sum_{j=1}^{n_1+n_2} Z_j^2}{n_1 + n_2} - m^2 \tag{3}$$

Now $\sum_{j=1}^{n_1+n_2} Z_i^2$ represents $\sum_{i=1}^{n_1} X_i^2 + \sum_{l=1}^{n_2} Y_l^2$

From (1)

$$\sum_{i=1}^{n_1} X_i^2 = (s_1^2 + m_1^2)n_1$$

and from (2)

$$\sum_{l=1}^{n_2} Y_l^2 = (s_2^2 + m_2^2)n_2$$

so

$$s^2 = \frac{(s_1^2 + m_1^2)n_1 + (s_2^2 + m_2^2)n_2}{n_1 + n_2} - m^2 \quad \text{using (3)}$$

But we know from *Example 1* of Section 2.7 that

$$m = \frac{n_1 m_1 + n_2 m_2}{n_1 + n_2}$$

so

$$s^2 = \frac{(s_1^2 + m_1^2)n_1 + (s_2^2 + m_2^2)n_2}{n_1 + n_2} - \frac{(n_1 m_1 + n_2 m_2)^2}{(n_1 + n_2)^2}$$

$$= \frac{(s_1^2 n_1 + m_1^2 n_1 + s_2^2 n_2 + m_2^2 n_2)(n_1 + n_2) - (n_1 m_1 + n_2 m_2)^2}{(n_1 + n_2)^2}$$

which, after manipulation, reduces to

$$s^2 = \frac{s_1^2(n_1^2 + n_1 n_2) + s_2^2(n_2^2 + n_1 n_2) + n_1 n_2 (m_1 - m_2)^2}{(n_1 + n_2)^2}$$

Example 2: Prove that

$$\frac{\Sigma (X_i - K)^2}{N}$$

is a minimum when $K = \bar{X}$.

Answer

Putting

$$y = \frac{\Sigma\,(X_i - K)^2}{N}$$

we differentiate to get

$$\frac{dy}{dK} = \frac{\Sigma - 2\,(X_i - K)}{N}$$

$$= \frac{-2\,\Sigma\,X_i}{N} + 2K$$

and

$$\frac{d^2y}{dK^2} = 2$$

Putting

$$\frac{dy}{dK} = 0$$

to find turning points we get

$$\Sigma\,(X_i - K) = 0$$

i.e. $\Sigma\,X_i - NK = 0$

giving $K = \dfrac{\Sigma\,X_i}{N} = \bar{X}$

Since

$$\frac{d^2y}{dK^2} > 0$$

this value of K will be a minimum.

Example 3: For the 45 college students of *Example 14* of Section 1.9 find the interquartile range, and comment.

Answer

The interquartile range is defined to be $Q_3 - Q_1$, so for *Example 14* of Section 1.9, we get $67{\cdot}39'' - 58{\cdot}97'' = 8{\cdot}42'' = IQR$

Fifty percent of the readings fall within the interquartile range and so the smaller it is the more densely packed the central items are, and, conversely, the larger it is the greater the variation of the central items. Thus it is a useful measure of dispersion.

Because Q_3 and Q_2 are positional averages and are not adversely affected by extreme items at the upper and lower ends of the data, the interquartile range is likewise unaffected. So, unlike the range, the interquartile range is more reliable in its characterisation of dispersion.

However, the fact that extreme values do not influence adversely the interquartile range is not only its strength but one of its weaknesses. Since all the items do not contribute to its calculation it cannot fully represent *all* the data. Another disadvantage of the interquartile range is that it does not refer to any average, therefore it does not show deviations about any average.

Example 4: For the 45 college students of *Example 14* of Section 1.9 find the semi-interquartile range, and comment.

Answer

The semi-interquartile range is defined to be

$$\frac{Q_3 - Q_1}{2},$$

so for the 45 college students we get

$$\frac{67{\cdot}39'' - 58{\cdot}97''}{2} = 4{\cdot}21'' = SIQR$$

The $SIQR$ is much more commonly used than the IQR. Although the remarks made in the previous example about the IQR apply also to the $SIQR$, the latter has one advantage over the IQR, namely, it can express the dispersion in association with the median, a measure of central tendency. The best example is the case of the normal distribution where Q_1 and Q_3 are equidistant from the median, Q_2.

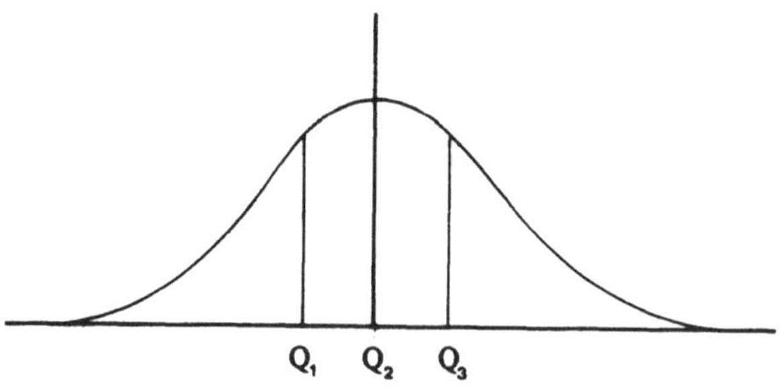

Fig. 3.7 (a)

It can be seen that 50% of the cases fall within the range $Q_2 \pm SIQR$. In the case of the 45 college students the median was found to be 63·17" (Section 2.5) and as this distribution is very nearly normally distributed we can say that 50% of the readings fall in the range 63·17 ± 4·21", i.e. 58·96" to 67·38".

In the case of skewed distributions it is only *approximately* 50% of the items that fall within the range $Q_2 \pm SIQR$. A modification of this idea so that it is applicable to skewed distributions is set in Exercise 3.

3.8 Review

We have now considered the graphing of data and the summarising of its important features – the most important of these being its centre and the way it is dispersed about this centre. The location of the centre is described in terms of the arithmetic mean, the median and the mode, and of these, two, the mode and median, are positional averages, while the arithmetic mean is a computed average.

When we come to dispersion we see that again they can be classified in two ways – those which are dependent on positions of items within the data, the range and the semi-interquartile range – and those which are computed and are averages of the deviations of the individual observations from some measure (usually the mean) of central tendency, the mean deviation and the standard deviation.

All these measures have their own individual characteristics and their use in different circumstances must reflect these characteristics.

We recall too that dispersion may be expressed in absolute terms i.e. in the units of the variable, grams, centimetres, and so on, or in relative terms. The range, standard deviation, etc., are examples of the former whilst the coefficient of variation was the one example of the latter considered in this text.

The arithmetic mean and the standard deviation are the two most commonly used statistics – despite the difficulty in the understanding of the standard deviation – because their mathematical properties are so superior to the others.

All these statistics, as we have seen, are attempts to describe data and a distribution is most adequately characterised when the features of average, dispersion and skewness are known.

We have now looked at the two stages in a statistical investigation which we called in the introduction the organisation and the analysis of data. These sections come under the general heading of *descriptive statistics* because no conclusions are drawn from the data – we are content to describe it accurately. However, the whole point of collecting data is so that not merely description can be carried out but predictions can be made and conclusions drawn. This drawing of conclusions and making predictions is called *statistical inference* and, to repeat what was said in the introduction, these predictions cannot be made with complete accuracy.

Let us amplify this point by considering the following situation. A university has just admitted a new intake which contained 1000 male students. The statistics lecturer on the staff measures the height of 100 of these students. Now in possession of his results a non-mathematician is enquiring what conclusions he can draw from his figures.

Non-mathematician: First of all, just what do your figures tell you?

Statistician: They tell me that the mean height of these students, those that I have measured, is 67″, and that the standard deviation of the distribution of heights is 3″.

NM: I understand the average height all right, but what does this standard deviation tell you?

S: Height is a variable that is normally distributed (he draws a graph) and so I know that roughly two-thirds of these students will be between 64″ and 70″, i.e. one standard deviation from the mean. Furthermore about 95% will have heights that fall between 61″ and 72″, and they practically all have heights between 58″ and 76″.

NM: And that is information solely about those students you measured?

S: Yes.

NM: But what about those you haven't measured? Do your figures tell you anything about them?

S: Yes. These results tell me that I can be pretty sure that all the male students of this year will have an average height of roughly 67″.

NM: You said 'pretty sure' and 'roughly', why can't you be certain?

S: Because in statistics we can never be *absolutely sure*. There's always the *possibility* that the students I picked were, in some way, a bad sample. The sample might just *by chance*, have contained a large number of taller than average students and so my figure would be higher than the true average of the population of first year students.

NM: What about those limits of 64″ and 70″ between which you said two-thirds of the sample heights lay? Will the same be true of the population?

S: Again rather roughly speaking, yes, you could say that. Perhaps another way of putting it might help you. I could say that if any one of the 1000 students were selected *at random* then the probability that he was between 64″ and 70″ would be two-thirds, or two out of three.

NM: How sure are you that your figures are right?

S: Taking into account that, most *likely*, the sample was a good one, I'd say I was 95% sure.

NM: 95% sure? What does that mean?

S: That 95 times out of a hundred I would be right but that 5 times out of a hundred I would be wrong!

NM: So this sample could be one of 95 good ones or one of the 5 bad ones?

S: That's right.

It will have been noticed that to start with the conversation was couched in the everyday language of probability, i.e. in terms of what was most likely, most probable and so on. But towards the end the statistician was putting a numerical estimate onto this everyday language. This now brings us to two important points.

First, as the statistician said, in statistics certainty is an impossibility and so we go for the next best thing – to be as sure as we can – and this entails thinking about *degrees* of probability. We must therefore take a closer look at the ideas of probability. We must examine them in a more detailed way.

The second point is that, as we have seen before, qualitative assessments are of little use in statistics and we must be more systematic and attempt to put the ideas of probability into mathematical terms, i.e. quantitative terms.

These two reasons explain why probability is so important in statistics and why probability has developed in a mathematical way.

Once we have greater knowledge of probability we can make inferences, take decisions, and make forecasts, knowing precisely what degree of risk is involved, and at the same time feel that our actions have a more logical rather than an intuitive basis.

Exercise 3

1.

		(a)	(b)	(c)	(d)	(e)
	X_i	f_i	f_i	f_i	f_i	f_i
	2	1	10	30	5	2
	4	1	10	20	10	3
	6	1	10	10	20	5
	8	1	10	5	20	10
	10	1	10	3	10	20
	12	1	10	2	5	30
Answers	mean deviation	3	3	2	2·14	2
	standard deviation	3·4	3·4	2·52	2·59	2·6

Find the mean deviation and the standard deviation of the above distributions. Keep all your working and compare the different distributions. Write out your comments on what points you notice.

To each X_i add (i) 10 (ii) 25 and then re-calculate the various statistics. What pattern emerges?

2. Find the standard deviation of the following distribution

X_i	20	22	24	26	28	30	32	34	36	38	40	42
f_i	3	22	51	60	73	60	52	34	22	14	·7	2

Answer

$s = 4{\cdot}5$

3. If the numbers 1, 2, 3, . . . , 10 occur with frequencies 1, 2, 3, . . . , 10 respectively, find the arithmetic mean, the mode and the standard deviation. Hence find Pierson's first coefficient of skewness. Explain why it is not possible to find Pearson's second coefficient of skewness.

$\bar{X} = 7$, mode $= 10$, $s = \sqrt{6}$, Pearson's $Sk_1 = -3{\cdot}88$

4. If the numbers 1, 2, 3, . . . , n occur with frequencies 1, 2, 3, . . . , n respectively, find Pearson's first coefficient of skewness.

Answer

$$\frac{\sqrt{2}(1 - n)}{\sqrt{n^2 + n - 2}}$$

5. Compute the median for *Example 1* of Section 3.6, and hence find Pearson's second coefficient of skewness. Account for any difference with Sk_1.

6. Show that for a symmetrical distribution

$$\frac{Q_1 + Q_2}{2} = \bar{X}$$

Explain why this is not so for a skewed distribution.

7. Give some examples like those in Section 3.4 where information regarding the standard deviation is necessary for a decision to be made.

8. Explain how the range of a set of raw data will differ when that same data is grouped into classes and tabulated in a frequency table.

9. Fifteen scores have a mean of 5 and the sum of their squares is (a) 165 (b) 1065. Find the variance of the scores in these two cases.

Answer
(a) $s^2 = 12\frac{2}{3}$ (b) $s^2 = 46$

10. Derive a coding method for computing the mean deviation.

11. If $d_i = X_i - A$, where A is an assumed mean, prove that

$$s^2 = \frac{\Sigma f_i d_i^2}{N} - \left(\frac{\Sigma f_i d_i}{N}\right)^2$$

12. Prove

$$s^2 = \frac{N_1 s_1^2 + N_2 s_2^2}{N_1 + N_2}$$

where N_1 is the number of scores in the set with mean m_1 and variance s_1^2, and N_2 is the number of scores in the set with mean m_2 and variance s_2^2, and s^2 is the variance of the combined groups, if and only if $m_1 = m_2$

13. Find the variance of the first n natural numbers

Answer

$$\frac{(n^2 - 1)}{12}$$

14. If the mean of 20 numbers is 5 and $\Sigma (x_i - \bar{x})^2 = 40$, show that $\Sigma x_i^2 = 540$, and find values of k such that $\Sigma (x_i - k)^2 = 220$.

Answer
$k = 8$ or 2

15. Four dice were tossed 100 times and the number of heads turning up for each throw were recorded as in the following table:

Number of heads	0	1	2	3	4
Number of throws	52	40	15	2	1

Find the standard deviation and comment on its suitability as a measure of dispersion for this data

Answer
0·84

16. A machine for filling boxes with powder can work at any preset arithmetic mean, but the variability in the amounts it puts into individual

boxes forms a normal curve with a standard deviation of 0·1 lb. If it is a legal requirement that the boxes must be certain to contain at least 1 lb of powder and the machine is set to work at an average of 1·1 lb to a box

(i) what proportion of boxes will contain less than the required minimum?

(ii) what mean setting would conform to the legal requirements for all boxes?

(iii) what would the chances be of getting an under weight box if the machine was set at a mean of 1 lb.

Answer

(i) approximately 15·87% (ii) 1·3 lb (iii) Fifty-fifty

17. The numbers 1, 2, 3, . . . , n occur with frequencies 1, 2, 3, . . . , n respectively. Find the standard deviation.

Answer

$$\sqrt{\frac{n^2 + n - 2}{18}}$$

18. The numbers 1, 2, 3, . . . , n occur with frequencies n, $(n - 1)$, $(n - 2)$, . . . , 3, 2, 1, respectively. Find the standard deviation.

Answer

$$\sqrt{\frac{6 + 9n - 47n^2 + 4n^3 - 8n^4}{18}}$$

19. When is the standard deviation an unsuitable measure of dispersion? Give examples.

20. Comment on the following:

(i) Life would be impossible if everything in the universe was completely random. It is because the variation within every aspect of life forms a pattern that existence is possible.

(ii) 'The range is a very crude measure of variability – I can't understand why it is so commonly used'.

21. Find Pearson's first coefficient of skewness for *Example 1* and *Example 2* of Section 1.9.

Answer

Example 1, $Sk_1 = -0{\cdot}43$ *Example 2*, $Sk_1 = -0{\cdot}29$

22. Find the mean deviation, the standard deviation, the arithmetic mean and the mode of Exercise 1 (question 7). Hence find Pearson's

first coefficient of skewness.

Answer

M.D. = 0·4, $s = 1{\cdot}32$, $\bar{X} = 1{\cdot}5$, mode = 1, $Sk_1 = -0{\cdot}3$

23. Show that $W \pm SIQR$ includes exactly 50% of the items of a skewed distribution if $W = Q_1 + SIQR$.

24. Can the IQR be found for a group formed by the combining of two smaller groups whose individual IQR's are known, solely by algebraic manipulation?

25. Discuss the algebraic qualities of the $SIQR$.

4 Set Theory and Probability

4.1 Introduction

We saw earlier that the mathematician prefers to deal with quantitative rather than qualitative assessments of situations and the theory of probability is no exception. We all know what we mean by such statements as, 'It will never happen in a thousand years', 'It could happen, but I doubt it'; 'It could easily happen'; 'More than likely it will happen'; 'It's an absolute certainty'; and it is this everyday notion of impossible, possible, probable, and certain that the mathematician seeks to make more precise. It will be noted that these statements express a graduation of opinion from impossibility through to certainty and the mathematician imposes upon this range a scale or measurement. He does this by assigning a number between zero and one in the following way:

Impossible	–	0
Perhaps	–	$\frac{1}{4}$
Probable	–	$\frac{3}{4}$
Certain	–	1

so that the closer the number assign is to zero, the less likely the event to which it refers will occur, and the closer the assigned number is to 1, the more likely the event to which it refers will occur. Some actual examples will help to clarify the idea.

Example 1: The probability that the next person seen in the street is over 9 feet tall — Probability 0

Example 2: The probability that the next person seen in the street is male — Probability $\frac{1}{2}$

Example 3: The probability that a person selected at random in a main street is under 55 — Probability $\frac{3}{4}$

Example 4: The probability that a ball kicked into the air comes down again Probability 1

In *Example 2*, the argument that preceeded that assignation of the number $\frac{1}{2}$ may have been like this. There are two possibilities regarding the next person seen (i.e. whether male or female) – as the population consists roughly of half male and half female, the chances that it will be a male who is observed is one out of two, hence $\frac{1}{2}$. We might continue this argument and say that the probability of seeing a female is also $\frac{1}{2}$. We note that $\frac{1}{2} + \frac{1}{2} = 1$.

The reader should work out the arguments used for the ascription of the figures in the other examples.

We might now consider the probability of rolling a 6 with a dice. Obviously the probability equals $\frac{1}{6}$. Similarly the probability of rolling a 1, or 2, or 3, or 4, or 5 will be $\frac{1}{6}$, and we note that $\frac{1}{6} + \frac{1}{6} + \frac{1}{6} + \frac{1}{6} + \frac{1}{6} + \frac{1}{6} = 1$. We shall have cause to examine this idea further in the following sections, but we note now that this shows that probabilities are assigned to events not independently, but in relation to other events connected with the same subject. Since probability is concerned with the occurrence or non-occurrence of events we must also make precise what we mean by an event and we do this in the next section.

4.2 Random Phenomena; Random Variable; Event

If a dice is rolled, the number which is on the top face when it comes to rest may be observed and recorded. The result is not known before the throw. Similarly with the next and subsequent throws. If the next person to walk through a certain door is selected and weighed, his weight will not be known beforehand. Similarly with the next and subsequent persons selected for weighing.

Such phenomena, because they exhibit this property of being unpredictable, are called *random phenomena*. Further examples of random phenomena are road deaths on any one day, peas in a pod, or apples on a tree in any one year.

Random phenomena may be better understood in contrast with non-random phenomena such as the sequence of lights in a traffic signal, or the distance travelled by a car if the car maintains a constant speed.

Although we have called some phenomena 'random', a qualification must be made. Within the randomness there is a sense of order. Although we can not predict the weight of someone selected at random, we do know that the result of the weighing will fit into the pattern of weights of human beings, i.e. the normal curve shape that comes from this and similar measurings. Thus we see that phenomena is not *totally* random in the sense of no pattern at all, but only random in the sense of having this element of unpredictability whilst at the same time fitting into a general pattern or order. It is the pattern of variation within the randomness that the statistician must investigate.

When investigating a random phenomenon it is necessary to measure it in some way. For instance, the height of a person could be measured in inches (amongst other measurements available), the peas in a pod will – usually – be counted in whole numbers, and the income of somebody could be measured in £'s.

The number of units of the measure which individual items in the investigation have, will vary from one to another – one man will be 72″ tall and another one will be 58″ tall – one man will earn £1000 per annum and another one will earn £1200 per annum. In each case we will be interested in a number which we give to each item. That number is a value assumed by what is called a *random variable.*

The *height* – when given in figures – of people is a random variable, the *number* of road deaths on any day is a random variable, the *number* of cars owned by men selected at random is a random variable. We are thus making a distinction between a random phenomenon and its measurement – the phenomenon occurs naturally and the measurement is imposed upon it by us. It will be instructive to consider the random phenomenon of the colour of peoples eyes. It is usually more convenient to consider random variables as numbers and, since the colour of peoples eyes is usually described in terms of colour, it is better to code the range of colours in terms of numbers, e.g. blue = 1, brown = 2, etc.

The student will note that this definition of a random variable is slightly different from the definition of a variable given in Section 1.9. This latter definition makes a distinction between a random phenomenon and a random variable which was not necessary at the earlier stage.

When investigating random phenomenon it is necessary to perform experiments and usually this means repeating a certain action, such as the rolling of a dice, or the tossing of a coin, a large number of times. Consider again the experiment of rolling a dice. There are six possible outcomes of this experiment, namely, 1, 2, 3, 4, 5, 6. If we now roll the dice and get a 4 then this is the occurrence of one of the possible outcomes of the experiment. Consider again the experiment of drawing a card from a normal pack. There are 52 possible outcomes and if we now draw a card and get the four of hearts then this is the occurrence of one of the possible outcomes of the experiment. This leads us to define an *event* as the occurrence of one of the possible outcomes of an experiment on a random phenomenon. Note that this is a narrower sense of the word than is usual in normal speech.

4.3 The Outcome Space

When investigating a random phenomenon, it is obvious that we should try to find out all possible outcomes of the experiments. With the rolling of a dice this is simply the set {1, 2, 3, 4, 5, 6} and with the drawing of a card it is {Ace of hearts, two of hearts, . . . , Queen of spades, King of spades}. The set which consists of all the possible outcomes of an experiment upon a random phenomenon is called the *outcome space.* This particular set has received many names and other ones that the reader may find elsewhere are *sample space, sample description space, universal set* or *universe of discourse.*

If the elements of the outcome space are whole numbers, it is called a discrete outcome space, and if the elements of the outcome space form a continuous set of numbers, then it is called a continuous outcome space. Note the connection with discrete and continuous variables.

Example 1: The outcome space of rolling a dice is discrete

Example 2: The outcome space for weights of human beings is continuous

Since, for the beginner, discrete outcome spaces are much easier to deal with than continuous ones, attention is for the moment confined to them alone.

N.B. The outcome space is the domain of the random variable associated with the random phenomenon.

4.4 Probability Measure

We take the outcome space of a random phenomenon and with each element of this space associate a number which is called the probability of the occurrence of the event associated with the element.

Example 1: Random phenomenon: rolling a dice

Outcome space: {1, 2, 3, 4, 5, 6}

Set of associated numbers $\{\frac{1}{6}, \frac{1}{6}, \frac{1}{6}, \frac{1}{6}, \frac{1}{6}, \frac{1}{6}\}$

This can be interpreted as the probability of $2 = \frac{1}{6}$ and shortened to $P(2) = \frac{1}{6}$. We also note that $P(1) = \frac{1}{6}$, $P(3) = \frac{1}{6}$, etc.

Since 'associate a number with every element of a set' is the definition of a function, this relationship between elements of the outcome space and the set of associated numbers can be thought of as a function. This process of associating a number with every element of the outcome space is called putting a *probability measure* onto the outcome space. The terms probability measure and probability function are used interchangeably.

Example 2: Put a probability measure onto the outcome space of the random phenomenon of tossing a coin.

Outcome space: {Heads, Tails}

Probability measure: $\{\frac{1}{2}, \frac{1}{2}\}$

i.e. $P(H) = \frac{1}{2}$ and $P(T) = \frac{1}{2}$.

We recall now the idea of a random variable (introduced in Section 1.9 and further explained in Section 4.2) in connection with descriptive statistics. We do so in order to look at the counterpart to this idea of a random variable, as it is defined in probability work.

Definition

If a variable **x** takes the values $x_1, x_2, \ldots, x_n$ with probabilities $P(x_1), P(x_2), \ldots, P(x_n)$ such that $\Sigma P(x_i) = 1$, then **x** is a *random variable*.

Furthermore if the outcome space of **x** consists of discrete elements then **x** is a *discrete* random variable. If the outcome space of **x** is a continuous set then **x** is a *continuous* random variable. The definition given above is of a discrete random variable – to define a continuous random variable requires the use of the calculus.

In the light of this it will be seen that *Example 1* is in fact a random variable. The particular concept of a random variable intended will be clear from the context where the term is used.

The beginner can easily be forgiven for being confused over this point as a random variable as just defined is also called a probability function, a chance variable, a stochastic variable and a variate.

4.5 Set Theory

We have now gone as far as we can without introducing explicitly set theory, but in order to pursue the ideas of probability further we must now look at this topic. The word 'set' has been used frequently in the text in such a way that the reader would understand it in its everyday sense of a collection of different objects. We confirm this sense now with the following definition:

A *set* is a collection of definite, well-distinguished objects of our perception or of our thought. (This is virtually the definition of a set given by Cantor (1845 – 1918), the founder of modern set theory). It is usual to enclose the members of a set, called elements, between two brace brackets as follows:

$$A = \{1, 21, 4, 77\}$$

and to refer to the set with a capital letter. In this example we say that the set A consists of the elements 1, 21, 4, and 77.

Example 1: B = {The members of Parliament in 1966}

Example 2: C = {The kings of England}

Example 3: D = {The numbers between 0 and 98}

There are two ways of indicating a set. The first is by displaying all the elements, as in the set A, and the second is to lay down a qualification for membership of the set, as in the sets B, C and D.

When the qualification method is used it is convenient to make the following abbreviations:

$$X = \{y \mid y \text{ is even}\}$$

this is read 'X is the set of elements y such that y is even', i.e. X is the set $\{2, 4, 6, \ldots\}$

It is usual to refer to elements of sets with small letters and to indicate that they belong to a set by use of the connective '$\in$' as follows:

$x \in A$ which is read 'x is an element of A'

N.B. Just as a plus sign, '+', is used meaningfully with numbers on either side, $4 + 7$, then the sign '$\in$' can only be used in a sense which has meaning if there is an element of a set on the left, and a set on the right of it.

Example 4: $21 \in A$ *Example 5*: King Harold $\in C$

Example 6: $55 \in D$ *Example 7*: $A \in D$ has no meaning

Order in which the elements of a set are indicated is immaterial.

Example 8: $\{1, 2, 3, 5, 88\}$ is the same as $\{1, 3, 2, 88, 5\}$

If elements of a set are repeated it does not alter the set.

Example 9: $\{1, 2, 3, 3, 4, 4, 5\}$ is the same as $\{1, 2, 3, 4, 5\}$ the reason for this is that elements of a set must be distinct. If x is not an element of the set D then the notation $x \notin D$ is used, and this is read, 'x is not an element of D'.

N.B. Do not confuse X as a set and X_1, X_2 and so on, as a variate.

4.6 Subsets

Example 1: Consider the set D = {The numbers between 0 and 98} and also the set {1, 2, 3, 4, 5, 6, 7, 8, 9} = E. We note that although E is a set in its own right, all its elements are also elements of D. This leads us to define: If every element of one set is also an element of a second set, then the first set is called a *subset* of the second.

Example 2: In any set consisting of a football team, the following subsets can be picked out:

(i) The subset of forwards
(ii) The subset of defenders
(iii) The subset of wingers
(iv) The subset of the goalkeeper.

N.B. A subset may consist of only one element
To indicate that H is a subset of J the connective $\subset$ is used, $H \subset J$, and again the point is made that the connective $\subset$ is only used with meaning if there is a set on each side of it, i.e. $x \subset G$ has no meaning.

If H is not a subset of J then the notation $H \not\subset J$ is used and this is read, 'H is not a subset of J'. If the symbol $\subset$ is reversed and used as follows, $H \supset J$, then this is read, 'H is a superset of J, or H contains J'. The meaning of $H \not\supset J$ follows naturally as 'H is not a superset of J'.

It is possible to consider H as a subset of itself since it will in this way satisfy the condition of a subset. In this context it is called an *improper* subset. All other subsets are *proper* subsets.

4.7 The Empty Set

It is convenient to postulate that there is a set which contains no elements, and it is usually referred to as *the empty set*, or as *the null set*. It is denoted by the symbol ϕ or by { }. Examples of null or empty sets are {All human beings over 300 years old}, {Triangles with two sides}, {Number of men on the sun}.

It is also convenient to consider the empty set as a subset of every set, i.e. $\phi \subset A$, regardless of A.

4.8 The Universal Set

When people discuss affairs they generally consider only one topic at a time and this topic may be called the *subject* of their discourse. This subject of discourse is referred to in set theory as the *universal set* i.e. the universal set is the set to which discussion or thought is temporarily restricted. As the conversation changes so will the universal set, thus for any particular instance the universal set needs defining.

Example 1: Universal set: {Members of the armed forces}. In this case the set {The Royal Navy} would be a subset of the universal set. Similarly with {the Army} and {the Royal Air Force}. If we now change our universal set to {the Royal Navy} then in this new case the Army and the Royal Air Force are excluded from the conversation. Subsets of this new universal set are {Men at Sea}, {Men on Frigates}, etc.

Example 2: Universal set {Europe}
Subsets {Great Britain}, {France, Holland}, etc.

4.9 Venn Diagrams

Sets may conveniently be demonstrated with Venn Diagrams – so named after John Venn, a 19th century mathematician – as follows:

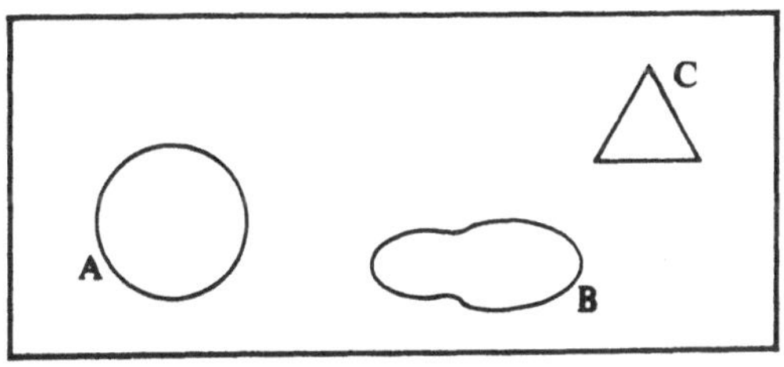

Fig. 4.9 (a)

The outside rectangle represents the universal set, and the shapes inside represent subsets of this universal set. To put this now into the probability context, the universal set may be thought of as the outcome space and the subsets of this outcome space as events.

If A is a subset of B, then the diagram is as follows:

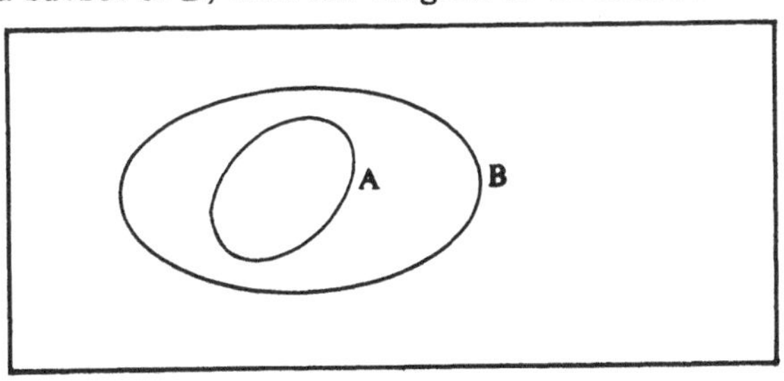

Fig. 4.9 (b)

4.10 The Complement

Example 1: Universal set: $S = \{1, 2, 3, 4, 5, 6, 7, 8, 9, 10\}$
$A = \{3, 5, 7, 9\}$
If we look at A and the universal set we note that all the elements 1, 2, 4, 6, 8, and 10 are in the universal set but not in A. It is sometimes useful to look at the set formed by these numbers and we therefore define: The *complement* of a set A is that set which contains all the elements in the universal set which are not in A. It is denoted by A', or A^c; for the above example

$$A' = \{1, 2, 4, 6, 8, 10\}$$

Example 2: universal set: $I = \{1, 3, 5, 7, 9\}$

$$A = \{3, 5, 7, 9\}$$

$$A' = \{1\}$$

Note that in both these examples set A is the same but A' varies. This is because the universal set varies and this is one reason why the universal set should be carefully defined in individual cases. In the following Venn diagram the area shaded represents A'.

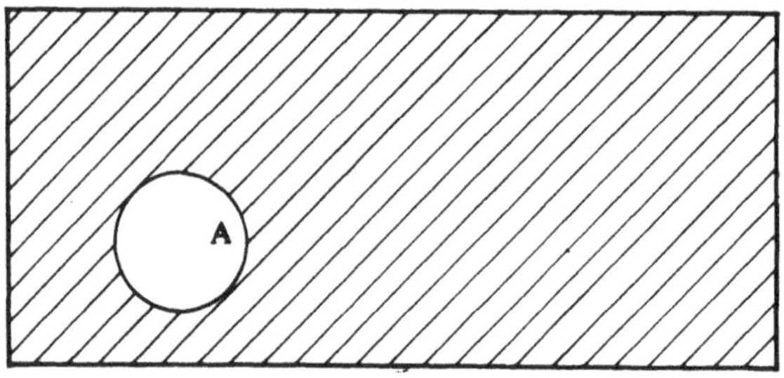

Fig. 4.10 (a)

Example 3: If we consider the experiment of rolling a dice, then the outcome space – universal set – is

$$S = \{1, 2, 3, 4, 5, 6\}$$

If we consider the event 'throwing a 5' then this may be represented by the subset $R = \{5\}$. $R' = \{1, 2, 3, 4, 6\}$ and is the event 'not throwing a five'.

4.11 The Union of Sets

One of the earliest operations we learn to perform is the addition of two numbers, e.g. $4 + 5 = 9$, and we now look at the operations that can be performed with sets. If we take two different sets one of the first things that suggests itself is the combining of these into a third.

Example 1: $A = \{1, 2, 3, 4, 5, 6\}$

$B = \{5, 6, 7, 8, 9\}$

If we now take all the elements in these two sets we get the set $\{1, 2, 3, 4, 5, 5, 6, 6, 7, 8, 9\}$ which we have seen is the same as $\{1, 2, 3, 4, 5, 6, 7, 8, 9\}$. This leads us to define:
The set made up of the elements which are contained *either* in A *or* B is called the *union* of A and B and is written $A \cup B$, read 'A union B'.

Example 2: C = {All red haired men}

D = {All blue eyed men}

$C \cup D$ = {All men who have red hair *or* blue eyes}

Venn diagram: The shaded area represents the set $A \cup B$

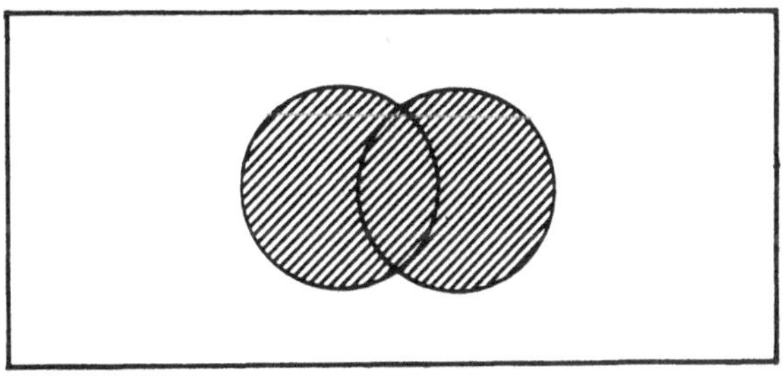

Fig. 4.11(a)

4.12 The Intersection of Sets

The second thing that suggests itself when dealing with two sets is to see which elements they have in common.

Example 1: $E = \{21, 31, 51, 42\}$

$F = \{27, 31, 42, 77, 88\}$

We see that E and F have the elements 31, and 42 in common.

Thus we define the set that is formed by taking the elements which two sets have in common as the *intersection* of the two sets. It is written $E \cap F$, read 'E intersection F', and is this example $E \cap F = \{31, 42\}$

Venn diagram: The area shaded in Fig. 4.12(a) shows the intersection of A and B

If two sets have no elements in common they are said to be *disjoint*.

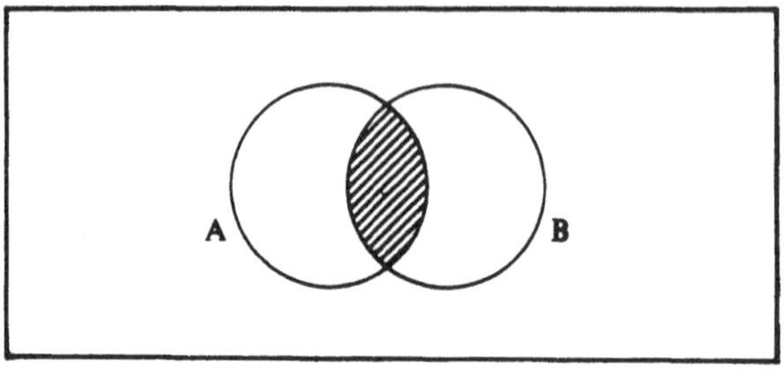

Fig. 4.12(a)

Example 2: L = {The set of even numbers}

M = {The set of odd numbers}

L and M are disjoint

Example 3: G = {All gas fires}

H = {All electric fires}

G and H are disjoint

The first diagram in Section 4.9 shows three disjoint sets. Sets which have common elements are called non-disjoint sets – see Fig. 4.12(a).

4.13 The Equality of Sets

Two sets A and B are said to be equal if, and only if, every element of A is also an element of B, and every element of B is also an element of A. Using the notation developed so far this may be written

$$A = B, \text{ if and only if } A \subset B \text{ and } B \subset A$$

Example 1: A = {All even numbers}

$B = \{2, 4, 6, 8, \ldots\}$

Every element of A is an element of B, therefore $A \subset B$
Every element of B is an element of A, therefore $B \subset A$, hence $A = B$.
Although the proof of the equality of the two sets in this example may seem rather pedantic, it is emphasised that the proof of equality of sets must have the two parts $A \subset B$ and $B \subset A$. It is not always as immediately obvious as in this example, that two sets are equal

Example 2: Prove that $(E \cup F)' = (E' \cap F')$

Proof: Let x be an element of $(E \cup F)'$

i.e. $x \in (E \cup F)'$
then $x \notin E$ and $x \notin F$
so $x \in E'$ and $x \in F'$

i.e. $x \in (E' \cap F')$

therefore $(E \cup F)' \subset (E' \subset F')$

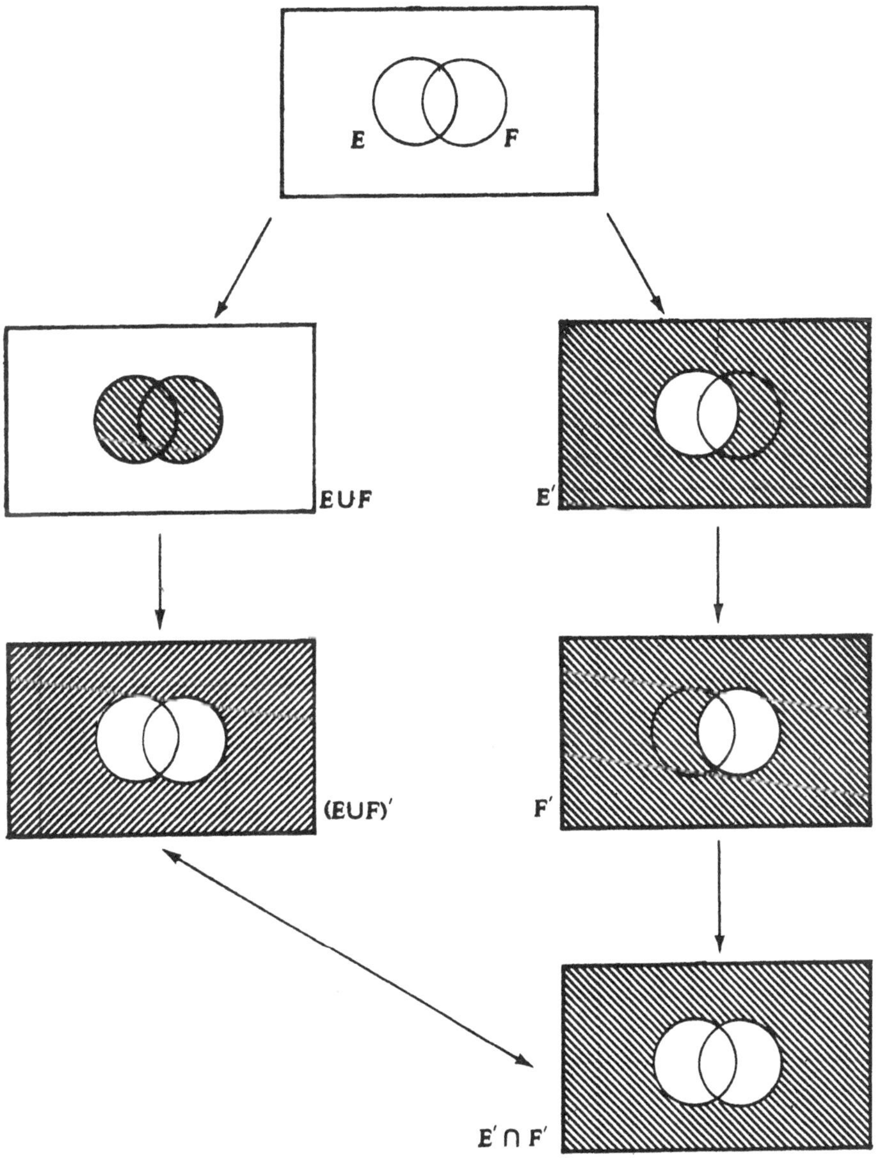

Fig. 4.13(a)

Similarly let $x \in (E' \cap F')$
then $x \in E'$ and $x \in F'$
so $x \notin E$ and $x \notin F$
and $x \notin (E \cup F)$
so $x \in (E \cap F)'$
therefore $(E' \cap F') \subset (E F)'$

It now follows that $(E \cup F)' = E' \cap F'$

A method of 'seeing' when two sets are equal is to use Venn diagrams. *Example 2* is illustrated in Fig. 4.13 (a).
Since the parts shaded in the final pictures are the same, and one represents $(E \cup F)'$, and the other $E' \cap F'$, the equality of $(E \cup F)'$ and $E' \cap F'$ follows. It is emphasised that diagrams do not in themselves represent a proof in the strictly mathematical sense, but they are useful in getting results which may then be proved with greater rigour.

4.14 Set Algebra

It is possible to examine how ordinary numbers behave when subjected to the four operations of addition, subtraction, multiplication and division, and to note certain features.

Example 1: $4 + 6 = 6 + 4$ or more generally $a + b = b + a$
$4 - 2 \neq 2 - 4$ or more generally $a - b \neq b - a$

in the first case we say that addition is commutative and in the second case that subtraction is non-commutative. By examining numbers in this fashion we can get a better idea of the structure of number.

Similarly we can examine how sets behave under the operations of union and intersection and this study is called the *algebra of sets* or *set algebra*. The most important results of this investigation are tabulated below.

For any universal set S, and subsets A, B, and C of S, the following laws hold.

A1. *Closure*

For any A, B, subsets of S, $A \cup B$ and $A \cap B$ exist and are unique subsets of S

A2. *Commutative laws*

$$A \cup B = B \cup A \qquad A \cap B = B \cap A$$

A3. *Associative laws*

$$(A \cup B) \cup C = A \cup (B \cup C) \qquad (A \cap B) \cap C = A \cap (B \cap C)$$

A4. *Distributive laws*

$A \cap (B \cup C) = (A \cap B) \cup (A \cap C) \qquad A \cup (B \cap C) = (A \cup B) \cap (A \cup C)$

A5. *Complimentary laws*

$A \cup A' = S \qquad A \cap A' = \phi$

A6. *Identity laws*

$A \cup \phi = A \qquad A \cap S = A$

The above axioms are such that all the other laws (theorems) of set algebra can be deduced from them, in much the same way as the theorems of geometry can be deduced from Euclid's axioms.

Example 2: Prove that $A \cap A = A$

Proof: $A = A \cap S$ (Identity of $\cap$ – A.6)
$= A \cap (A \cup A')$ (A5)
$= (A \cap A) \cup (A \cap A')$ (Distributive law)
$= (A \cap A) \cup \phi$ (A5)
$= A \cap A$ (A6)

The student should convince himself of the self evidence of the above axioms – either by checking that both sides of the equalities contain the same elements, or by looking at Venn diagrams – and the useful results, immediately derivable from them as in *Example 2* below, should be worked through in detail.

1. $A \cup A = A$
2. $A \cup S = S \qquad A \cap \phi = \phi$
3. $(A')' = A$
4. $S' = \phi \qquad \phi' = S$
5. $(A \cup B)' = A' \cap B' \qquad (A \cap B)' = A' \cup B'$
6. $(A \cup B \cup C \cup \ldots \cup K)' = A' \cap B' \cap C' \cap \ldots \cap K'$
   $(A \cap B \cap C \cap \ldots \cap K)' = A' \cup B' \cup C' \cup \ldots \cup K'$
7. $A \cap (B \cup C \cup D \cup \ldots \cup K) = (A \cap B) \cup (A \cap C) \cup (A \cap D) \cup \ldots \cup (A \cap K)$
   $A \cup (B \cap C \cap D \cap \ldots \cap K) = (A \cup B) \cap (A \cup C) \cap (A \cup D) \cap \ldots \cap (A \cup K)$

4.15 Number in a Set

Frequently it must be known how many elements there are in a set.

Example 1: $A = \{$John, Mary, Paul$\}$
A contains 3 elements

Example 2: $B = \{\square, \Delta\}$
B contains 2 elements

We refer to the number of elements in a set A by using the notation $N(A)$, read 'the number of elements in A'.
From *Example 1*, $N(A) = 3$, and from *Example 2*, $N(B) = 2$
N.B. A is a set, but $N(A)$ is a number and may be treated in the way that numbers are normally treated, i.e. added and subtracted etc. Note $N(\phi) = 0$

If we wish to refer to the number of elements in the set $A \cup B$ we do so as before by using the notation $N(A \cup B)$, read, 'the number of elements in the set $A \cup B$'.

Example 3: Form $A \cup B$ from *Example 1* and *Example 2* and find $N(A \cup B)$

$$(A \cup B) = \{\text{John, Mary, Paul}, \square, \Delta\}$$

therefore $$N(A \cup B) = 5$$

Note that $N(A \cup B) = N(A) + N(B)$. Will this always be the case?

Example 4: Consider
$$C = \{1, 2, 3, 4, 5\}$$
$$D = \{3, 4, 5, 6\}$$
$$C \cup D = \{1, 2, 3, 4, 5, 6\}$$
$$N(C) = 5, \quad N(D) = 4, \quad N(C \cup D) = 6$$

so in this case since $6 \neq 5 + 4$

$$N(C \cup D) \neq N(C) + N(D)$$

The difficulty here is that when sets are united under the operation of union repeated elements are not counted twice, thus the result will always differ by the number of repeated elements. In this example, there are 3 repeated elements, 3, 4, and 5. But the repeated elements are just those elements in the intersection of the two sets. Thus we can say in this case that

$$6 = 5 + 4 - 3$$

giving

$$N(C \cup D) = N(C) + N(D) - N(C \cap D) \qquad (1)$$

It will be readily seen that (1) will apply in all cases. If, as in *Example 3* $A \cap B = \phi$, then $N(A \cap B) = 0$, and in these cases (1) reduced to the form given in *Example 3*.

Example 5: In a group of 50 people 35 have brown hair, and 26 wear glasses. How many have brown hair and wear glasses?

Answer

$$N(B \cup G) = N(B) + N(G) - N(B \cap G)$$

i.e. $$50 = 35 + 26 - N(B \cap G)$$

therefore $$N(B \cap G) = 61 - 50 = 11.$$

Hence 11 people wear glasses and have brown hair. This may be exhibited diagrammatically (see Fig. 4.15 (a))

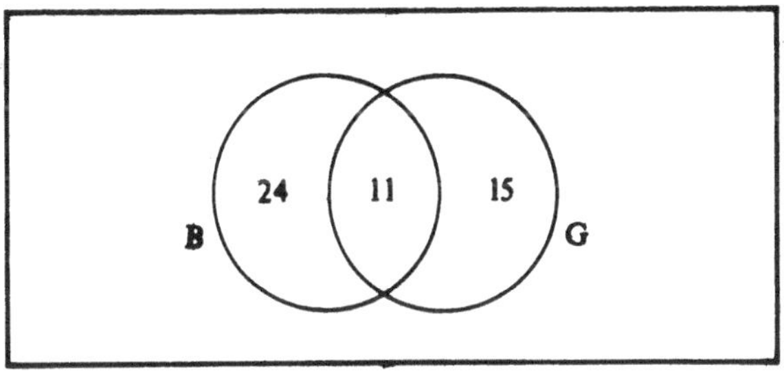

Fig. 4.15(a)

The student may be further convinced of (1) by considering the following argument. Let the *area* of a set drawn in a Venn diagram represent the *number* in the set. Then in the diagram below the number in A is represented by the shaded area:

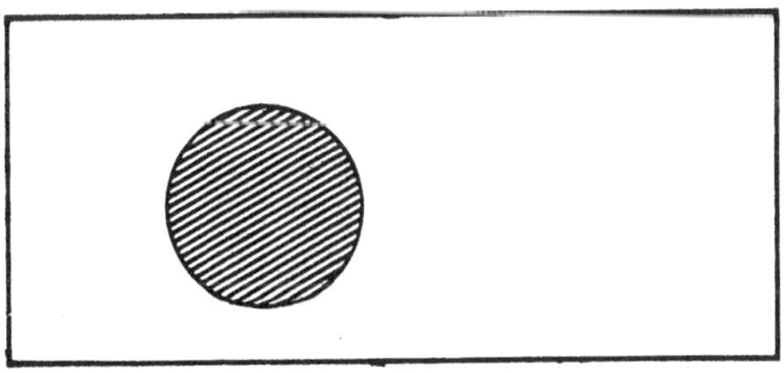

Fig. 4.15(b)

If another set is now drawn so that it intersects with A and the *area* of this second set B is also representative of the *number* in B then the diagram will look as follows:

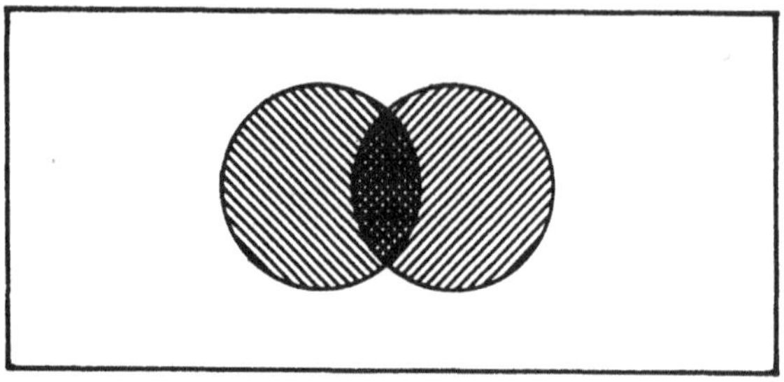

Fig. 4.15(c)

The area of $A \cup B$ will also represent the number in $A \cup B$ and that is the area shaded below:

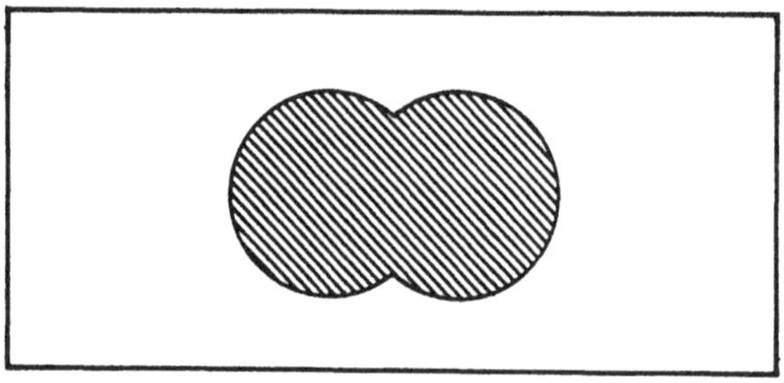

Fig. 4.15(d)

the difference in shading in Figs. 4.15(c) and 4.15(d) for the area which represents the number in $A \cup B$ is that in Fig. 4.15(d), the shading covers the area once, whereas in Fig. 4.15(c) the shading covers the area twice in the part which represents $A \cap B$. Thus in order to make the two figures correspond one layer of shading will have to be removed from the area which represents $A \cap B$. This removal of shading represents the subtraction of $N(A \cap B)$ in (1).

(1) can be extended from two sets to three to give the following result:

$$N(A \cup B \cup C) = N(A) + N(B) + N(C) - N(A \cap B) - N(A \cap C) - N(B \cap C) + N(A \cap B \cap C) \quad (2)$$

Either of the above two arguments can be extended to get this result.

Example 6: A group of 100 people were questioned about their eating habits in relation to Apples, Bananas and Chocolate and the following results obtained.

25 ate none of them, 15 ate only apples, 18 ate only bananas, 11 ate only chocolate, 9 ate both apples and bananas, 7 ate both bananas and

chocolate and 3 at both apples and chocolate. How many ate all three?

Answer

In the following diagram the outside rectangle represents the 100 people and the other information is shown as given. The $N(A \cap B \cap C)$ is not known so this is put in as x.

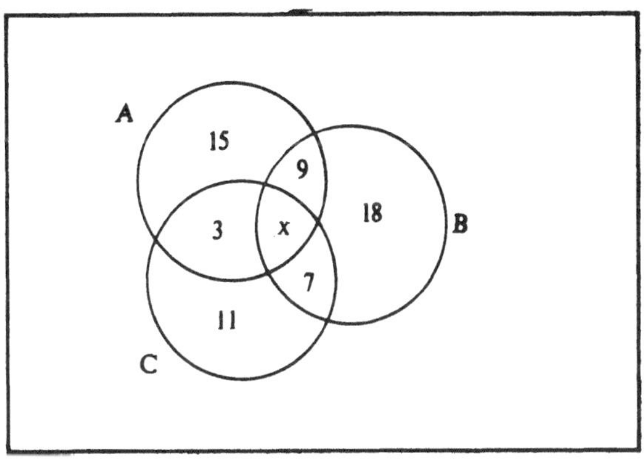

Fig. 4.15(e)

The area outside the three sets A, B and C represents the 25 people who eat none of the three commodities.
The $N(A)$ will be $15 + 3 + 9 + x = 27 + x$ and $N(A \cap B) = 9 + x$
The $N(B)$ will be $18 + 7 + 9 + x = 34 + x$ and $N(A \cap C) = 3 + x$
The $N(C)$ will be $11 + 7 + 3 + x = 21 + x$ and $N(B \cap C) = 7 + x$
Substituting these results in (2) gives

$$\begin{aligned} 75 &= (27 + x) + (34 + x) + (21 + x) - (9 + x) - (3 + x) - (7 + x) + x \\ &= (82 + 3x) - (19 + 3x) + x \\ &= 63 + x \end{aligned}$$

giving $x = 12$
Therefore we can say that 12 people eat all three products.

In the examples considered so far in this section the sets were finite, i.e. their elements could be counted and the result expressed as a finite number. There are however sets whose elements cannot be so counted.

Example 7: The set $\{1, 2, 3, 4, \ldots\}$ consists of an infinite number of elements.

Example 8: The set $\{1, 3, 5, 7, \ldots\}$ consists of an infinite number of elements.

Example 9: The set of all *real* numbers between 0 and 1 cannot be counted so this is an infinite set.

We thus say that a set A is an *infinite* set if the elements cannot be counted and the result expressed as a finite number.

4.16 Set Theory and Probability

In this and subsequent sections, we will see how set theory is applied to probability. We let the outcome space be the universal set S, and the elements of S represent the different outcomes of the experiment upon the random phenomenon. A single element may be associated with an event – in the case of the dice, the element 4 from the sample space $\{1, 2, 3, 4, 5, 6\}$ is associated with the event, 'the rolling of a 4'. More than one element may be associated with an event – in the case of a dice, the elements 5 and 6 from the outcome space are associated with the event, 'the rolling of a number greater than 4'. Thus an event may be associated with more than one outcome of the outcome space. These elements, single, double, triple, etc., form subsets of the outcome space and thus a subset of an outcome space may serve to define an event. The subspace $\{1, 2, 3\}$ serves to define the event, 'the rolling of a number less than 4'.

We now look to see how the probabilities of events defined by subsets with more than one element may be calculated.

Example 1: Find the probability that in the rolling of a dice a 5 or a 6 will be rolled.

Answer

The subset of the outcome space for this is $\{5, 6\}$. It thus seems reasonable to say that the probability of a 5 or a 6 will be $\frac{1}{3}$. i.e. Probability $(\{5, 6\}) = P(\{5, 6\}) = \frac{1}{3}$

Example 2: Repeat *Example 1* with various subsets of S.

$$P(\{1, 2\}) = \tfrac{1}{3} \qquad P(\{3, 4\}) = \tfrac{1}{3}$$
$$P(\{1, 2, 3\}) = \tfrac{1}{2} \qquad P(\{3, 4, 5\}) = \tfrac{1}{2}$$
$$P(\{1, 2, 3, 4\}) = \tfrac{2}{3} \qquad P(\{2, 3, 4, 5\}) = \tfrac{2}{3}$$
$$P(\{1, 2, 3, 4, 5\}) = \tfrac{5}{6}$$

If we now take the whole of the sample space and consider it as a subset of itself, then, because of the construction of the outcome space, at least one of the outcomes is certain to occur. Therefore, for the dice, $P(\{1, 2, 3, 4, 5, 6\}) = 1$, and generalising this,

$$P(S) = 1$$

where S is any outcome space.

Also since $S' = \phi$ $P(S') = P(\phi) = 0$, thus the event associated with S' is impossible.

We now confirm what is implicit in the above work, that in the notation $P(\ )$, what is put inside the bracket is a subset of the outcome space.

4.17 Ascription of Probabilities

Hitherto we have taken a 'common sense' view in ascribing probabilities – it seems perfectly reasonable to say that the probability of getting a head upon the flip of a coin is $\frac{1}{2}$, i.e. $P(H) = \frac{1}{2}$, but what would happen if we took a coin tossed it four times and got three heads and one tail? No doubt the reply would be that the coin should be tossed a greater number of times. Let us suppose that this is done and that out of one hundred tosses, seventy four heads appeared; and out of one thousand tosses, seven hundred and fifty heads appeared – what then? The reply to this might well be that the coin in question is not a 'fair' coin – it is biased towards head by virtue of some uneveness in its density. But what does this imply? It implies that we have decided that a coin ought to come down heads roughly one half of the number of times of tossing and any marked deviation from this result in experiments will be an indication *not that we are incorrect in our assessment* but that the coin is defective in some way.

We have thus ascribed probabilities without initially taking any account of experience, and such probabilities are called *a priori* probabilities. The full import of this may be seen in a definition of probability which runs as follows:

If an event can happen in x ways and fail to happen in y ways, all of which are equally likely, then the probability of the event happening is

$$\frac{x}{x+y},$$

i.e. in the case of a coin – heads may happen in 1 way, and fail to happen in 1 way, therefore the probability of heads occurring is

$$\frac{1}{1+1} = \frac{1}{2}.$$

Clearly by defining the coin to be 'fair', or by saying that the ways an event can happen or fail to happen are equally likely, there is circularity. The result is laid down in advance by virtue of the conditions imposed at the beginning. This does not of itself, invalidate this procedure, in fact it can be most useful. If we ascribe *a priori* probabilities to a subject, then experiment, how far the results differ from what is expected has very useful application. More of this will be seen later.

Although there are many situations where it seems reasonable to apply *a priori* probabilities, there are many situations when it is not possible to do this. What is the probability of a 35 year old man living until he is 70? What is the probability that a baby will die at birth? To these and many other questions like them there is no *a priori* answer possible, and in these cases we have to use what is called *a posteriori* or *empirical* probability. These are calculated by actually looking at the events and trials themselves. If for example, out of every 1000 babies born, 4 died at birth, we would say that the probability of a baby dying at birth is $\frac{4}{1000}$. If, over 40 games of tennis between A and B, A won 25 games and B won 15, then we would say that the probability that A will win the next game is $\frac{25}{40} = \frac{5}{8}$. Thus we define empirical probability as

$$\frac{\text{the number of occurrences of the event in question}}{\text{the total number of trials/observations}}$$

and the greater the total number of trials the more reliable will be the figure reached. The taking of a large number of trials is important as will be seen in the following example.

Example 1: A coin was tossed 20 times and the number of heads recorded as follows

Number of tosses	1	2	3	4	5	6	7	8	9	10	11	12	13	14	15	16	17	18	19	20
Number of heads	0	1	2	2	2	2	3	3	4	4	4	5	6	6	7	8	9	10	11	11

and the results are graphed in Fig. 4.17(a) in the form of the ratio

$$\frac{\text{number of heads}}{\text{number of tosses}}$$

Two things are obvious from the following graph. First, that the ratio differs very markedly from a $\frac{1}{2}$ after only a few tosses, and, secondly, that the greater the number of tosses the closer the ratio tends towards $\frac{1}{2}$. In this experiment only twenty flips were given but the form of the graph suggests that if more flips were given, the ratio would tend closer to $\frac{1}{2}$. The results of this experiment are in accordance with the common sense thinking that the smaller the sample the less likely it is to be accurate, and the larger the sample the better the result will be.

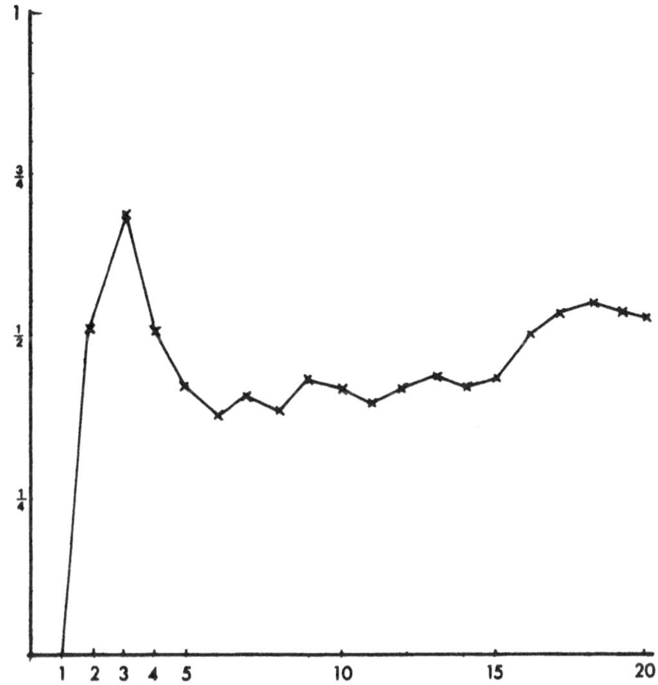

Fig. 4.17 (a). Graph to show the ratio $\frac{\text{number of heads}}{\text{number of tosses}}$ in twenty tosses of a coin

A more sophisticated definition can now be given if we admit the idea of letting the number of trials get larger and larger and tend towards infinity. This is

$$P(E) = \lim_{N \to \infty} \frac{\text{number of occurrences of } E}{N}$$

which reads, 'The probability of an event E is the limit of the fraction

$$\frac{\text{number of occurrences of } E}{N}$$

where N is the number of observations, as N gets larger and larger and approaches infinity'. This is only making more precise the definition of empirical probability given above, and is called the *relative frequency definition of probability.*

Exercise 4

1. Find more examples like those in Section 4.1. Ascribe a probability value to them and discuss the method by which you obtained the result.

2. Find more examples of random phenomena and non-random phenomena like those in Section 4.2. Say how you could measure them. Can you measure the same phenomena in more than one way? Give examples. Show clearly the difference between the random phenomena and the random variable in your examples.

3. For those examples you picked in Question 2 show the outcome spaces. Say whether they are discrete or continuous.

4. Where possible, in your examples used in Questions 2 and 3, find a set to indicate the probability values of the individual elements of the outcome spaces.

5. Write out in full the following sets:

(i) {The continents of the world}
(ii) {The first ten letters of the alphabet}
(iii) {The integers between -4 and $+6$.}

Answer

(iii) $\{-3, -2, -1, 0, 1, 2, 3, 4, 5\}$. Note -4 and $+6$ are not included because the requirement is for those numbers *between* -4 and 6.

6. Write the sets of Question 5 in the qualification method

Answer

(i) $\{x \mid x \text{ is a continent of the world}\}$
(ii) $\{y \mid y \text{ is a letter of the alphabet before } k\}$
(iii) $\{x \mid x \text{ is integral and } -3 \leqslant x \leqslant 5\}$

7. State in words and then write out the following in full:

(i) $A = \{x \mid x \text{ is even, integral and } 2 \leqslant x < 12\}$
(ii) $B = \{x \mid x \text{ is a vowel}\}$
(iii) $C = \{x \mid x + 4 = 10\}$
(iv) $D = \{x \mid x^2 - 5x + 6 = 0\}$
(v) $E = \{x \mid x \text{ is odd, positive and } x < 8\}$

Answer

(i) A is the set of even whole numbers bigger than or equal to 2 but less than 12. $\{2, 4, 6, 8, 10\}$.
(iii) C is the set of numbers which when added to 4 give 10. $\{6\}$
(v) E is the set of positive odd numbers less than 8. $\{1, 3, 5, 7\}$

8. Which of the following are incorrectly written and why?

(1) $x \in A$ (2) $B \in y$ (3) $x + A$ (4) $x \in y$

(5) $y \in Z$ (6) $y \notin Y$ (7) $A - y$

Answer

(1) correct (3) incorrect because adding a letter to a set in arithmetic fashion has no meaning in set theory. (5) correct (7) incorrect because subtracting a letter from a set in arithmetic fashion has no meaning in set theory.

9. Let $A = \{a, b, c, d\}$. State whether the following are correct or not:

(i) $b \in A$ (ii) $\{a, b\} \in A$ (iii) $\{a, b\} \subset A$ (iv) $a \subset A$

(v) $a \in A$ (vi) $A \supset \{a, b, c\}$ (vii) $\phi \in A$ (viii) $\{a, b, c, d\} \not\subset A$

Answer

(i) correct (ii) incorrect $\{a, b\}$ is a set and the connective to use between it and A is $\subset$ (iii) correct (iv) incorrect. a is an element of a set and the correct connective to use between it and A is $\in$
(v) correct (vi) correct (vii) incorrect (viii) incorrect

10. If (i) $A = \{a\}$ (ii) $B = \{a, b\}$ (iii) $C = \{a, b, c\}$ how many subsets do these sets contain? (Don't forget ϕ) What pattern forms? Can you predict the number of subsets for sets with any given number of elements?

Answer

(i) 2 (ii) 4 (iii) 8. For any set with n elements there are 2^n subsets.

11. Draw Venn diagrams of a universal set S with subsets A, B, and D, showing the following:

(i) $A \subset B$ (ii) $A \not\subset B$ (iii) $A \subset B$ and $B \subset D$ (iv) $A \subset B$ and $B \subset A$

12. For the diagram are the following correct:

(i) $A \subset B$ (ii) $C \subset A$ and $C \subset B$ (iii) $E \subset D$ (iv) $D \subset E$ (v) $D \subset A$

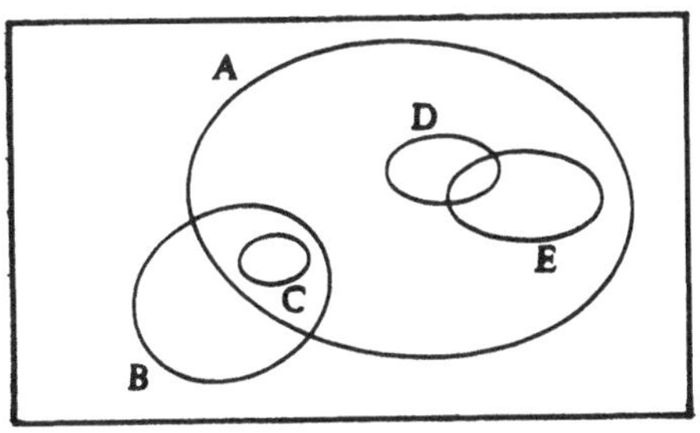

Answer

(i) incorrect (ii) correct (iii) incorrect (iv) incorrect (v) correct

13. On a Venn diagram draw two sets A and B, and shade $A \cup B$. How many different diagrams can you draw?

Answer

Six which are essentially different.

14. Repeat Question 13 but use 3 sets A, B and C. Shade (i) $A \cup B$ (ii) $A \cup C$ (iii) $B \cup C$ (iv) $A \cup B \cup C$

15. Extend Question 14 to four sets A, B, C and D.

16. On a Venn diagram draw two sets A and B and shade $A \cap B$. Is it always possible to shade $A \cap B$? How many different diagrams can you draw?

17. Repeat Question 16 but use 3 sets A, B and C, and shade (i) $A \cap B$ (ii) $A \cap C$ (iii) $B \cap C$ (iv) $A \cap B \cap C$

18. Extend Question 17 to four sets A, B, C and D

19. Let $I = \{1, 2, 3, \ldots, 10\}$ $A = \{1, 2, 3, 4, 5\}$ $B = \{6, 7, 8, 9, 10\}$ $D = \{2, 4, 6, 8\}$ $E = \{1, 3, 5, 7, 9\}$ $F = \{4, 5, 6, 7\}$
Find (i) $A \cup B$ (ii) $A \cup D$ (iii) $D \cup B$ (iv) $A \cup E$ (v) $B \cup F$ (vi) A' (vii) B' (viii) D' (ix) E' (x) $A \cap B$ (xi) $A \cap D$ (xii) $E \cap F$ (xiii) $A' \cup B$ (xiv) $A' \cup D$ (xv) $B' \cup F$ (xvi) $B' \cap E$ (xvii) $B' \cap D$ (xviii) $E' \cap F$ (xix) $A' \cap D'$ (xx) $A' \cap B'$ (xxi) $A' \cap F'$ (xxii) $A' \cap E'$ (xxiii) $(A \cup B)'$ (xxiv) $(A \cup D)'$ (xxv) $(B \cup D)'$.

Which of these are the same? How many other possible combinations have been omitted?

Answer

(i) $A \cup B = I$ (iii) $D \cup B = \{2, 4, 6, 7, 8, 9, 10\}$
(v) $B \cup F = \{4, 5, 6, 7, 8, 9, 10\}$ (vii) $B' = A$ (ix) $E' = D$
(x) $A \cap B = \phi$ (xiii) $A' \cup B = B$ (xvi) $B' \cap E = \{1, 3, 5\}$
(xix) $A' \cap D' = \{7, 9\}$ (xxiii) $(A \cup B)' = \phi$ (xxv) $(B \cup D)' = \{1, 3, 5\}$

20. Given $I = \{x \mid x \text{ is a letter of the alphabet}\}$ and $A = \{a, b, c\}$, $B = \{b, c, d, e\}$, and $C = \{x, y, z, w\}$, verify that (i) $A \cup B = B \cup A$ (ii) $A \cap B = B \cap A$ (iii) $(A \cup B) \cup C = A \cup (B \cup C)$ (iv) $(A \cap B) \cap C = A \cap (B \cap C)$ (v) $A \cap (B \cup C) = (A \cap B) \cup (A \cap C)$ (vi) $A \cup (B \cap C) = (A \cup B) \cap (A \cup C)$ (vii) $A \cup A' = I$ (viii) $A \cap A' = \phi$ (ix) $B \cup B' = I$ (x) $B \cap B' = \phi$ (xi) $A \cap I = A$ (xii) $A \cup I = I$

21. In a football team, four players smoke, five players drink beer and five are both teetotal and non-smoking. How many both drink beer and smoke?

Answer

2

22. In a class of 30 children 15 have no pet, 6 have dogs only as a pet, four have a dog and a cat as pets, and the remainder have cats only as a pet. How many have cats?

Answer

5

23. Out of 100 people interviewed 27 drink tea only, 17 drink coffee only and 19 drink cocoa only. 10 drink tea and cocoa, 12 drink cocoa and coffee, and 8 drink tea and coffee – (None of these necessarily at the same time!). If 32 drink coffee, how many drink (a) all three (b) drink neither tea, coffee, nor cocoa?

24. A tetrahedron (four sided die) has the numbers 1 to 4 painted on the faces. When it is thrown the underface is noted when it comes to rest. Write out the outcome space and the set of associated probabilities. Find (a) $P(1)$ (b) the probability of throwing either 1 or 2 (c) $P(\{1, 4\})$ (d) $P(\{2, 3, 4\})$.

Answer

$S = \{1, 2, 3, 4\}$ Associated probabilities $\{\frac{1}{4}, \frac{1}{4}, \frac{1}{4}, \frac{1}{4}\}$

(a) $\frac{1}{4}$ (b) $\frac{1}{2}$ (c) $\frac{1}{2}$ (d) $\frac{3}{4}$

25. A six sided die has the 5 and 6 removed and replaced by 2 and 3 respectively. Find (a) $P(2)$ (b) the probability of throwing 1 or 2 (c) $P(\{2, 3\})$ (d) the probability of throwing either 1, 2 or 3 (e) $P(\{2, 3, 4\})$ (f) $P(\{1, 2, 3, 4\})$

Answer

(a) $\frac{2}{3}$ (b) $\frac{1}{2}$ (c) $\frac{2}{3}$ (d) $\frac{5}{6}$ (e) $\frac{5}{6}$ (f) 1

26. Given the die of the previous question and $A = \{1\}$ $B = \{1, 2\}$, $C = \{2, 3, 4\}$. Find (a) $P(A \cup B)$ (b) $P(A \cap B)$ (c) $P(A \cup B \cup C)$ (d) $P(A \cap B \cap C)$

Answer

(a) $A \cup B = B$, therefore $P(A \cup B) = P(B) = \frac{1}{2}$ (b) $\frac{1}{6}$ (c) 1 (d) 0

27. Which of the following must have probabilities ascribed to them by using empirical probability methods. In all cases where appropriate look up actual data and find a numerical value for the probability:

(a) the probability a person will survive an appendix operation

(b) the probability that a person chosen at random will be taller than average

(c) the probability a person will survive (i) a heart (ii) a kidney transplant operation

(d) the probability that two sixes will appear when two dice are thrown

(e) the probability that a page will have a misprint on it

(f) the probability that a machine will produce a defective item

(g) the probability that a man under 25 years of age will have a car accident

(h) the probability that it will rain tomorrow

(j) the probability that a book will be a best seller

Answer

(a), (c), (e), (f), (g), (h), (j)

28. Explain in your own words the two uses of the phrase 'a random variable'. Also discuss the idea of a 'random variable' as used in probability, together with the idea of a relative frequency graph as used in descriptive statistics.

5 Permutations and Combinations

5.1 A Fundamental Theorem

Many problems in statistics require, as we have seen, the complete enumeration of the outcome space, and in the simple cases that we have seen there has been no difficulty. However not all cases are as simple as this and we now require methods that will enable us to determine the outcome space in these more difficult cases. We approach the problem by example. Suppose a man can travel from A to B by either train, bus, or car, and from B to C by either bus or car. How many different ways can he travel between A and C?

Answer

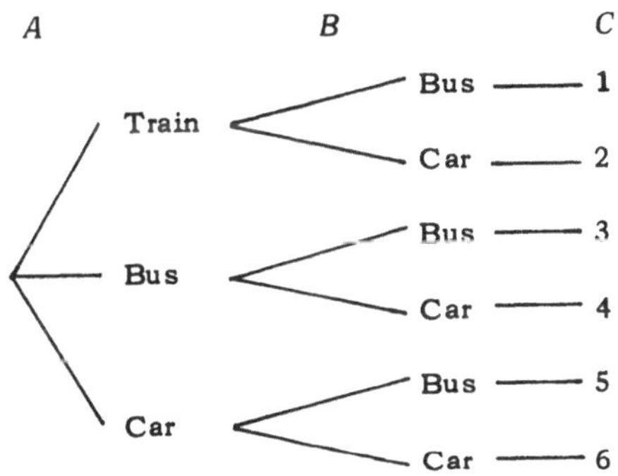

Fig. 5.1 (a)

From the diagram it can easily be seen that there are six different ways. If we consider the set {Train, Bus, Car} for the first part of the journey, and the set {Bus, Car} for the second part, it can be seen that every element in the first set is combined with every element in the second set.

Example 2: An experiment consists of rolling a die and then flipping a coin. Find the outcome space.

Solution:

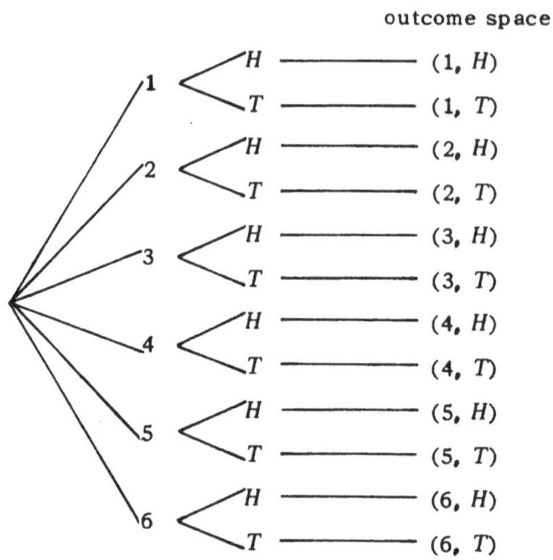

Fig. 5.1 (b)

Using the same method as in the first example we get the above solution. One thing that is immediately apparent is that the solution space does not consist of the simple elements that we have seen in previous problems. The elements are in fact pairs, and in this case the first place in the pair is occupied by a number, and the second place is occupied by a letter. We are now in a position to make the following definition:

If we take two sets, A and B, and form the set of ordered pairs (x, y) such that x is an element of A, and y is an element of B, then the set so formed is called the product set of A and B and is written $A \times B$, and read 'A cross B'. Note that such pairs are called ordered pairs and that order matters insofar as $(x, y) \neq (y, x)$ except in a few special cases.

Example 3: What is the product set $C \times D$, where

$$C = \{a, b, c\} \quad \text{and} \quad D = \{1, m, n, p\}$$

Answer

$$\begin{aligned} C \times D = \{&(a, 1)\ (a, m)\ (a, n)\ (a, p) \\ &(b, 1)\ (b, m)\ (b, n)\ (b, p) \\ &(c, 1)\ (c, m)\ (c, n)\ (c, p)\} \end{aligned}$$

From the examples so far seen it will be noted that since every element in the first set is associated with every element in the second set, the number of elements in the product set will be found by multiplying together the numbers which represent the numbers of elements in the two sets. In *Example 2*, this is $6 \times 2 = 12$, and in *Example 3*, it is $3 \times 4 = 12$. More generally this becomes

$$N(A \times B) = N(A) \times N(B)$$

A study of *Example 3* will show that $C \times D \neq D \times C$, and in general $A \times B = B \times A$, although $N(A \times B) = N(B \times A)$.

This concept can be extended to three and more sets. The set of ordered triples formed by taking elements of the form (x, y, z), where $x \in A$, $y \in B$, $z \in C$, is called the product set of A, B and C, written $A \times B \times C$.

Example 4: An experiment consists of throwing a die and then tossing two coins. Find the outcome space.

Answer

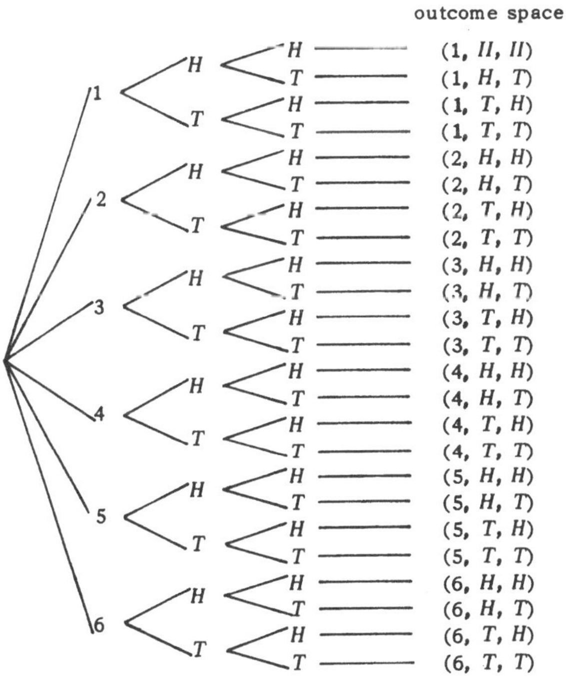

Fig. 5.1(c)

Since there are six elements in the first set, two in the second, and two in the third, a total of $6 \times 2 \times 2 = 24$ ordered triples can be formed.

Thus a natural extension of the rule for the number of elements in a product set for two sets gives us

$$N(A \times B \times C) = N(A) \times N(B) \times N(C)$$

More generally if we have sets $A_1, A_2, A_3, \ldots, A_i$, then there are $N(A_1) \times N(A_2) \times N(A_3) \times \ldots \times N(A_i)$ ways of forming ordered i tuples. In less formal language we might say that if we have sets $A_1, A_2, A_3, \ldots, A_i$, then there are $N(A_1) \times N(A_2) \times N(A_3) \times \ldots \times N(A_i)$ ways in which one can first select an element of A_1, and then an element of $A_2, \ldots$, and finally an element of A_i. We can now use this to find how many elements there will be in outcome spaces of a more complicated kind.

Example 5: If three dice and five coins are used in an experiment, how many elements will there be in the outcome space:

Answer

$A_1 = 6 \quad A_2 = 6 \quad A_3 = 6 \quad A_4 = 2 \quad A_5 = 2 \quad A_6 = 2 \quad A_7 = 2$
$A_8 = 2$

Therefore the outcome space will consist of

$$6 \times 6 \times 6 \times 2 \times 2 \times 2 \times 2 \times 2 = 6912 \text{ elements}$$

The diagrams used in the above section are called 'twig' or 'tree' diagrams and are useful in determining outcome spaces in simple cases. They can also be useful in determining probabilities as will be seen later.

5.2 Outcome Space Diagrams

It is often useful to have some sort of diagramatic representation of an outcome space and we now look at some examples. The simple one dimensional outcome spaces can be represented by points on a line.

Example 1:

Diagramatic representation of the outcome space of the random phenomenon 'rolling a die'.

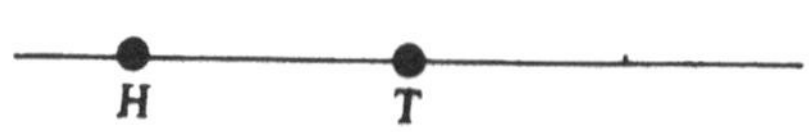

Diagramatic representation of the outcome space of the random phenomenon 'tossing a coin'.

The more complicated outcome spaces have to be shown on a diagram which has the same dimension as the elements of the outcome space. In the case of 'rolling a die and then tossing a coin', we saw that the elements of the outcome space consisted of ordered pairs, i.e. two dimensional elements, and a two dimensional diagram is needed.

Example 3: Show diagramatically the outcome space of the experiment of rolling a die and then tossing a coin.

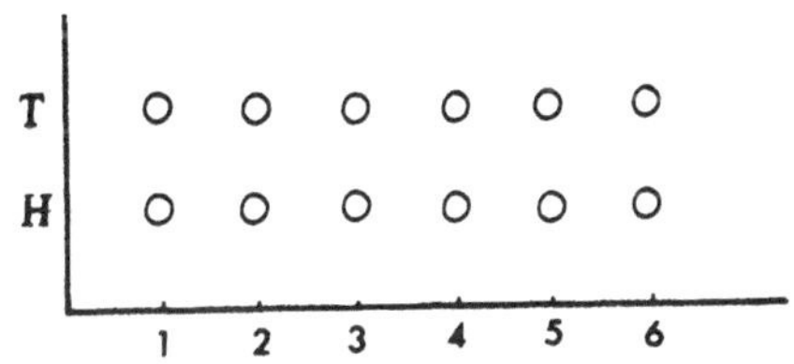

Fig. 5.2 (a)

This diagram is in fact called the graph of the product set Die × Coin. The point representing (3, *T*) i.e. throwing a 3, and tossing a tail, is found by first finding the 3 on the horizontal axis and then the *T* on the vertical axis.

Example 4: Show diagramatically the outcome space of the experiment 'rolling a die and then tossing two coins'. See Fig. 5.2 (b).

In order that the diagram should not be confused only a few of the 24 points have been put in. To find the point which represents (4, *H*, *H*), first find 4 on the axis which comes towards the left foreground, then *H* on the horizontal axis which goes to the right, and finally, find the *H* on the vertical axis.

Physical representation of outcome spaces whose elements are of dimension greater than 3, is, of course, impossible, although it is possible to give a complete enumeration of the elements in the space.

Example 5: Show the elements of the outcome space for the experiment 'rolling 4 dice'.

Answer

$$S = \{(1, 1, 1, 1), (1, 1, 1, 2), (1, 1, 2, 1), \ldots, (6, 6, 6, 6)\}$$

Diagrams are also useful for showing subsets of the outcome space.

Example 6: The outcome space for the experiment of 'rolling two dice' is shown below. See Fig. 5.2 (c). What event does the subspace indicated by the broken line represent.

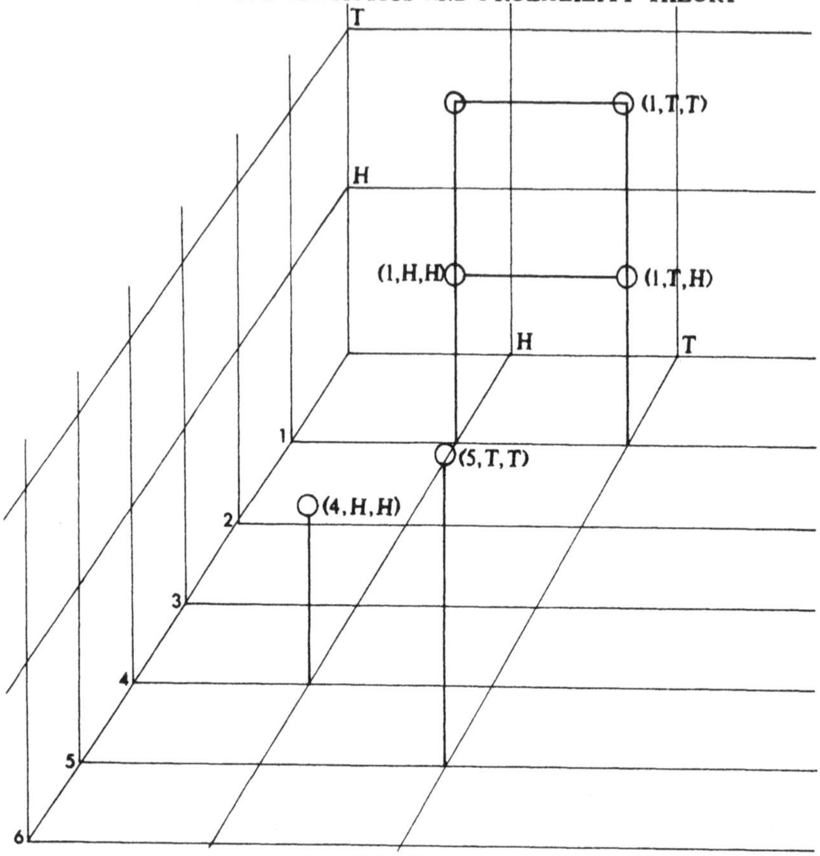

Fig. 5.2(b)

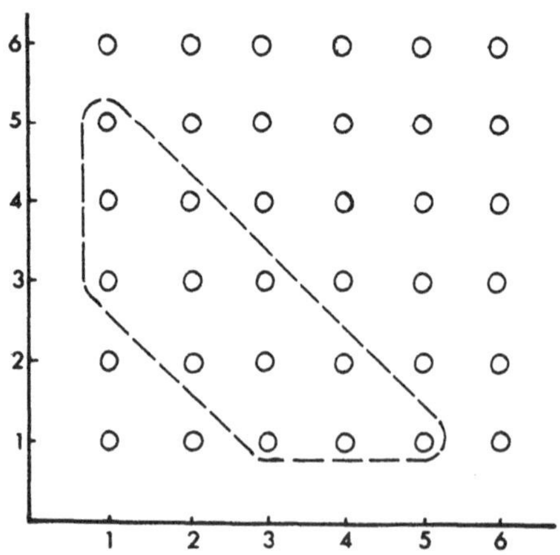

Fig. 5.2(c)

Answer

The dotted line surrounds all those points where the sum of the digits is equal to 4, 5, or 6, thus the event the subspace represents is 'the throw where the sum of the digits is more than 3 but less than 7'.

5.3 Permutations

Having found a general principle for combining elements of one set with elements of another in every possible arrangement, we now seek to find a general principle for arranging the elements of a single set in every possible way.

Example 1: A man has a wireless set, a television, and a record player and wishes to arrange them on a shelf. How many different ways may he do this?

Answer 1

We may experiment and list the possibilities as follows:

$$\begin{array}{lll} W\ T\ R & & W\ R\ T \\ T\ R\ W & & T\ W\ R \\ R\ T\ W & & R\ W\ T \end{array}$$

Answer 2

We can argue as follows: When the shelf is empty we have a choice of three objects to go into the first place. As soon as we place the first object in the first place we have two objects left to fill the second place, and when one of these is placed on the shelf, there is only the choice of the one remaining object left.

i.e. for 1st place we have a choice of	3
2nd	2
3rd	1

Therefore the number of arrangements can be found with the aid of the following diagram: and it can be seen from this diagram – and also from the argument – that the total number of ways can be found by multiplying $3 \times 2 \times 1 = 6$, and we see that this agrees with the number of arrangements in answer 1.

So far we have used the neutral word 'arrangement', and we note that in these arrangements order is important, i.e. $W\ R\ T$, is not the same as, $R\ T\ W$. We now give the mathematical word for such situations.

Definition: If the elements of a set are arranged in some specific order, then such an arrangement is called a *permutation*

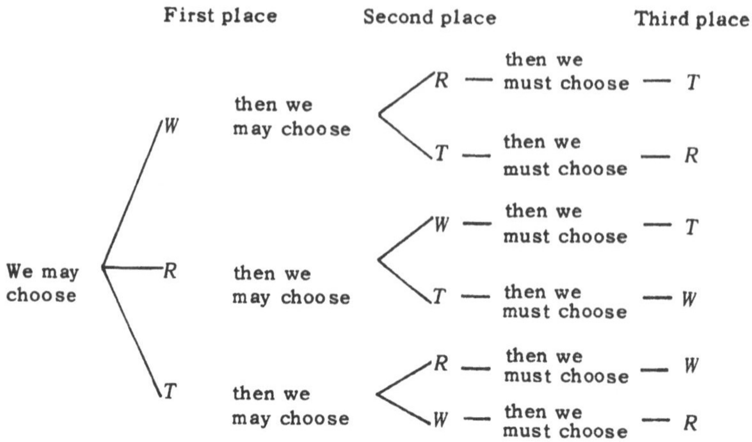

Fig. 5.3(a)

Example 2: How many permutations are there of the letters

(i) $A\ B$ (ii) $A\ B\ C$ (iii) $A\ B\ C\ D$

Answer

Answer

Arguing as above gives numbers as below:

(i)	$A\ B$	$B\ A$			$2 \times 1 = 2$
(ii)	$A\ B\ C$	$A\ C\ B$			
	$B\ A\ C$	$B\ C\ A$			$3 \times 2 \times 1 = 6$
	$C\ A\ B$	$C\ B\ A$			
(iii)	$A\ B\ C\ D$	$B\ A\ C\ D$	$C\ A\ B\ D$	$D\ A\ B\ C$	
	$A\ B\ D\ C$	$B\ A\ D\ C$	$C\ A\ D\ B$	$D\ A\ C\ B$	
	$A\ C\ B\ D$	$B\ C\ A\ D$	$C\ B\ A\ D$	$D\ B\ A\ C$	
	$A\ C\ D\ B$	$B\ C\ D\ A$	$C\ B\ D\ A$	$D\ B\ C\ A$	$4 \times 3 \times 2 \times 1 = 24$
	$A\ D\ B\ C$	$B\ D\ A\ C$	$C\ D\ A\ B$	$D\ C\ A\ B$	
	$A\ D\ C\ B$	$B\ D\ C\ A$	$C\ D\ B\ A$	$D\ C\ B\ A$	

We have seen that the multiplication of numbers in descending order occurs quite frequently and it would therefore be convenient to have a shorthand notation for this.

Definition:

2×1 is written $2!$ and read 'factorial 2'.

$3 \times 2 \times 1$ is written $3!$ and read 'factorial 3'.

$4 \times 3 \times 2 \times 1$ is written $4!$ and read 'factorial 4'.

$n(n-1)(n-2) \ldots . 2 \times 1$ is written $n!$ and read 'factorial n'.

Thus we may now say:

The number of different permutations of the elements of a set S containing n elements is $n!$

In the above work it has been assumed that all the elements of the set are distinct and thus it is applicable to situations with distinct objects. Occasionally, however, situations arise where all the objects are not distinct.

Example 3: How many different permutations can be made with the letters of the word 'see'.

Answer

Let us for the moment distinguish between the two e's by using subscripts i.e. s, e_1, e_2, and we get

$$\begin{array}{ll} s\,e_1\,e_2 & s\,e_2\,e_1 \\ e_1\,s\,e_2 & e_1\,s\,e_2 \\ e_1\,e_2\,s & e_2\,e_1\,s \end{array}$$

the 3! arrangements as before. If we now drop out the subscripts we get

$$\begin{array}{ll} s\,e\,e & s\,e\,e \\ e\,s\,e & e\,s\,e \\ e\,e\,s & e\,e\,s \end{array}$$

and it can be seen that there are only three different permutations possible.

Let us now take the letters '$s\ e\ e\ e$' and repeat the above.

$$\begin{array}{llllll} s\,e_1\,e_2\,e_3 & s\,e_1\,e_3\,e_2 & s\,e_2\,e_1\,e_3 & s\,e_2\,e_3\,e_1 & s\,e_3\,e_1\,e_2 & s\,e_3\,e_2\,e_1 \\ e_1\,s\,e_2\,e_3 & e_1\,s\,e_3\,e_2 & e_2\,s\,e_1\,e_3 & e_2\,s\,e_3\,e_1 & e_3\,s\,e_1\,e_2 & e_3\,s\,e_2\,e_1 \\ e_1\,e_2\,s\,e_3 & e_1\,e_3\,s\,e_2 & e_2\,e_1\,s\,e_3 & e_2\,e_3\,s\,e_1 & e_3\,e_1\,s\,e_2 & e_3\,e_2\,s\,e_1 \\ e_1\,e_2\,e_3\,s & e_1\,e_3\,e_2\,s & e_2\,e_1\,e_3\,s & e_2\,e_3\,e_1\,s & e_3\,e_1\,e_2\,s & e_3\,e_2\,e_1\,s \end{array}$$

dropping the subscripts gives

$$\begin{array}{llllll} s\,e\,e\,e & s\,e\,e\,e & s\,e\,e\,e & s\,e\,e\,e & s\,e\,e\,e & s\,e\,e\,e \\ e\,s\,e\,e & e\,s\,e\,e & e\,s\,e\,e & e\,s\,e\,e & e\,s\,e\,e & e\,s\,e\,e \\ e\,e\,s\,e & e\,e\,s\,e & e\,e\,s\,e & e\,e\,s\,e & e\,e\,s\,e & e\,e\,s\,e \\ e\,e\,e\,s & e\,e\,e\,s & e\,e\,e\,s & e\,e\,e\,s & e\,e\,e\,s & e\,e\,e\,s \end{array}$$

Studying these we note that, in the case of $s\ e\ e$ each pair with subscripts yields only one permutation without subscripts, and in the case of $s\ e\ e\ e$ each set of 6 with subscripts yields only 1 without subscripts. Thus factorial 3 reduces to 3, and factorial 4 reduces to 4. To reduce 3!

to three we divide by 2!, i.e. 3!/2! = 3, and to reduce 4! to four we divide by 3!, i.e. 4!/3! = 4. Since adding extra elements to a set increases the number of permutations multiplicatively, then reducing the number of distinct elements will reduce the number of permutations by the inverse process of multiplication, i.e. division.

Example 4: Consider the word 'success'. With subscripts to distinguish the c's and the s's there will be 7! permutations. If however the subscripts on the s's are dropped then there will be 6 = 3! permutations yielding only 1 permutation; therefore without subscripts on the s's there will be 7!/3! permutations. If now the subscripts on the c's are dropped then 2! = 2 permutations will yield only 1 permutation; therefore without subscripts on the c's there will be

$$\frac{7!}{3! \times 2!} = 420$$

different permutations of the letters in the word 'success'.

We can now generalise this result into:

If in a set of n elements where k_1 are alike, k_2 others alike, ..., and k_t others alike, then the number of permutations will be

$$\frac{n!}{k_1!\, k_2!, \ldots, k_t!}$$

In the above work every element of the set was selected each time, and we now look at the question of what permutations can be formed if only a few of the elements are taken at a time.

Example 5: If we have a set containing 6 elements, $\{a, b, c, d, e, f\}$ and we wish to form all the permutations of these 6 elements taken 2 at a time we may use an argument similar to that used in *Example 1*, answer 2.

Consider the following:

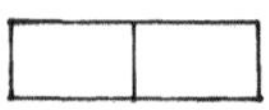

For the first vacant place we have a choice of 6 elements. Having put one of these elements in the first place there remains 5 elements to be selected for the second place. Now any of the 6 ways of filling the first place may be combined with any of the 5 ways of filling the second place, so there are 6 × 5 = 30, ways of filling the two places. The following diagram will make this clear. See Fig. 5.3 (b).

Reading from the top in this diagram we get $a\,b$, $a\,c$, $a\,d$, ... right through to ... $f\,e$, for the 30 different permutations.

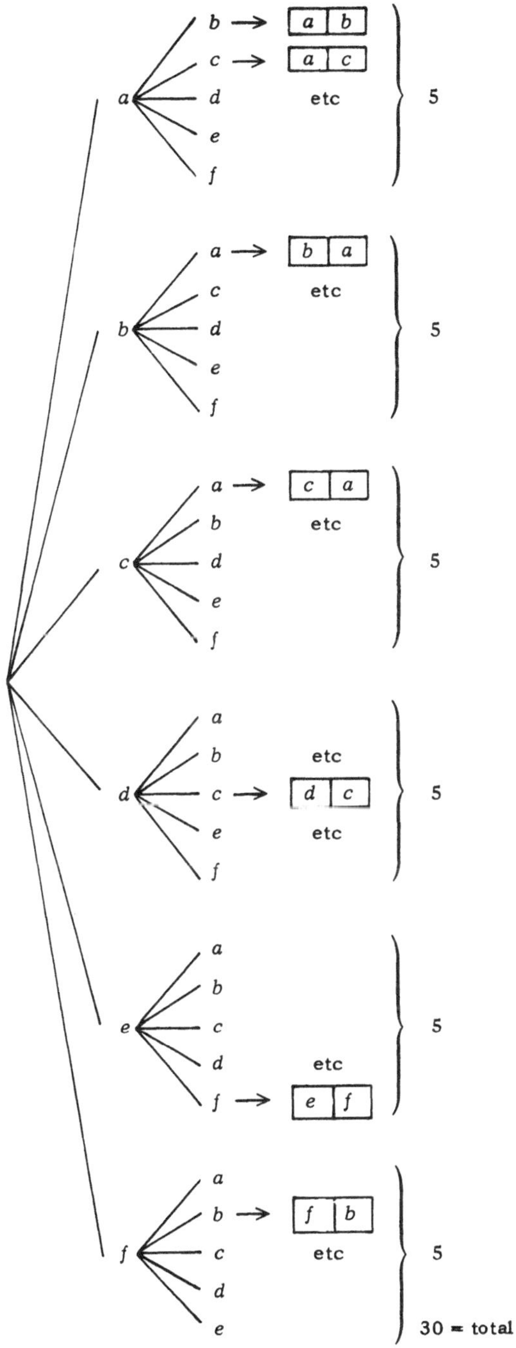
a
b → a b
c → a c
d etc
e
f
5
b
a → b a
c etc
d
e
f
5
c
a → c a
b etc
d
e
f
5
d
a
b etc
c → d c
e etc
f
5
e
a
b
c
d etc
f → e f
5
f
a
b → f b
c etc
d
e
5
30 = total

Fig. 5.3 (b)

A similar argument will show that if we now select 3 of the elements at a time then we will be able to form

$$6 \times 5 \times 3 = 90 \text{ permutations.}$$

Now consider:

Number of elements in the set

6 Number of permutations formed when 2 elements selected at a time $= \underbrace{6 \times 5}$ permutations

Note —— 2 factors

6 Number of permutations formed when 3 elements selected at a time $= \underbrace{6 \times 5 \times 4}$ permutations

Note —— 3 factors

We may now generalise this to say, that if from a set of n elements, r at a time are selected, then

$$\underbrace{n(n-1)(n-2)\ldots(n-[r-1])}_{r \text{ factors}}$$

permutations will be formed.

The notation for the number of permutations of r distinct elements selected from a set of n elements is nPr; other notations used are ${}^nP_r$ and $P(n, r)$. i.e.

$$nPr = n(n-1)(n-2)\ldots(n-[r-1]).$$

We now make use of the following device:

$$5 \times 4 = \frac{5 \times 4 \times 3 \times 2 \times 1}{3 \times 2 \times 1}$$

and so

$$n(n-1)(n-2)\ldots(n-[r-1])$$

$$= \frac{\overbrace{n(n-1)(n-2)\ldots(n-[r-1])}^{r \text{ factors}}\overbrace{(n-r)(n-r+1)\ldots 3 \times 2 \times 1}^{(n-r) \text{ factors}}}{\underbrace{(n-r)(n-r+1)\ldots 3 \times 2 \times 1}_{n \text{ factors}}} = \frac{n!}{(n-r)!}$$

Therefore we may write

$$nPr = \frac{n!}{(n-r)!}.$$

Example 6:

$$5\,P\,3 = \frac{5!}{(5-3)!} = \frac{5!}{2!} = 60$$

$$14\,P\,2 = \frac{14!}{(14-2)!} = \frac{14!}{12!} = 182$$

5.4 Combinations

Suppose we select the elements *a, b, c* from the set {*a, b, c, d, e*} then we have seen that they will yield 3! permutations, i.e. *a b c, a c b,* etc.; if we select the elements *a, b, c, d,* they will yield 4! permutations, *a b c d, a b d c,* etc. Suppose now that we disregard order in these selections and consider *a b c, a c b,* etc., to be the same – how will this effect the number of selections? Such selections are called *combinations*, and the notation used is $n\,C\,r$ – this symbol denotes the number of ways of selecting r distinct objects from n disregarding order.

Example 1: How many ways may two of *A, B, C* be selected?

Answer

A B, A C, B C $\quad 3\,C\,2 = 3$

Example 2: How many ways may two of *A, B, C, D,* be selected?

Answer

A B, A C, A D, B C, B D, C D $\quad 4\,C\,2 = 6$

Example 3: How many ways may three of *A, B, C, D,* be selected?

Answer

A B C, A B D, A C D, B C D $\quad 4\,C\,3 = 4$

We note in *Example 1*, that each of the combinations of 2 yields 2! permutations, and thus we can say $(3\,C\,2) \times 2!$ would give the number of permutations of 2 elements from 3. i.e.

$$(3\,C\,2) \times 2! = 3 \times 2! = 3! = \frac{3!}{1!} = \frac{3!}{(3-2)!} = 3\,P\,2$$

Similarly in *Example 3*, each combination of 3 yields 3! permutations and

$$(4\,C\,3) \times 3! = 4 \times 3! = 4! = \frac{4!}{(4-3)!} = 4\,P\,3$$

gives the number of permutations of 3 elements from 4. Generalising this we can say that if r distinct elements are selected from a set of n, then each of these $n\,C\,r$ combinations will yield $r!$ permutations. Thus we can say that $(n\,C\,r) \times r!$ will give the number of permutations of r

elements from n. i.e.

$$(n\ C\ r) \times r! = n\ P\ r$$

but
$$n\ P\ r = \frac{n!}{(n-r)!}$$

therefore
$$(n\ C\ r) \times r! = \frac{n!}{(n-r)!}$$

giving
$$n\ C\ r = \frac{n!}{(n-r)! \times r!}$$

Example 4: How many combinations of 7 elements are there in a set of 9 elements?

Answer

$$9\ C\ 7 = \frac{9!}{(9-7)! \times 7!} = \frac{9!}{2! \times 7!} = \frac{9 \times 8}{2} = 36$$

Example 5: Evaluate (i) 10 C 3 (ii) 10 C 4 (iii) 9 C 9

Answer

(i)
$$10\ C\ 3 = \frac{10!}{(10-3)! \times 3!} = \frac{10!}{7! \times 3!}$$
$$= \frac{10 \times 9 \times 8}{3 \times 2 \times 1} = 120$$

(ii)
$$10\ C\ 4 = \frac{10!}{(10-4)! \times 4!} = \frac{10!}{6! \times 4!}$$
$$= \frac{10 \times 9 \times 8 \times 7}{4 \times 3 \times 2 \times 1} = 210$$

(iii) We adopt the convention that $0! = 1$, then

$$9\ C\ 9 = \frac{9!}{(9-9)!\ 9!} = \frac{9!}{0!\ 9!} = 1.$$

5.5 Some Useful Results

(1)
$$n\ C\ r = n\ C(n-r)$$

Proof 1:

$$n\ C(n-r) = \frac{n!}{[n-(n-r)]!\ (n-r)!} = \frac{n!}{r!\ (n-r)!}$$
$$= n\ C\ r$$

Proof 2: We may argue as follows:
If we have a set of 6 elements and take 2 of them we will leave 4 behind – also *each time* we take 2 of them we will leave 4 behind. So there will be just as many ways of selecting 4 from 6 as there is of selecting 2 from 6. Therefore

	$6\,C\,2 = 6\,C\,4$	Note $2 + 4 = 6$
Similarly	$6\,C\,1 = 6\,C\,5$	$1 + 5 = 6$
and	$6\,C\,3 = 6\,C\,3$	$3 + 3 = 6$
and	$6\,C\,4 = 6\,C\,2$	$4 + 2 = 6$

Generalising this now, if we have a set of n elements and select r at a time, each time we take r, we will leave $n - r$ behind. Thus there are just as many ways of selecting $n - r$ from n as there are of selecting r from n, hence

$$n\,C\,r = n\,C(n - r)$$

(2) $$(n\,C\,r) + (n\,C\,r + 1) = (n + 1\,C\,r + 1)$$

Proof:

$$(n\,C\,r) + (n\,C\,r + 1)\frac{n!}{(n - r)!\,r!} + \frac{n!}{[n - (r + 1)]!\,(r + 1)!}$$

$$= \frac{n!}{[n - (r + 1)]!\,r!}\left\{\frac{1}{(n - r)} + \frac{1}{(r + 1)}\right\}$$

$$= \frac{n!}{[n - (r + 1)]!\,r!}\left\{\frac{r + 1 + n - r}{(n - r)(r + 1)}\right\}$$

$$= \frac{n!}{[n - (r + 1)]!\,r!}\left\{\frac{(n + 1)}{(n - r)(r + 1)}\right\}$$

$$= \frac{(n + 1)!}{(n - r)!\,(r + 1)!} = (n + 1\,C\,r + 1)$$

Note: A verbal argument – as in proof 2 above – may also be used.

(3) $n\,C\,n = 1$ i.e. there is only one way of selecting all the elements of a set if all are to be taken

(4) $n\,C\,0 = 1$ i.e. there is one way of selecting 'no elements' from any set

5.6 Permutations, Combinations and Probability

We are now in a position to take another look at the intuitive idea that the probability of an event can be found by dividing the total number of outcomes favourable to the event by the total number of outcomes.

Example 1: A panel of 3 men and 2 women have to form a committee of 3. If three àre selected at random what is the probability that the committee will consist of 3 men?

Step 1 Total number of ways of selecting 3 from 5 is

$$5\,C\,3 = \frac{5!}{2!\;3!} = 10$$

Step 2 Total number of ways of selecting 3 men from 3 men is

$$3\,C\,3 = 1$$

Step 3 Probability that if three people are selected at random from the panel they will all be men

$$= \frac{3\,C\,3}{5\,C\,3} = \frac{1}{10}$$

Example 2: If in *Example 1*, it is desirable (but not compulsory) that 1 woman be on the committee, and again the 3 members of this committee are selected at random, what is the probability that 1 woman will be selected?

Step 1 As before

Step 2 If 1 woman fills one place this may be done in $2\,C\,1 = 2$ ways. If two men fill the other two places this may be done in $3\,C\,2 = 3$ ways. Thus the total number of ways of selecting 3 people from the panel of 5 so that 1 is a woman and 2 are men is $(2\,C\,1) \times (3\,C\,2) = 2 \times 3 = 6$

Step 3 The probability that if three people are selected at random from the panel there will be one woman selected

$$= \frac{(2\,C\,1) \times (3\,C\,2)}{5\,C\,3} = \frac{6}{10} = \frac{3}{5}$$

Example 3: If in *Example 1*, it is desirable that *at least* 1 woman be on the committee, and again the members are selected at random, what is the probability that *at least* 1 woman will be selected?

Step 1 As before

Step 2 At least 1 means *1 or more*, i.e. either 1 or 2. We saw in *Example 2*, that if 1 woman is on the committee then there are 6 ways of selecting 3 from 5 to include 1 woman. If now 2 places are filled by women then this may be done in $2\,C\,2 = 1$ way, and the remaining place may be filled by a man in $3\ C\ 1 = 3$ ways. Therefore the total number of ways of selecting 3 from the 5 so that 2 are women is $(2\ C\ 2) \times (3\ C\ 1) = 1 \times 3 = 3$. Therefore the total number of ways of selecting 3 from the 5 so that either 1 woman or 2 women are selected is $3 + 6 = 9$.

Step 3 The probability that if three people are selected at random from the panel there will be at least 1 woman

$$= \frac{[(2\ C\ 1) \times (3\ C\ 2)] + [(2\ C\ 2) \times (3\ C\ 1)]}{5\ C\ 3} = \frac{9}{10}$$

5.7 The Binomial Theorem

Algebraic expressions consisting of 2 terms are called *binomial* expressions. The following are all binomial expressions

$$a^2 + 36 \qquad dk - 3t^3 \qquad az^{36} + 999 \qquad 77 + 12$$

For convenience of work with binomial expressions it is convenient to denote the general binomial expression by

$$a + b$$

Algebraic expressions with more than 2 terms are called polynomials. We are now going to investigate what happens when $(a + b)$ is multiplied by itself 2, 3, 4, . . . , n times.

First factor Second factor

$$(a + b)\ (a + b) \qquad = (a + b)^2 = aa + ab + ba + bb$$
$$= a^2 + \quad 2ab \quad + b^2$$

Let us now examine the terms of this resulting polynomial. The first term consists of a^2 and is obtained by taking the a from the first factor and then the a from the second factor and multiplying the two together. A similar remark holds for b^2. The second term, $2ab$, is obtained by first taking the a from the first factor and multiplying it by the b from the second factor, then, taking the b from the first factor and multiplying it by the a from the second factor, and then, finally, adding them – ab and ba – together.

This might be put another way by saying that there is only one way to select a from the first factor *and* a from the second factor and so a^2 has a coefficient of 1. Also there is only one way of selecting b from the first factor *and* b from the second factor and so the coefficient of b^2 is 1. But there are two ways of selecting a and b from this product – a from the first factor and b from the second, and b from the first factor and a from the second, and so the coefficient of ab is 2.

Let us now try the same thing with $(a + b)^3$.

First factor	Second factor	Third factor	
$(a + b)$	$(a + b)$	$(a + b)$	$= (a + b)^3$

$$= aaa + aab + aba + baa + abb + bab + abb + bbb$$

$$= a^3 \quad + \quad 3a^2b \quad + \quad 3ab^2 \quad + \quad b^3$$

The first term of this resulting polynomial is obtained by taking a from the three factors and multiplying them together. The second term is obtained by taking a from the first two factors and b from the third factor and multiplying them together, then taking a from the first and third factors and the b from the second factor and multiplying them together, then taking b from the first factor and a from the second and third factors and multiplying them together, and finally adding these three results. The third term is obtained in a similar fashion but this time two b's are selected and only one a. The final factor b^3 is found in precisely the same fashion as a^3.

Again we might put this another way by saying that there is only one way to select a from the first factor, a from the second factor and a from the third factor, and so the coefficient of a^3 is 1. For the second term we say that there are three ways that two a's and a b may be selected from the three factors and so the coefficient of a^2b is three. Similar remarks hold for the last two terms.

Let us now generalise these remarks to the case of $(a + b)^n$.

First factor	Second factor		nth factor	
$(a + b)$	$(a + b)$	.....	$(a + b)$	$= (a + b)^n$

We find the first term as follows. We select a from each of the n factors and multiply them together – this will give us a^n. Now there is only one way of selecting an a from each factor so the coefficient of a^n will be one.

We find the second term as follows. We select a from $(n - 1)$ factors and b from the remaining factor and multiply them together – this will give us $a^{n-1}b$. Now we have to consider how many ways this selection can be made. Each time we select $(n - 1)$ a's from $(n - 1)$ factors that will leave one factor to select a b, so the number of times this can be done is the number of times b can be selected from n factors, i.e. n times. In the notation of previous sections we can say that the number of ways of selecting one object from n objects one at a time is $nC1$ and so the coefficient of $a^{n-1}b$ is $n\,C\,1$.

We find the third term as follows. We select from $(n - 2)$ factors an a and from the remaining factors we select two b's, and multiply them together. This gives us $a^{n-2}b^2$. We find the coefficient of this terms by reasoning similar to that used previously: each time we select $n - 2$ factors for a's this leaves 2 factors from which to select b's. Thus the coefficient will be the number of ways of selecting two b's from n factors, i.e. $n\ C\ 2$.

If we continue to argue as above we finally get

$$(a+b)^n = a^n + (n\ C\ 1)\ a^{n-1}b + (n\ C\ 2)\ a^{n-2}b^2 + (n\ C\ 3)\ a^{n-3}b^3 + \ldots\ldots (n\ C\ r)\ a^{n-r}b^r \ldots\ldots + (n\ C\ n)\ b^n.$$

Note the pattern in these terms. The power of the first term starts with n and 'winds down' through $n - 1$, $n - 2$, . . . to 0, whilst the second term starts with a power 0 and 'winds up' through 1, 2, 3, . . . up to n. The power of a gives the two numbers for the combination sign, i.e. when a has the power $n - 2$ the combination sign reads $n\ C\ 2$. The powers of a and b when added together for each term come to n. The binomial expansion outlined above is called the binomial theorem and provides a quick way of expanding any given binomial expression. It will be seen later that the binomial theorem is greatly used in statistics.

Example 1: Put $a = b = \frac{1}{2}$, $n = 5$.

$$\begin{aligned}(\tfrac{1}{2}+\tfrac{1}{2})^5 &= 5\ C\ 0(\tfrac{1}{2})^5(\tfrac{1}{2})^0 + 5\ C\ 1(\tfrac{1}{2})^4(\tfrac{1}{2})^1 + 5\ C\ 2(\tfrac{1}{2})^3(\tfrac{1}{2})^2 \\ &\quad + 5\ C\ 3(\tfrac{1}{2})^2(\tfrac{1}{2})^3 + 5\ C\ 4(\tfrac{1}{2})^1(\tfrac{1}{2})^4 + 5\ C\ 5(\tfrac{1}{2})^0(\tfrac{1}{2})^5 \\ &= \tfrac{1}{32} + \tfrac{5}{32} + \tfrac{10}{32} + \tfrac{10}{32} + \tfrac{5}{32} + \tfrac{1}{32} \\ &= \tfrac{32}{32} - 1 \\ (\tfrac{1}{2}+\tfrac{1}{2}) &= (1)^5 = 1\end{aligned}$$

Example 2: Put $a = b = 1$, $n = 4$

$$\begin{aligned}(1+1)^4 &= 4\ C\ 0(1)^4(1)^0 + 4\ C\ 1(1)^3(1)^1 + 4\ C\ 2(1)^2(1)^2 \\ &\quad + 4\ C\ 3(1)^1(1)^3 + 4\ C\ 4(1)^0(1)^4 \\ &= 1 + 4 + 6 + 4 + 1 \\ &= 16 \\ (1+1)^4 &= (2)^4 = 16\end{aligned}$$

Example 3: Put $a = b = 1, n = n$

$$
\begin{aligned}
(1+1)^n &= n\,C\,0(1)^n(1)^0 + n\,C\,1(1)^{n-1}(1)^1 + \ldots \\
&\quad + n\,C\,r(1)^{n-r}(1)^r + \ldots + n\,C\,n(1)^0(1)^n \\
&= n\,C\,0 + n\,C\,1 + \ldots + n\,C\,r + \ldots + n\,C\,n \\
&= \sum_{r=0}^{n} n\,C\,r
\end{aligned}
$$

Thus

$$(1+1)^n = 2^n = \sum_{r=0}^{n} n\,C\,r$$

5.8 Supplementary Examples

Example 1: A die is rolled twice. What is the probability that (a) there will be a four on the first roll and a three on the second (b) there will be a two on the second roll (c) there will be either a two on the first roll or a five on the second.

Answer

The outcome space diagram is shown in Fig. 5.2(c). The outcome space consists of the set $\{(1, 1), (1, 2), \ldots, (6, 6)\}$ and there will be $6 \times 6 = 36$ ordered pairs. (Since any ordered pair has the same chance as any other of appearing each one may be assigned the probability of $\frac{1}{36}$.)

(a) This event is represented by the ordered pair (4, 3) and this is the only pair of the outcome space favourable to the occurrence of this event, so the probability,

$$\frac{\text{number of favourable ways}}{\text{total number of ways}}, \text{ is } \frac{1}{36}.$$

(b) This event is represented by the ordered pairs (1, 2), (2, 2), (3, 2), (4, 2), (5, 2), (6, 2) and so there are six pairs of the outcome space favourable to the occurrence of this event, so we get $\frac{6}{36} = \frac{1}{36}$ for the probability.

(c) A two on the first throw gives us the ordered pairs (2, 1), (2, 2), (2, 3), (2, 4), (2, 5), (2, 6) and a throw of a five on the second throw gives us the ordered pairs (1, 5), (2, 5), (3, 5), (4, 5), (5, 5), (6, 5). It will be seen that the ordered pair (2, 5) appears twice and so the total number of favourable pairs is 11. Hence we get a probability of $\frac{11}{36}$.

Example 2: Two dice are rolled and the results added. What is the probability that (a) the total is 5 (b) the total is larger than 3 but smaller than 7.

Answer

The outcome space (for two dice being rolled) is shown in Fig. 5.2(c). If, as well as the diagram of the outcome space of the rolling of two dice, we draw a diagram of the totals, we get:

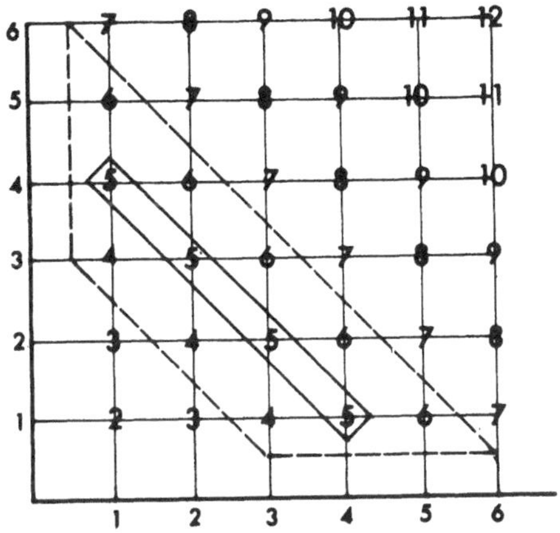

Fig. 5.8(a)

Note: for this experiment the outcome space is {2, 3, 4, . . . , 12}, i.e. a set of single elements. These single elements are formed as a result of the addition of the ordered pairs.

(a) There are four points in Fig. 5.8(a) which show a sum of 5, thus the probability is $\frac{4}{36} = \frac{1}{9}$.

(b) The sum more than three but less than seven is represented by 12 points in Fig. 5.8(a), and so the probability is $\frac{12}{36} = \frac{1}{3}$.

Example 3: How many three digit numbers can be formed using the digits 1, 2, 3, 4, 5, if (a) repetitions are not allowed (b) repetitions are allowed (c) the number formed must be less than 430, repetitions being allowed.

Answer

(a)

Method 1

This is equivalent to asking how many permutations can be made from a group of five objects taking three at a time, so we get

$$5P3 = \frac{5!}{2!} = 60$$

Method 2

The first digit – i.e. the one in the hundreds column – may be any one of five digits. The second digit may be any one of the four digits left, and the last digit may be any one of the three digits left.

Therefore 5.4.3 = 60

(b) The first digit may be any one of five digits.

The second digit may be any one of five digits since repetitions are allowed. Similarly the third digit may be any one of five digits. Thus 5.5.5 = 125 different numbers may be formed.

(c) The first digit – i.e. the one in the hundreds column – must be 4 or less, therefore it can only be one of four digits.

The second digit must be *less than* three, so it may be any one of the two digits 1 and 2. Since the digits 0, 9, 8, 7, and 6 are not available for the units column the question is effectively asking for the numbers less than 426. This makes the digits 1 to 5 available for the units column.

Thus we get 4.2.5 = 40 different numbers formed

Example 4: A pack consists of 5 red and 5 white cards numbered 1 to 5, together with 10 blue cards numbered 1 to 10 and 12 green cards numbered 1 to 12.

Four cards are chosen at random. What is the probability that (a) all are 1's (b) two are 1's and two are 5's (c) two are 2's and two are 9's (d) three are blue and one is red (e) two are white, one is red and one is green.

Answer

There are 32 cards all together. We can pick 4 cards from 32 in 32 C 4 different ways, i.e.

$$\frac{32!}{28!4!} = 35960$$

(a) there is only one way of selecting four cards so that we get four 1's, thus the probability is

$$\frac{1}{35960}$$

(b) there are four 1's and four 5's so we can select two 1's and two 5's in (4 C 2) × (5 C 2) ways, i.e. 6 × 10 = 60 ways. Therefore

$$P(\text{two 1's and two 5's}) = \frac{60}{35960} = \frac{1}{597}$$

(c) there are four 2's and two 9's so we can select two 2's and two 9's in $(4\ C\ 2) \times (2\ C\ 2)$ ways, i.e. $6 \times 1 = 6$ ways. Therefore

$$P(\text{two 2's and two 9's}) = \frac{6}{35960} = \frac{1}{5970}$$

(d) there are ten blue cards and five red ones, so we can select three blue ones and one red one in $(10\ C\ 3) \times (5\ C\ 1) = 120 \times 5 = 600$ ways. Therefore

$$P(\text{three blue and one red card}) = \frac{600}{35960} = \frac{10}{597}$$

(e) Arguing as before we see P(two white, one red and one green card)

$$= \frac{(5\ C\ 2) \times (5\ C\ 1) \times (12\ C\ 1)}{(32\ C\ 4)} = \frac{10 \times 5 \times 12}{35960} = \frac{10}{597}$$

Example 5: A retailer received a consignment of 100 light bulbs containing 6 defective bulbs. He decided to test the consignment by selecting 3 bulbs at random and testing them. What is the probability that he selects (a) 3 good bulbs (b) one defective and 2 good bulbs.

Answer

(a) P(selecting 3 good bulbs)

$$= \frac{\text{number of ways of selecting 3 from 94}}{\text{number of ways of selecting 3 from 100}}$$

$$= \frac{94\ C\ 3}{100\ C\ 3} = \frac{\dfrac{94!}{91!3!}}{\dfrac{100!}{97!3!}} = \frac{94!\ 97!}{91!100!} = 0{\cdot}84$$

(b) P(selecting 1 defective and 2 good bulbs)

$$= \frac{\text{number of ways of selecting one defective and two good bulbs}}{\text{number of ways of selecting three bulbs}}$$

$$= \frac{(6\ C\ 1) \times (94\ C\ 2)}{100\ C\ 3} = \frac{6 \times \dfrac{94!}{92!2!}}{\dfrac{100!}{97!3!}} = \frac{6 \times 94! \times 97! \times 3!}{92! \times 2! \times 100!}$$

$$= 0{\cdot}16$$

Exercise 5

1. A filing system is coded from AA/001 to ZZ/999. How many items may be filed in it?

Answer

675999

2. During the 1939–1945 war the Government issued every person with a National Identity Number. Typical of those issued was RCPQ/189/8. Discuss why this type of number would be chosen.

3. Find a typical example of a National Insurance number and discuss why it has the form it does.

4. How many numbers greater than 300 can be formed from the digits 0, 1, 2, 3, 4, 5?

Answer

90

5. How many four digit (a) even numbers (b) odd numbers can be formed from the digits 0, 1, 2, 3, 4, 5, 6?

Answer

(a) 1176 (b) 882

6. What is the number of ways of forecasting the results of five football matches if (a) each result can be a home win, a draw, or an away win, (b) as well as the above results the possibility of matches being abandoned is included.

Answer

(a) 243 (b) 1024

7. Given $A = \{a, b\}$, find (i) $A \times A$ (ii) $A \times A \times A$ (iii) $A \times A \times A \times A$

Answer

(i) $\{(a, a), (a, b), (b, a), (b, b)\}$

8. Given $A = \{a, b\}$, and $B = \{x, y, z\}$, find (i) $A \times B$ (ii) $A \times A \times B$ (iii) $A \times B \times B$ (iv) $A \times A \times B \times B$

Answer

(ii) $\{(a, a, x), (a, a, y), (a, a, z), (a, b, x), (a, b, y), (a, b, z), (b, a, x), (b, a, y), (b, a, z), (b, b, x), (b, b, y), (b, b, z)\}$.

9. Can you find sets for which $A \times B = B \times A$?

10. Does $A \times (B \times C) = (A \times B) \times C$?

11. Draw the diagram of the outcome space for the experiment of tossing a coin and throwing a die. How does it differ from Fig. 5.2(a)?

12. Draw the diagram of the outcome spaces, and write out the outcome spaces themselves, for the experiment of (a) tossing two coins (b) tossing three coins.

Answer

(b) $\{(H, H, H), (H, H, T), (H, T, H), (T, H, H), (H, T, T), (T, H, T), (T, T, H), (T, T, T)\}$

13. Write out the outcome space for the experiment of tossing four coins.

14. In Question 12 above, on the diagram of the outcome space show the points that represent the appearance of one head in a throw.

15. For Question 13 above, write out the subset of the outcome space which represents the throws where two heads only appear.

16. Two four sided dice (tetrahedra) are thrown and the numbers on the underfaces are subtracted – in each case the lower is taken from the higher. Draw the diagram of the outcome space for the throwing of the dice. Draw a similar two dimensional diagram showing the results of the subtractions. Hence show the outcome space of the experiment. What is the probability of getting (a) 0 (b) 1 (c) 2?

Answer

(a) $\frac{1}{4}$ (b) $\frac{6}{16}$ (c) $\frac{1}{4}$

17. The numbers 1, 2, 3, are put on cards in one box and the numbers 3, 4, 5, 6, are put on cards and placed in another box. One card is then drawn from each box. Draw a diagram of the outcome space. Write out the outcome space. If the two numbers are added what is the probability that the total is (a) 4 (b) 7 (c) 6? If the two numbers are multiplied what is the probability that the result is (d) 4 (e) 7 (f) 6?

Answer

(a) $\frac{1}{12}$ (b) $\frac{1}{4}$ (c) $\frac{1}{4}$ (d) $\frac{1}{12}$ (e) 0 (f) $\frac{1}{6}$

18. Evaluate (a) $5\,P\,1$ (b) $5\,P\,2$ (c) $5\,P\,3$ (d) $5\,P\,4$ (e) $5\,P\,5$ (f) $10\,P\,4$ (g) $13\,P\,3$ (h) $20\,P\,5$

Answer

(a) 5 (c) 60 (e) 120 (f) 5040 (h) 1660 480

19. How many different permutations are there using all the letters of the words (a) diathermy (b) equilibrium?

20. There are 4 seats on a bus and 10 people standing. How many ways can those standing use the four seats? In what proportion of these ways will one person be involved?

Answer
5040

21. There are three seats in a row. How many ways can two men and one woman be seated if (a) no restrictions are imposed (b) men must occupy the outside seats (c) a man must occupy the centre seat?

Answer
(a) 6 (b) 2

22. Repeat the previous question using three men and two women.

Answer
(a) 5 P 3 (b) 12 (c) 60

23. Topic: take the situation described in the two previous questions and vary the number of men, women and seats available. Vary the conditions (suggested example: men on even numbered seats, women on odd numbered seats). Work systematically and discuss any patterns you come across.

24. Topic: investigate the ways books may be arranged on a shelf. Vary the conditions by making two books be either together or at opposite ends etc.

25. Topic: investigate arranging coloured cards in a row. Start with a small number of one colour, then increase the number. Then use two colours with small numbers, then increase the numbers. Then number the cards (or find some other method of distinguishing them) repeat, and note any differences.

26. Evaluate (a) 5 C 2 (b) 5 C 3 (c) 7 C 5 (d) 11 C 7 (e) 13 C 8 (f) 16 C 9

Answer
(a) 10 (c) 21 (e) 1287

27. How many different hands of 5 cards can be formed from a normal deck?

Answer
52 C 5

28. In how many ways can a sub-committee of 5 be formed from a committee of 9 people if (a) no restrictions are imposed (b) the committee chairman *must* be on the sub-committee (c) either the chairman or the secretary of the committee must be on the sub-committee – but not both, (d) the chairman must *not* be on the sub-committee?

Answer

(a) 126 (c) 140

29. A class of 10 children is to be split between two teachers A and B. A is to have 4 children and B 6. How many different ways could the class be split?

Answer

210

30. Prove that $n\,C\,1 + n\,C\,2 + n\,C\,3 + \ldots + n\,C\,n = 2^n - 1$

31. From 6 teachers and 5 students a committee of 3 teachers and 2 students is to be formed. How many ways can this be done if (a) there are no restrictions (b) one particular teacher must always be on the committee (c) one particular teacher and one particular student must not be on the committee together?

Answer

(a) 200 (c) $[(5\,C\,2) \times (4\,C\,2)] + [(5\,C\,3) \times (4\,C\,2)] + [(5\,C\,3) \times (4\,C\,1)]$

32. A box contains 5 white and 4 black marbles. Two are drawn at random. What is the probability that (a) both are white (b) both are black (c) one is black and the other white?

Answer

(a) $\dfrac{5\,C\,2}{9\,C\,2}$ (b) $\frac{6}{36}$ (c) $\frac{5}{9}$

33. In the previous question three marbles are drawn. Find the probability that (a) 3 are white (b) 2 are white and 1 black (c) 1 is white and 2 are black (d) 3 are black.

Answer

(a) $\frac{5}{42}$ (b) $\dfrac{(5\,C\,2) \times (4\,C\,4)}{9\,C\,3}$

34. In question 32 eight marbles are drawn. Find the probability of (a) 5 white and 3 black marbles (b) 4 white and 4 black marbles. Find two ways of answering (b).

Answer

(a) $\dfrac{(5\,C\,5) \times (4\,C\,3)}{9\,C\,8}$

35. Take the idea of the previous three questions and vary the number of marbles in the box and the number drawn. Work systematically and discuss any points of interest which arise.

36. Take a box containing an unknown number of marbles which are of two colours only. Draw one ball from the box, replace it and draw another. Repeat this successively until you can answer the question; 'What proportion of the marbles are of one colour, and what proportion are of the other colour?'

Repeat the experiment but draw two marbles instead of one. Note any differences.

37. Repeat question 36 but use a box containing three different coloured marbles. Then go on to four different colours. Write up any points that interest you.

38. Two dice are thrown. What is the probability of getting a double 6.

Answer

$\frac{1}{36}$

39. Three dice are thrown. What is the probability that the sum of the upper faces is (a) 4 (b) 5 (c) 6 (d) 10 (e) 15?

Answer

(a) $\frac{1}{72}$ (c) $\frac{10}{216}$ (e) $\frac{7}{216}$

40. Invent questions for yourself similar to those of questions 38 and 39. Write out the full outcome spaces and if possible draw a diagram of them.

41. Four cards are drawn from a pack. What is the probability that (a) they are all spades (b) they are all Jacks (c) either aces or kings only (d) there is one card from each suit (e) there are only cards from two suits?

Answer

(a) $\frac{11}{4165}$ (c) $\frac{2}{7735}$

42. Take three cards numbered 1, 2, and 3. Place them at random in a line face downwards, then turn them over and note their positions. Continue in this way until you can give an experical probability value for the probability that they will be placed in order. Confirm your empirical result by finding the *a priori* probability.

43. Repeat the previous question but vary the conditions: find the probability that, though not in order, they may be in cyclic order i.e. 123, 231, 312 – find the probability that a card occupies its proper position.

44. Repeat the ideas of the previous two questions but vary the number of cards.

45. Expand (a) $(\frac{1}{2} + \frac{1}{2})^n$ (b) $(\frac{1}{4} + \frac{3}{4})^n$ (c) $(\frac{1}{3} + \frac{2}{3})^n$
(d) $(\frac{3}{4} + \frac{1}{4})^n$ (e) $(\frac{2}{3} + \frac{1}{3})^n$ (f) $(\frac{2}{3} + \frac{2}{3})^n$
(g) $(\frac{3}{4} + \frac{3}{4})^n$ (h) $(1 + 1)^n$ (i) $(\frac{5}{2} + \frac{5}{2})^n$
(j) $(\frac{1}{10} + \frac{9}{10})^n$ (k) $(\frac{9}{10} + \frac{1}{10})^n$

In each case let $n = 2, 3, 4, \ldots$ and work as many as necessary to see what pattern forms. Compare (c) and (e) and other similar pairs.

46. Expand $(1 + x)^n$, and then by putting $x = -1$ show that

$$n\,C\,0 - n\,C\,1 + n\,C\,2 - n\,C\,3 + \ldots + (-1)^n n\,C\,n = 0$$

47. Prove that $4\,C\,2 + 2(4\,C\,3) + 4\,C\,4 - 6\,C\,4 = 0$

48. Prove that $n\,C\,1 + 2(n\,C\,2) + n\,C\,3 - (n + 2\,C\,3) = 0$

49. In question 1 what is the probability that in a chance selection of 1 card from the filing system, it is a card (a) with code WT/437 (b) with a number bigger than 500 (c) has letters AB (d) with either a number bigger than 500 or letters AB (or both)?

Answer
(b) $\frac{337999}{675999}$ (d) $\frac{37611}{75111}$

50. Three digits are selected consecutively at random from 1, 2, 3, 4, 5, 6, 7, and used to form the hundreds, tens and units columns of a three digit number. If repetitions are allowed, what is the probability that (a) it is bigger than 200 (b) it is even (c) it is odd (d) it is less than 700?

Answer
(a) $\frac{6}{7}$ (b) $\frac{4}{7}$

51. Using the outcome space of question 13, find the probability that in one throw (a) four heads appear (b) two heads and two tails appear (c) at least two heads appear (d) at least one head appears.

Answer
(a) $\frac{1}{16}$ (b) $\frac{3}{8}$ (c) $\frac{11}{16}$ (d) $\frac{15}{16}$

52. In question 19(a) what is the probability that a random shuffle of the letters will produce a sequence (i) starting with a vowel (ii) ending with a vowel (iii) starting and ending with a vowel?

Answer
(i) $\frac{1}{3}$ (ii) $\frac{1}{12}$

53. Repeat question 52 for question 19(b)

Answer

(i) $\frac{5}{11}$ (iii) $\frac{(6\ C\ 2) \times 8!}{11!}$

54. Set yourself a probability question based upon questions 21, 22 and 23.

55. Set yourself a probability question based upon question 24.

56. A 'one armed bandit' machine has three rotating drums on each of which are painted the figures

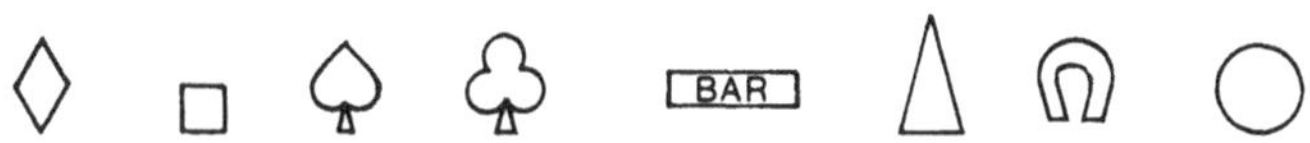

When the drums come to rest the three figures shown in the window □□□ determine the prize: (a) how many different results are possible? (b) if three ○ are the jackpot, how often would you expect it to come up in the long run? (c) what is the probability of a jackpot? (d) if stake money is not returned and a win gives a player twice his stake, how many results must the owner make non-prize results in order to *just* make a profit? (e) discuss the profitability of the machine with varying stakes and winning combinations.

Answer

(a) $8^3 = 512$ (b) once every 512 goes (c) $\frac{1}{512}$ (d) 257

6 More Probability Theory

6.1 Addition of Probabilities

We are now going to make explicit certain ideas which have been used previously in an intuitive fashion. In the experiment which consists of rolling a die we saw that the probability of throwing a 5 was $\frac{1}{6}$, and the probability of throwing a 2 was also $\frac{1}{6}$. The question we next ask is, 'What is the probability of throwing a 5 *or a* 2?' Intuitively we see that the probability is $\frac{2}{6}$ or $\frac{1}{3}$. What relationship have these three probabilities? It can be seen that

$$\frac{1}{6} + \frac{1}{6} = \frac{1}{3}$$

i.e. $$P(5) + P(2) = P(5 \text{ or a } 2).$$

Arguing similarly we can see that

$$P(5 \text{ or a } 2 \text{ or a } 6) = P(5) + P(2) + P(6),$$

i.e. $$\frac{1}{2} = \frac{1}{6} + \frac{1}{6} + \frac{1}{6}$$

We may now say – the probability that an event, which consists of several outcomes, will occur, is the sum of the probabilities of the individual outcomes.

In terms of set theory we say – for an outcome space S, where A and B are subsets of S, that

$$P(A \cup B) = P(A) + P(B) \qquad (1)$$

This is not yet quite the full story however. Let us consider the following. Let us again take the experiment of rolling a die. Here S will be $\{1, 2, 3, 4, 5, 6\}$. Let $A = \{1, 2, 3\}$ i.e. the event of rolling either a 1 or a 2 or a 3. Let $B = \{2, 3, 5\}$, i.e. the event of rolling either a 2 or a 3 or a 5.

Then $P(A) = \frac{1}{2}$, and $P(B) = \frac{1}{2}$. $A \cup B = \{1, 2, 3, 5\}$, and $P(A \cup B) = \frac{2}{3}$. Now in this case

$$P(A \cup B) \neq P(A) + P(B) \text{ since } \frac{2}{3} \neq \frac{1}{2} + \frac{1}{2}.$$

Why is there this discrepancy? The answer to this is that some of the elements of A are common to B and when $A \cup B$ is formed they are not counted twice. Thus the equation will fail to balance by the probability associated with the elements common to both A and B. Thus we finally get

$$P(A \cup B) = P(A) + P(B) - P(A \cap B)$$

which is

$$\tfrac{2}{3} = \tfrac{1}{2} + \tfrac{1}{2} - \tfrac{1}{3}$$

since

$$A \cap B = \{2, 3\}, \text{ and } P(A \cap B) = \tfrac{1}{3}.$$

The reader will, no doubt, notice that this situation is exactly analagous to the situation in Section 4.15 (page 124) where the number in a set was considered. This result can be extended to three subsets of S as follows,

$$P(A \cup B \cup C) = P(A) + P(B) + P(C) - P(A \cap B) - P(A \cap C) - P(B \cap C) + P(A \cap B \cap C)$$

This situation where subsets of the outcome space are non-disjoint leads us to consider the notion of mutually exclusive events. Two events A and B are said to be *mutually exclusive* if the occurence of any one of them prevents the occurence of the other.

Example 1: The outcome space of the experiment tossing a coin consists of two mutually exclusive events, i.e. heads and tails. The occurrence of a head prevents the occurrence of a tail.

If two events, A and B, are mutually exclusive then $A \cap B = \phi$ and $P(A \cap B) = 0$.

It should be noted that an experiment can give rise to both types of situation. Consider the rolling of a die. If we choose subsets $A = \{1, 2\}$, and $B = \{3, 4\}$, then A and B are disjoint and therefore the events represented by them are mutually exclusive.

Example 2: If $A = \{\text{Ace}\}$, $B = \{\text{Three}\}$, and $S = \{\text{A pack of playing cards}\}$ determine the probability of drawing either an ace or a three in drawing a single card from the pack?

Answer

Since A and B are disjoint we may use (1) and get

$$P(A \cup B) = P(A) + P(B) = \tfrac{1}{13} + \tfrac{1}{13} = \tfrac{2}{13}$$

Example 3: If $A = \{\text{Ace}\}$, $C = \{\text{Hearts}\}$, and S is as above, what is the probability of drawing either an ace or a heart in drawing a single card from the pack?

Answer

Since A and C are non-disjoint we must use the general equation,

$$P(A \cup C) = P(A) + P(C) - P(A \cap C) = \tfrac{1}{13} + \tfrac{1}{4} - \tfrac{1}{52}$$
$$= \tfrac{4}{52} + \tfrac{13}{52} - \tfrac{1}{52} = \tfrac{16}{52} = \tfrac{4}{13}$$

We again consider the experiment of rolling a die and ask, 'What is the probability of rolling a 1, or a 2, or a 3, or a 4, or a 5, or a 6, i.e. $P(1 \text{ or } 2 \text{ or } 3 \text{ or } 4 \text{ or } 5 \text{ or } 6)$?' Since these outcomes are mutually exclusive $P(1 \text{ or } 2 \text{ or } 3 \text{ or } 4 \text{ or } 5 \text{ or } 6) = P(1) + P(2) + P(3) + P(4) + P(5) + P(6) = \tfrac{1}{6} + \tfrac{1}{6} + \tfrac{1}{6} + \tfrac{1}{6} + \tfrac{1}{6} + \tfrac{1}{6} = 1$. This accords with the fact that one of these outcomes is certain to occur and we saw in Section 4.1 that a certain event is given probability 1. In practice, when probabilities are ascribed the whole of the outcome space has to be known, and the probabilities assigned to the individual elements of the sample space in such a fashion as will make their total unity.

Example 4: An experiment consists of throwing a 12 sided die. Given $A = \{1, 2\}$, $B = \{3, 4, 5, 6\}$, $C = \{7, 8, 9\}$, $D = \{4, 5\}$, $E = \{9, 10, 11, 12\}$, find (a) $P(A \cup B)$ (b) $P(C \cup E)$ (c) $P(A \cup B \cup C)$ (d) $P(A \cup C \cup E)$ (e) $P(B')$ (f) $P([C \cup D]')$

Answer

Since each outcome is equally likely we assign to each element of the outcome space a probability of $\tfrac{1}{12}$.

(a) *Method 1*:

$$A \cup B = \{1, 2\} \cup \{3, 4, 5, 6\} = \{1, 2, 3, 4, 5, 6\}$$

Therefore

$$P(A \cup B) = P(\{1, 2, 3, 4, 5, 6\}) = \tfrac{1}{2}.$$

Method 2:

$$P(A \cup B) = P(A) + P(B) - P(A \cap B)$$
$$= \tfrac{1}{6} + \tfrac{1}{3} - 0 \text{ (since } A \text{ and } B \text{ are disjoint)}$$
$$= \tfrac{1}{2}$$

(b)
$$P(C \cup E) = P(C) + P(E) - P(C \cap E)$$
$$= \tfrac{1}{4} + \tfrac{1}{3} - \tfrac{1}{12} \text{ (since } C \cap E = \{9\})$$
$$= \tfrac{1}{2}.$$

(c)
$$A \cup B \cup C = \{1, 2\} \cup \{3, 4, 5, 6\} \cup \{7, 8, 9\}$$
$$= \{1, 2, 3, 4, 5, 6, 7, 8, 9\}$$

therefore $P(A \cup B \cup C) = \frac{3}{4}$.

(d) $P(A \cup C \cup E) = P(A) + P(C) + P(E) - P(A \cap C) - P(A \cap E) - P(C \cap E) + P(A \cap C \cap E)$

$= \frac{1}{6} + \frac{1}{4} + \frac{1}{4} - 0 - 0 - \frac{1}{12} + 0$

(since $A \cap C = \{9\}$ and $A \cap C \cap E = \phi$)

$= \frac{7}{12}$

(e) *Method 1*:

$B' = \{1, 2, 7, 8, 9, 10, 11, 12\}$

therefore $P(B') = P(\{1, 2, 7, 8, 9, 10, 11, 12\})$

$= \frac{2}{3}$

Method 2:

$P(B') = 1 - P(B)$

$= 1 - \frac{1}{3} = \frac{2}{3}$

(f) $P([C \cup D]') = 1 - P(C \cup D)$

$= 1 - \frac{5}{12} = \frac{7}{12}$

6.2 Multiplication of Probabilities I – Independent Events

We saw in Section 5.1 that the outcome space for the experiment of rolling a die and then tossing a coin contains 12 elements, each one being an ordered pair. The probability associated with each element is $\frac{1}{12}$. If we consider these experiments separately we see that the probability of throwing, say a 3, is $\frac{1}{6}$, and that the probability of tossing, say a head, is $\frac{1}{2}$. Since the probability of throwing a 3 and tossing a head when the experiments are combined into one experiment is $\frac{1}{12}$, we see that P(throwing a 3 *and* tossing a head) $= P(3) \times P(H)$, i.e. $\frac{1}{6} \times \frac{1}{2} = \frac{1}{12}$. We also note that the rolling of the dice is independent of the tossing of the coin.

We now state the general result that if A and B are two *independent* events the probability that they will both occur is found by multiplying together their separate probabilities, i.e. $P(A \cap B) = P(A) \times P(B)$. This result can be easily extended to three or more independent events.

It will have been noted by the student in Sections 5.1 and 5.2 that in the construction of the outcome space for experiments involving two or more separate and independent experiments that this multiplication idea was used.

Example 1: A bag contains 3 white and 2 red balls, what is the probability that a ball drawn will be white? What is the probability that if a ball is drawn, replaced, and another ball drawn that two white balls were drawn?

Answer

$P(W) = \frac{3}{5}$.

$P(W)$ on first draw is $\frac{3}{5}$, and $P(W)$ on second draw is $\frac{3}{5}$, therefore the

$$P(W \cap W) = \frac{3}{5} \times \frac{3}{5} = \frac{9}{25}.$$

Note that the two separate draws were independent.

Example 2: A card is drawn from an ordinary deck and noted. It is then replaced and a second card is drawn and noted. Likewise a third card is drawn. What is the probability that three aces are drawn?

Answer

Because the cards are replaced before subsequent drawings each draw is independent of the others. Therefore the P(drawing 3 aces) = P(drawing an ace) × P(drawing an ace) × P(drawing an ace) = $\frac{4}{52} \times \frac{4}{52} \times \frac{4}{52} = \frac{1}{2197}$

Generally for events $A_1, A_2, \ldots, A_n$ then, if they are all independent of the other $n - 1$ events

$$P(A_1 \cap A_2 \cap \ldots \cap A_n) = P(A_1) \times P(A_2) \times \ldots \times P(A_n)$$

providing $P(A_i) \neq 0$.

6.3 Multiplication of Probabilities II – Dependent Events

In example 1 in the last section the first ball drawn was replaced before the second ball was drawn. What would have happened if the first ball had not been replaced? If the first ball drawn had been a white one there would have been 2 white and 2 red left for the second draw, but if the first one drawn had been a red one it would have left 3 white and only 1 red for the second draw. Such situations, where one stage is *dependent* on what has immediately preceeded it, also use the idea of the multiplication of probabilities.

Example 1: If a bag contains 3 white and 2 red balls what is the probability that if two balls are drawn in succession – the first one not being replaced – they will be drawn in the order W, R?

Answer

$P(W)$ is drawn first is $\frac{3}{5}$. We now assume that a white ball has been chosen and consider the probability of drawing a red on the second draw.

$P(R)$ on the second draw is $\frac{1}{2}$, since there are two white and two red left after a white one has been removed. Therefore the probability that two balls will be drawn in the order $W,R = \frac{3}{5} \times \frac{1}{2} = \frac{3}{10}$. Multiplication is again used as this the probability that one event *and* another event occur together.

We now introduce the notation $P(A \mid B)$, which is read, 'the probability of the event A occurring *given* that the event B has occurred'. If the occurrence or non-occurrence of B does not effect A then A and B are independent and the results of the previous section apply. In the above example we saw that $P(R \mid W)$ i.e. the probability that a red ball was drawn given that a white ball has been drawn was $\frac{1}{2}$. It will also be seen in the above example that $P(W \cap R) = P(W) \times P(R \mid W)$, i.e. $P(W \cap R) = \frac{3}{5} \times \frac{1}{2} = \frac{3}{10}$.

We now state generally that if A and B are two dependent events then $P(A \cap B) = P(A) \times P(B \mid A)$, which is read, 'the probability of A and B is equal to the probability of A multiplied by the probability of B given A has occurred. Note that in set theory no order temporal or otherwise is implied with $A \cap B$ but in the context of dependent events there is the notion of order to be taken into account, i.e. one of the events must preceed the other and have some effect on the outcome of the second one.

This result may be extended to three, or more, events. In the case of three events A, B, and C occurring in that order we get $P(A \cap B \cap C) = P(A)\, P(B \mid A)\, P(C \mid A \cap B)$.

Example 2: A bag contains 4 Red, 2 White, and 3 Blue balls. (a) If three balls are drawn with replacement, what is the probability that (i) they are drawn in the order R, W, B (ii) they are drawn in the order W, B, R (iii) that at least 2 balls are red? (b) If three balls are drawn without replacement, what is the probability that they are (i) drawn in the order R, W, B (ii) they are drawn in the order W, B, R (iii) 2 Red balls are drawn?

Answer

(a) (i) Since the balls are replaced each draw is independent, therefore

$$P(R \cap W \cap B) = \frac{4}{9} \times \frac{2}{9} \times \frac{3}{9} = \frac{8}{243}$$

$$\text{(ii) } P(W \cap B \cap R) = \frac{2}{9} \times \frac{3}{9} \times \frac{4}{9} = \frac{8}{243}$$

(iii) At least 2 balls are red means 2 *or* three balls drawn are red.

$$P(R \cap R \cap \text{not } R) = \frac{4}{9} \times \frac{4}{9} \times \frac{5}{9} = \frac{80}{729}$$

$$P(R \cap R \cap R) = \frac{4}{9} \times \frac{4}{9} \times \frac{4}{9} = \frac{64}{729}$$

Therefore the probability of at least 2 red balls is $\frac{80}{729}+\frac{64}{729}=\frac{144}{729}$

(b) (i) $P(R \cap W \cap B) = P(R) \times P(W \mid R) \times P(B \mid R \cap W)$

$$= \frac{4}{9} \times \frac{2}{8} \times \frac{3}{7} = \frac{1}{21}$$

(ii) $P(W \cap B \cap R) = P(W) \times P(B \mid W)\, P(R \mid W \cap B)$

$$= \frac{2}{9} \times \frac{3}{8} \times \frac{4}{7} = \frac{1}{21}$$

(iii) Two Red balls may be drawn in three ways, R, R, not$R$; R, not$R$, R; not$R$, R, R. With

$$P(R \cap R \cap \text{not}R) = P(R) \times P(R \mid R)\, P(\text{not}R \mid R \cap R) = \frac{4}{9} \times \frac{3}{8} \times \frac{5}{7} = \frac{5}{42}$$

$$P(R \cap \text{not}R \cap R) = P(R) \times P(\text{not}R \mid R) \times P(R \mid \text{not}R \cap R) = \frac{4}{9} \times \frac{5}{8} \times \frac{3}{7} = \frac{5}{42}$$

$$P(\text{not}R \cap R \cap R) = P(\text{not}R) \times P(R \mid \text{not}R) \times P(R \mid \text{not}R \cap R) = \frac{5}{9} \times \frac{4}{8} \times \frac{3}{7} = \frac{5}{42}$$

Therefore the probability that 2 red balls are drawn is the sum of these three possibilities, i.e. $\frac{15}{42} = \frac{5}{14}$

6.4 The Probability of an Event Not Occurring

In the experiment of rolling a die the probability that a 6 will occur is $\frac{1}{6}$. The probability that a 6 will not occur will be the same as the probability that a 1, 2, 3, 4, or 5 will occur, i.e. $\frac{5}{6}$. Thus we see that the $P(\text{not } 6) = P(\{1, 2, 3, 4, 5\}) = \frac{5}{6} = 1 - \frac{1}{6} = 1 - P(6)$.

Generalising this we get

$$P(A') = 1 - P(A)$$

read 'the probability of not-A is equal to one minus the probability of A' where A is a subset of the outcome space S.

Summary: When considering the problem of the occurrence of one event *or* another event the respective probabilities are added using

$$P(A \cup B) = P(A) + P(B) - P(A \cap B)$$

and watch has to be kept for mutually exclusive events (disjoint sets) or otherwise.

When considering the problem of the occurrence of one event *and* another event the respective probabilities are multiplied using either $P(A \cap B) = P(A)P(B)$ or $P(A \cap B) = P(A)P(B \mid A)$ in accordance with the question of the independence of A and B, or their dependence.

N.B. OR goes with $\cup$ and AND goes with $\cap$.

Most problems are a mixture of addition and multiplication of probabilities, and this addition and multiplication must be carried out in accordance with the ideas laid down above.

6.5 Tree Diagrams and Probabilities

Tree diagrams may be used to determine probabilities as follows. Write on the 'branch' of the tree the probability associated with the event for that particular branch. This is illustrated below with reference to the experiment of rolling a die:

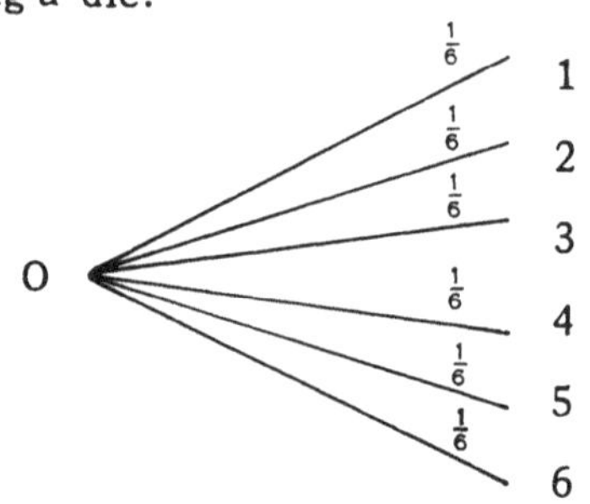

Fig. 6.5(a)

i.e. the probability of throwing a 3 is $\frac{1}{6}$, so $\frac{1}{6}$ is written on the branch that is concerned with the event of throwing a three. Similarly for the other events.

If we now wish to calculate the probability of throwing *either* a 3 *or* a 4 *or* a 5, we merely have to *add* the probabilities of the appropriate branches; in this case $\frac{1}{6} + \frac{1}{6} + \frac{1}{6} = \frac{1}{2}$.

For compound experiments the probabilities have to be written on the branches as shown in Fig. 6.5(b).

This diagram refers to the experiment of rolling a die and then tossing a coin. To calculate the probability of, say, rolling a 2 *and* then tossing a Tail, the probabilities on the two branches are *multiplied*, i.e. $\frac{1}{6} \times \frac{1}{2} = \frac{1}{12}$.

To calculate the probability of getting *either* $(2, T)$ *or* $(3, H)$, first find the probability of getting $(2, T) = \frac{1}{12}$, then find the probability of getting $(3, H) = \frac{1}{12}$, then *add* the two together, i.e. $\frac{1}{12} + \frac{1}{12} = \frac{1}{6}$.

There is no need, as the student will discover for himself, to write out the whole 'tree' to calculate one probability. If, for example, it is wished to calculate the probability of 'rolling a 3, then tossing a Head, then tossing a Tail, and finally rolling a 4', the following diagram would suffice:

$$0 \text{---} \tfrac{1}{6} \longrightarrow 3 \text{---} \tfrac{1}{2} \longrightarrow H \text{---} \tfrac{1}{2} \longrightarrow T \text{---} \tfrac{1}{6} \longrightarrow 4$$

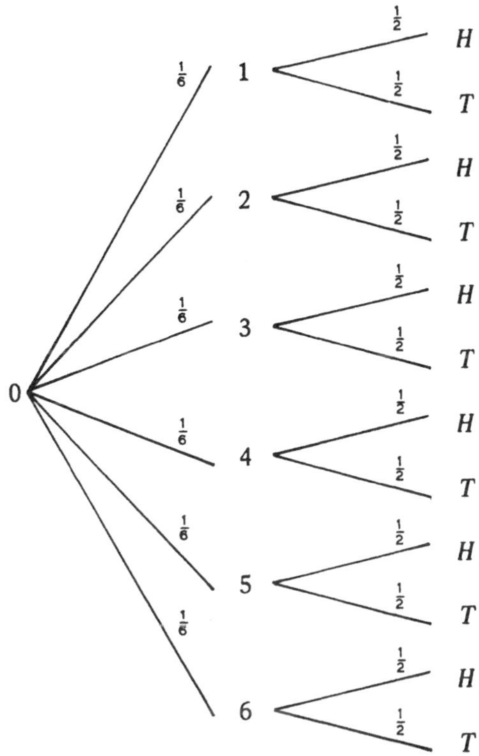

$\frac{1}{6} \times \frac{1}{2} = \frac{1}{12}$.

Fig. 6.5(b)

To calculate the probability then we multiply

$$\frac{1}{6} \times \frac{1}{2} \times \frac{1}{2} \times \frac{1}{6} = \frac{1}{144}$$

Note that in this experiment the outcome space consists of 144 ordered 4-tubles.

6.6 Probabilities and Graphs

We can now use the idea of graphs, developed in chapter one in connection with the recording of data, to help clarify the ideas of probability.

Example 1: Draw a graph of the experiment of rolling a die.

Answer

Outcome space = $\{1, 2, 3, 4, 5, 6\}$; associated set of probabilities $= \{\frac{1}{6}, \frac{1}{6}, \frac{1}{6}, \frac{1}{6}, \frac{1}{6}, \frac{1}{6}\}$

Graph

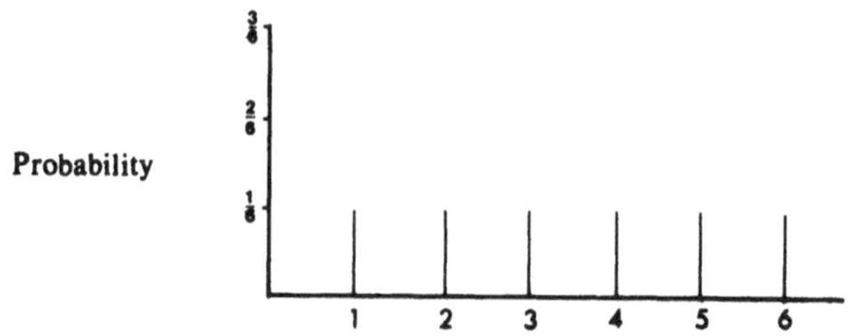

Note that the outcome space is put on the horizontal axis and the probability on the vertical axis. The vertical axis becomes the measure of the probability of the individual elements of the outcome space in the same way as it was the measure of the frequencies of the elements of the outcome space when concerned with random variables. The height of the lines at the points 1, 2, 3, etc., represents the probability that they will occur, i.e. $\frac{1}{6}$. Since all the elements of the outcome space have equal probabilities the lines are all of equal length. The total length of the lines is 1 which mirrors the fact that the sum of the probabilities is unity. In just the same way as the graphs of distributions enables us to 'see' how they were distributed the probability graphs enable us to 'see' how the probabilities are distributed.

Example 2: Draw a line graph of the experiment of tossing 3 pennies.

Answer

Since this experiment has an outcome space consisting of ordered triples such as (H, H, H) we have got to convert the situation to a form that will allow us to use a line graph. We do this by considering the question of 'the number of heads on one throw'.

This gives us the outcome space $\{0, 1, 2, 3\}$ and the associated set of probabilities $\{\frac{1}{8}, \frac{3}{8}, \frac{3}{8}, \frac{1}{8}\}$ the elements of which are found in the way previously described. Therefore we get

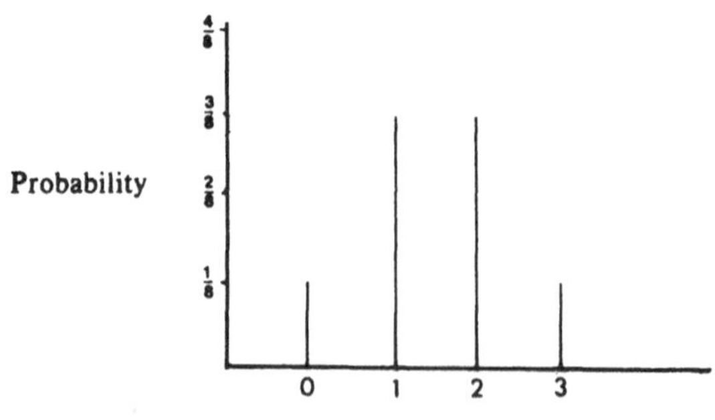

All the features commented upon in *Example 1* are again present here.

Example 3: 3 pennies are tossed. What is the probability of getting (a) 1 head (b) 1 or 2 heads (c) at least 1 head?

Answer

Using the graph of *Example 2*, we get

(a) $P(1) = \frac{3}{8}$

(b) $P(1 \text{ or } 2) = P(1) + P(2) = \frac{3}{8} + \frac{3}{8} = \frac{3}{4}$

(c) The probability of at least one head means the probability of one or more heads, i.e. $P(1, 2 \text{ or } 3 \text{ heads})$. Therefore

$$\begin{aligned} P(\{1, 2, 3\}) &= P(1) + P(2) + P(3) \\ &= \frac{3}{8} + \frac{3}{8} + \frac{1}{8} \\ &= \frac{7}{8} \end{aligned}$$

The line graph is appropriate in the examples considered here because these were discrete distributions. A similar development can be made for continuous distributions by using continuous lines, i.e. for the histogram

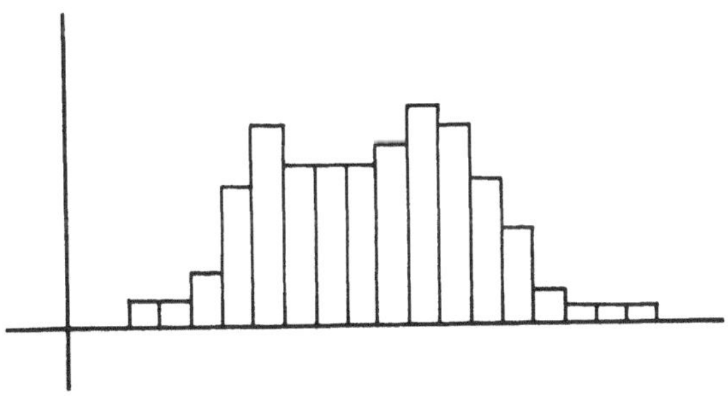

we will use the continuous curve

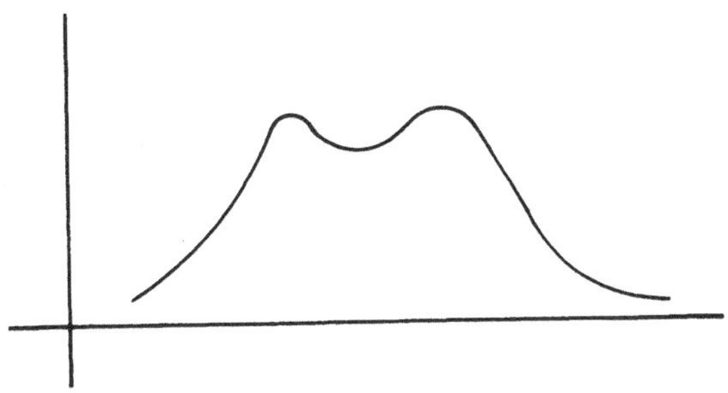

However this involves the use of the calculus and is not pursued here.

Example 4: How many times must a coin be tossed so that the probability of getting 1 or more heads is bigger than 0·98.

Answer

Method 1: Draw line graphs for one toss, two tosses, three tosses, etc., then add the probabilities given by the graphs for one or more heads. When this is gigger than 0·98 the number can be found from the graph.

Method 2: Since $P(0) + P(1) + P(2) + \ldots + P(n) = 1$ the probability of getting one or more is

$$P(1) + P(2) + \ldots P(n)$$

and this is equal to $1 - P(0)$. Hence we must find when

$$1 - P(0) > 0{\cdot}98$$

i.e. when

$$P(0) < 0{\cdot}02$$

Now $P(0) = (\frac{1}{2})^n$ so we need to know the value of n where

$$(\tfrac{1}{2})^n < 0{\cdot}02 = \tfrac{1}{50}$$

Since $(\frac{1}{2})^5 = \frac{1}{32}$ and $(\frac{1}{2})^6 = \frac{1}{64}$ we can see that we need 6 tosses or more to make the probability of getting 1 or more heads bigger than 0·98.

6.7 Review

In the first three chapters we were largely concerned with the different facets of descriptive statistics. It was when we wished to move from describing data to making inferences about the population from which the data came that the necessity for considering probability arose. Having now met the fundamental ideas of probability we can reconsider the necessity for them in statistics. The reader should now re-read the Introduction and Section 3.8.

We recall that much phenomena in the physical world exhibits a degree of randomness. It is this randomness which makes it impossible to predict or take decisions with *certainty*. If we cannot predict with certainty then we must do the next best thing – predict or decide so that we are wrong on as few occasions as possible. We will be in error on the least number of occasions if we know how probable certain events or outcomes are, and hence we return to the notion of probability.

But before we consider probability we must look again at randomness as this is a prior notion – it is upon randomness that probability is founded.

Different types of phenomena exhibit their own type of randomness. If a fair dice is thrown then, *over a long run*, each digit will appear roughly the same number of times and count for one sixth of the total. If however we select a human being and measure his height, then, *over a long run*, we do not get different heights appearing an equal number of times and forming one sixth of the total. The pattern that emerges, as we have seen, is roughly a normal distribution where certain numbers occur with greater frequency than others. Therefore the type of randomness of these phenomena differ.

It is when we know the type of randomness which a phenomenon exhibits that we are in a position to assign probability values, and once we assign probability values we can consider making predictions with a specified *degree of risk*. If, for example, we have a machine which produces 10% defective items and we decide to accept all it produces, then we can say that *in the long run* we will be right nine cases out of ten and wrong one case out of ten. This is the essence of statistical decision making – knowing what degree of risk is involved in taking a particular decision. It is this idea that lies behind efforts to classify risks in making decisions and is dealt with in *statistical estimation* and *statistical decision theory*.

Underlined above were phrases like 'in the long run' and it is through this that we see randomness and probability are closely linked to the idea of large numbers. It is only when we have a large number of items that we can see what pattern of randomness a phenomenon exhibits. It is only *to* large numbers of items that we may predict in probability terms. It is impossible to predict the outcome of a single trial using information supplied by large numbers. The best we can say is that whatever the outcome of this trial it will fit into its own pattern of randomness.

Thus if we have a sample with, say, a mean of 21″ we say that we can be 95% sure that the population mean lies in the interval 91″ to 23″ knowing that in statistics this means that in the long run we would be right 95 times out of 100.

Finally a word about the interpretation of the various examples used in the text. The reader may have wondered why so many examples in this (and other) texts on probability are concerned with rolling dice, tossing pennies, and drawing marbles from urns. The answer is that these activities form models of real situations. A bag containing 90 white marbles and 10 black marbles can be used as a model for a machine producing 10% defective items, it can be used as a model for considering the problem where 10% of a population catch a contageous disease after exposure to it, it can be used as a model for car accident figures, and so on. It is by seeing what happens to the model (called a probability model) that we can predict what will happen in the real life situation.

Exercise 6

1. An experiment consists of rolling a normal die. Given

$$A = \{1, 2\}, \quad B = \{3, 4, 5\}, \quad C = \{6\}, \quad D = \{2, 3, 4, 5\},$$

find (a) $P(A \cup B)$ (b) $P(A \cup C)$ (c) $P(A \cup D)$ (d) $P(B \cup D)$ (e) $P(A \cup B \cup C)$ (f) $P(A \cup B \cup D)$ (g) $P(B \cup C \cup D)$ (h) $P(A \cup B \cup C \cup D)$ (j) $P(A')$ (k) $P(D')$ (l) $P([A \cup B]')$ (m) $P([B \cup D]')$ (n) $P([A \cup D]')$.

Answer

(a) $\frac{5}{6}$ (c) $\frac{5}{6}$ (e) 1 (g) $\frac{5}{6}$ (j) $\frac{2}{3}$ (l) $\frac{1}{6}$ (n) $\frac{1}{6}$

2. A die is biased so that $P(1) = \frac{1}{12}$, $P(2) = \frac{1}{6}$, $P(3) = P(4) = \frac{1}{4}$, $P(5) = P(6) = \frac{1}{8}$. Using these probabilities repeat question 1.

Answer

(b) $\frac{7}{8}$ (d) $\frac{19}{24}$ (f) $\frac{7}{8}$ (h) 1 (k) $\frac{5}{24}$ (m) $\frac{5}{24}$

3. Two coins are tossed. What is the probability of getting (a) 1 head (b) at least 1 head (c) 1 tail (d) 2 tails?

Answer

(a) $\frac{1}{2}$ (b) $\frac{3}{4}$ (c) $\frac{1}{2}$ (d) $\frac{1}{4}$

4. Two coins are tossed. If a head counts 1 and a tail 0, what is the probability of getting (a) 1 (b) 2 (c) 0?

Answer

(a) $\frac{1}{2}$ (b) $\frac{1}{4}$ (c) $\frac{1}{4}$

5. Two coins are tossed and a head counts 4 while a tail counts 7. If the figures are added at the end of a throw, what is the probability of getting a total of (a) 8 (b) 11? If the lower figure is subtracted from the higher figure what is the probability of (c) zero?

Answer

(a) $\frac{1}{4}$ (b) $\frac{1}{2}$ (c) $\frac{1}{2}$

6. Two dice are thrown and the totals added. What is the probability that the total is (a) 2 (b) 4 (c) either 6 or 10 (d) either 5 or 7 or 9 (e) at least 10 (f) at most 5?

Answer

(a) $\frac{1}{36}$ (b) $\frac{1}{12}$ (c) $\frac{1}{4}$ (e) $\frac{1}{6}$ (f) $\frac{5}{18}$

7. Two dice are thrown and the totals added. Given $A = \{2, 3, 4, 5\}$, $B = \{6, 7, 8, 9\}$, $C = \{10, 11, 12\}$, $D = \{4, 5, 6, 7, 8, 9, 10\}$, find (a) $P(A)$ (b) $P(B)$ (c) $P(C)$ (d) $P(D)$ (e) $P(A \cup B)$ (f) $P(A \cup C)$ (g) $P(A \cup D)$ (h) $P(B \cup C)$ (j) $P(B \cup D)$ (k) $P(C \cup D)$ (l) $P(A \cap B)$ (m) $P(B \cap D)$ (n) $P(A \cup B \cup C)$ (o) $P(A \cup B \cup D)$ (p) $P(B \cup C \cup D)$ (q) $P(A')$ (r) $P(B')$ (s) $P(C')$ (t) $P(D')$ (u) $P([A \cup B]')$ (v) $P([A \cap B \cap D]')$ (w) $P([A \cap D]')$ (x) $P([C \cap D]')$

Answer

(a) $\frac{5}{18}$ (b) $\frac{5}{9}$ (c) $\frac{1}{6}$ (d) $\frac{5}{6}$ (e) $\frac{5}{6}$ (g) $\frac{11}{12}$ (j) $\frac{5}{6}$ (l) 0 (n) 1 (p) $\frac{11}{12}$ (r) $\frac{4}{9}$ (t) $\frac{1}{6}$ (v) $\frac{1}{12}$ (x) $\frac{35}{36}$.

8. Two dice are thrown and the lower score subtracted from the higher one. Given $A = \{1\}$, $B = \{2\}$, $C = \{3\}$, $D = \{4\}$, $E = \{5\}$, $F = \{0\}$, $G = \{1, 2\}$, $H = \{2, 3, 4\}$, find (a) $P(A)$ (b) $P(B)$ (c) $P(C)$ (d) $P(D)$ (e) $P(E)$ (f) $P(F)$ (g) $P(G)$ (h) $P(H)$ (j) $P(A \cup B)$ (k) $P(A \cup G)$ (l) $P(C \cup G)$ (m) $P(B \cup C)$ (n) $P(E \cup F)$ (o) $P(A \cup B \cup C)$ (p) $P(D \cup E \cup F)$ (q) $P(A \cup B \cup C \cup D)$ (r) $P(A \cup H)$ (s) $P(C \cup H)$ (t) $P(A')$ (u) $P([A \cup E]')$ (v) $P(G \cup H)$ (w) $P([G \cup H]')$

Answer

(a) $\frac{5}{18}$ (c) $\frac{1}{6}$ (e) $\frac{1}{18}$ (g) $\frac{1}{2}$ (j) $\frac{1}{2}$ (l) $\frac{2}{3}$ (n) $\frac{2}{9}$ (p) $\frac{1}{3}$ (r) $\frac{14}{19}$ (t) $\frac{13}{18}$ (v) $\frac{14}{19}$

9. Consider the experiment of throwing two dice together and (a) multiplying the two scores together (b) divide the smaller into the larger and take the remainder (c) add the scores together and for an even total count 1 and for an odd total count 0. Find the sample spaces and draw diagrams of the sample spaces. Invent for yourself probability questions based on these experiments. Can you think of other similar experiments for yourself?

10. Write out in words the result $P(A \cap B \cap C) = P(A)P(B \mid A)P(C \mid A \cap B)$.

11. Find an expression for $P(A \cap B \cap C \cap D)$ similar to that in no. 10 and write out in words what it means.

12. Discuss the question of order in $P(A \cap B)$ for the three cases (a) A and B independent and consecutive (b) A and B independent and simultaneous (c) A and B dependent.

13. A bag contains 2 white and 2 red marbles. If two of them are drawn with replacement, what is the probability of (a) 1 white marble (b) two white marbles? Draw the tree diagram to confirm your answers.

Answer

(a) $\frac{1}{2}$ (b) $\frac{1}{4}$

14. Repeat no. 13 for a bag containing (i) 3 white and 3 red marbles (ii) 4 white and 4 red marbles. What conclusions do you draw?

Answer

(i) (a) $\frac{1}{2}$ (b) $\frac{1}{4}$.

15. Repeat no. 13 for a bag containing x white marbles and x red marbles.

16. A bag contains 4 white and 2 red marbles. If two are drawn with replacement, what is the probability of (a) 1 white (b) 2 white marbles?

Answer

(a) $\frac{4}{9}$ (b) $\frac{4}{9}$

17. Repeat no. 16 for a bag containing (i) 5 white and 2 red marbles (ii) 6 white and 2 red marbles (iii) 7 white and 2 red marbles. Discuss any patterns in the working.

Answer

(i) (a) $\frac{20}{49}$ (b) $\frac{25}{49}$ (ii) (a) $\frac{3}{8}$ (b) $\frac{9}{16}$ (iii) (a) $\frac{28}{81}$ (b) $\frac{49}{81}$.

18. Repeat no. 16 for a bag containing x white and y red marbles.

Answer

(a) $\dfrac{2xy}{(x+y)^2}$ (b) $\dfrac{x^2}{(x+y)^2}$

19. A bag contains 2 white and 2 red marbles. If three of them are drawn with replacement, what is the probability of (a) 3 white (b) 2 white and one red marble?

Answer

(a) $(\frac{1}{2})^3$ (b) $3(\frac{1}{2})^3$

20. Repeat no. 19 for a bag containing (i) 3 white and 2 red marbles (ii) 4 white and 2 red marbles. Extend the question further for yourself.

Answer

(i) (a) $(\frac{3}{5})^3$ (b) $3(\frac{3}{5})^2(\frac{3}{5})$

(ii) (a) $(\frac{2}{3})^3$ (b) $3(\frac{2}{3})^2(\frac{1}{3})$

21. Repeat no. 19 for a bag containing x white and y red marbles.

Answer

(a) $\left(\dfrac{x}{x+y}\right)^3$ (b) $3\left(\dfrac{x}{x+y}\right)^2\left(\dfrac{y}{x+y}\right)$

22. A bag contains 5 blue and 4 yellow balls. Discuss the similarities and differences of the following situations:

(a) drawing three balls simultaneously

(b) drawing three balls consecutively with replacement

(c) drawing three balls consecutively without replacement.

23. An urn contains 10 red, 10 white and 10 blue marbles. Three are drawn consecutively without replacement. (a) Put into probability notation (i) The probability of drawing 3 reds (ii) The probability of a red, white and blue (iii) The probability of drawing a red, white and blue in that order (iv) The probability the third is red given that the first two were blue (b) Translate the following into words
(i) $P(R \cap R \cap W)$ (ii) $P(W \mid R \cap R)$ (iii) $P([R \cap R \cap R]')$

24. Two cards are drawn form an ordinary deck. Find the probability that (a) they are both aces (b) the first card is an ace but the second is not (c) the cards are the same suit (d) the cards are not the same suit (e) they are not picture cards (f) at least one is a picture card (g) the second is a picture card given the first was not a picture card.

Answer

(a) $\frac{1}{221}$ (b) $\frac{16}{221}$ (c) $\frac{4}{17}$ (e) $\frac{10}{17}$ (f) $\frac{12}{51}$

25. Consider the drawing of three cards from an ordinary deck. Invent questions similar to those of no. 24, and solve them.

26. Explain the statement, 'If two events are mutually exclusive they can't be independent'.

27. Two urns are arranged so that U_1 contains 3 white and 2 black balls, while U_2 contains 5 white and 5 black balls. A coin is tossed – if it comes down heads two balls are removed from U_1, if it comes down tails two balls are removed from U_2. What is the probability that the two balls are white?

Answer

$\frac{47}{180}$

28. In the previous question 3 balls are removed. What is the probability that they are 2 white and 1 black balls?

Answer

$\frac{61}{120}$

29. A box contains 3 white and 2 black balls. X and Y draw alternately without replacement from the box. X wins as soon as he draws a white and Y wins as soon as he (Y) draws a black. If X draws first write down the sequence of draws that gives A a win. Hence find the probability that X wins. If drawing is with replacement and the rules are the same, what is the probability that Y wins?

Answer

W, BWW, $BWBWW$. $P(X \text{ wins}) = \frac{9}{10}$ $P(Y \text{ wins}) = \frac{4}{19}$, (Hint: the sum of a geometric progression is required here)

30. A box contains 10 balls coloured with white or black but it is not known how many of each there are. If the probability of drawing 2 white ones is $\frac{1}{15}$, how many white ones are there?

Answer

3.

31. Cards marked 1 to 4 are put in a box. Three are drawn without replacement and the scores added. What is the probability of a total of 8.

Answer

$\frac{1}{4}$.

32. How many times must a die be thrown in order that the probability of rolling 2 sixes is exactly $\frac{125}{648}$.

Answer

5.

33. How many times must a die be thrown in order that the probability of rolling 1 or more sixes is bigger than a half.

Answer

4.

34. Discuss the similarities and difference between rolling 1 die four times and rolling four dice once.

35. Comment on the similarities between a relative frequency graph and a probability graph.

36. A red die and a green die are thrown. The score on the red die is subtracted from the green die – allowing negative answers. Find the outcome space for this experiment. Draw a line graph showing the distribution of probabilities. Find $P(0)$.

Answer

$\frac{1}{6}$.

37. Draw a line graph showing the probability distributions of the following experiments:

(a) two dice are rolled and the totals added.

(b) two dice are rolled and the totals multiplied.

(c) two coins are tossed and the number of heads counted.

(d) two coins are tossed and the number of tails counted.

(e) four coins are tossed and the number of heads counted.

38. A box contains equal numbers of black and white marbles. How many must I draw on the average so that two different colours are drawn?

Answer

3.

39. Extend the previous question to (a) three different colours and three marbles drawn (b) four different colours and four marbles drawn.

Answer

(a) Mathematically the answer is 5·5 but common sense boggles at drawing 0·5 of a ball so it can be rounded up to 6. (b) Similarly $8\frac{1}{3}$ rounds up to 9.

40. Two coins are tossed and a die thrown. The number of heads is counted and then subtracted from the number shown on the die. Write out the outcome space for the resulting number and find $P(0)$ and $P(4)$.

Answer

$\frac{1}{9}$ and $\frac{1}{6}$.

41. Consider various combinations of dice and coins and invent experiments similar to that of the previous question.

42. X tosses 5 coins and Y tosses 3 coins. Who has the best chance of getting 2 heads?

Answer

Y.

43. An urn U_1 contains x_1 red, x_2 white and x_3 blue balls. A similar urn U_2 contains x_4 red, x_5 white and x_6 blue balls. A coin is tossed and if heads appears two balls are selected from U_1 but if a tail appears two balls are chosen from U_2. If there are 30 balls in each urn and drawing is without replacement, show that the probability both balls drawn are the same colour is

$$\frac{1}{1740}\left[\sum_{i=1}^{6} x_i^2 - 60\right].$$

Show further that if drawing is with replacement the probability is

$$\frac{1}{1800}\left(\sum_{i=1}^{6} x_i^2\right).$$

7 An Axiomatic Approach to Probability Theory

7.1 Introduction

In the definition of probability where the notion of 'equally likely' was used (Section 4.17) we noticed that there was circularity since probability was being, in essence, defined in terms of itself. For this reason mathematicians have sought a better basis for a development of probability theory.

The definition of probability in terms of relative frequency, though very useful in practice, has the difficulty – from a mathematical point of view – that a unique limit may not really exist, and for this reason this definition has been rejected.

Modern probability theory has thus developed axiomatically and probability is defined in terms of a function. It is not uncommon for mathematical situations to develop in the way suggested by the previous paragraphs. Mathematical ideas and concepts are first developed by their practical use and then mathematicians look for a minimum set of 'self evident' assumptions from which they may deduce these notions as theorems. A typical and well known case is that of geometry. This was first developed practically and then Euclid was one of the first to formalise it in terms of theorems derived from postulates. It will be seen in the following sections how the notions of probability developed in previous chapters may be deduced as theorems from three axioms.

Before we proceed further we need one further concept in set theory. Consider the set $S = \{1, 2, \ldots 10\}$ and the subsets of S as follows: $A = \{1, 2, 3\}$ $B = \{4\}$ $C = \{5, 6, 7\}$ $D = \{8, 9, 10\}$. What do we notice about these subsets? First they are all disjoint, and second, between them they have used all the elements in S. We are thus led to the following definition: A *partition* of a set S consists of subsets A, B, $C, \ldots K$, which satisfy the following two conditions,

(a) they are mutually disjoint, and

(b) $A \cup B \cup C \cup \ldots \cup K = S$

Example 1: Let $A = \{1, 2, \ldots 10\}$ then the following are two more possible partitions of A

(i) $A = \{1, 2, 3, 4, 5\}$ $B = \{6, 7, 8, 9, 10\}$

(ii) $A = \{1\}$ $B = \{2\}$ $C = \{3\}$ $D = \{4\}$

$E = \{5, 6, 7\}$ $F = \{8\}$ $G = \{9, 10\}$

Example 2: If S is considered as a subset of itself, then S together with ϕ forms a partition on S since (a) $S \cup \phi = S$ and (b) $S \cap \phi = \phi$, showing S and ϕ are mutually exclusive.

7.2 Function – Set Function

A *function* is a rule whereby elements of one set, A, are associated with elements of another set B. If f denotes this rule we write $f: A \to B$, which is read, 'f is a function of A to B'. F, G, g and h are other commonly used letters along with f. A is called the *domain* of the function, and B is called the *co-domain* of the function. If x is an element of A, then the element in B associated with it is called the *image* of x and is written $f(x)$.

Example 1:

Let A = the set of positive integers
Let B = the set of positive integers
Let f = assign to each element in A its square,

i.e. $f = x^2$

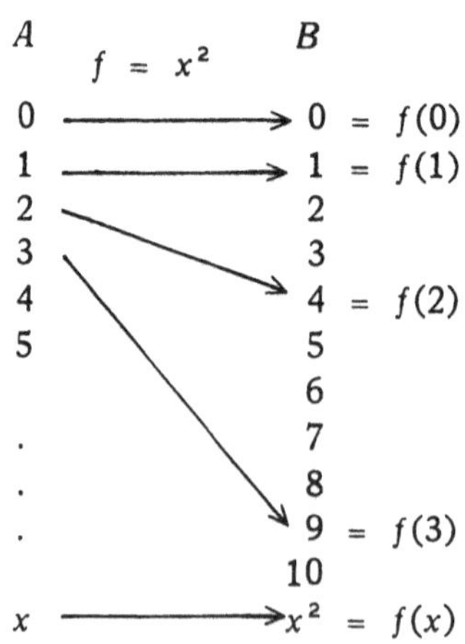

Fig. 7.2(a)

If for each $x \in A$, there is one and only one element $f(x) \quad B$, then f is called a 1 : 1 – read 'one to one' – function.

If for several elements of A there is only one element in B, then f is called a *many-one* function.

Example 2:

Let A = the set of positive integers
Let B = $\{0, E\}$
Let f = assign to every even element the letter E, and assign to every odd element the letter 0.

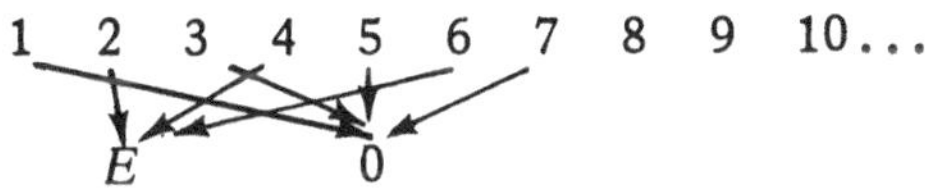

The diagram shows clearly that f is a many-one function.

If for one element in A there is more than one element in B, then f is called a one-many function.

Example 3:

Let A = the set of real numbers
Let B = the set of real numbers
Let f = take the square root, i.e. $f = \sqrt{x}$.

For $4 \in A$ there are two elements in B, namely $+2$ and -2, hence f is a one-many function.

If every element in B is the image of some element in A, then f is called an *onto* function.

Example 4: If A and B are as in *Example 3*, then $f = x + 1$ is an *onto* function.

If there are some elements in B which are not images of elements in A then f is called an *into* function. In *Example 1*, $3 \in B$ is not the image of any element in A, therefore $f = x^2$, in this case, is an into function.

It is not necessary that elements in the sets A and B be restricted to numbers. If A is the set of people and B is the set of ages, and F is the function 'assign to each person his age' then F is a perfectly good function.

It is sometimes useful to look at not only the images of the individual elements of A but to look at the image of a subset of A. In *Example 1*, the set $\{1, 2, 3\}$ is a subset of A and has an image set $\{1, 4, 9\}$, and we write $f(\{1, 2, 3\}) = \{1, 4, 9\}$. Thus in the functional notation $f(\ )$ the bracket may be occupied by a single element of A or by a subset of A.

It does not always follow that the image of a *subset* of A will be a *subset* of B since this will depend on the function. It may well be that the image of $X \subset A$ is a single element of B.

Example 5:

Let A = the set of positive integers
Let B = the set of positive integers
Let g = assign to each subset of A the highest number in the subset.

Then

$$g(\{1, 2, 3\}) = 3$$
$$g(\{40, 99\}) = 99$$
$$g(\{1, 2, 3, 4, 5, 6\}) = 6$$

Functions where the elements of A are themselves sets while their images in B are real numbers are called *set functions* and in what follows we shall be more interested in set functions than in ordinary functions. We have already seen in fact that, in assigning probabilities to subsets of the outcome space, that we have been using set functions.

7.3 The Axioms of Probability

Now we have the concept of a set function we can give a definition of what we mean by the probability of an event. First we refer to a discrete finite, or infinite, outcome space S, and define the function P on subsets A of S such that $P(A)$ is a real number, and this real number we call the probability of the event represented by A. The function P gives the measure of the probability of the various subsets A of S and is sometimes called a probability measure. Second we stipulate that the set function P must satisfy the following axioms:

$A\,1$: $0 \leqslant P(A) \leqslant 1$ for every $A \subset S$

$A\,2$: $P(S) = 1$

$A\,3$: $P(A_1 \cup A_2 \cup A_3 \cup \ldots) = P(A_1) + P(A_2) + P(A_3) + \ldots$

where A_i is a finite or infinite sequence of disjoint subsets of S.

It is important to notice that these axioms do not specify how the probabilities are to be assigned to the various subsets of S, and in practice they are assigned in the ways discussed in Section 4.17.

7.4 Some Theorems in Probability

We now show how the theorems already used in Chapter 6 may be deduced logically from the above axioms.

Theorem 1: $P(A) + P(A') = 1$

Proof: A and A' are disjoint and $A \cup A' = S$

Hence $P(A \cup A') = P(S) = 1$

and $P(A) + P(A') = 1$

This also gives us $P(A) = 1 - P(A')$ which was used in Section 6.3

Theorem 2: $P(\phi) = 0$

Proof: We recall that ϕ is a subset of every set

S and ϕ are disjoint and $S \cup \phi = S$

Hence $P(S \cup \phi) = P(S) = 1$

and $P(S) + P(\phi) = 1$

giving $P(\phi) = 0$

Theorem 3: $P(A \cup B) = P(A) + P(B) - P(A \cap B)$

Proof: We use the fact that

$A \cup B = (A \cap B') \cup (A \cap B) \cup (A' \cap B)$

and the 3 sets on the right hand side are disjoint.

This enables us to apply $A\ 3$ to

$P(A \cup B) = P((A \cap B') \cup (A \cap B) \cup (A' \cap B))$ to get

$P(A \cup B) = P(A \cap B') + P(A \cap B) + P(A' \cap B)$

Now adding and subtracting $P(A \cap B)$ on the right-hand side, we get

$$P(A \cup B) = [P(A \cap B\ ) + P(A \cap B)] - P(A \cap B) + [P(A \cap B) + P(A' \cap B)]$$

But $A = (A \cap B') \cup (A \cap B)$ and $B = (A \cap B) \cup (A' \cap B)$

and $P(A) = P(A \cap B') + P(A \cap B)$ and $P(B) = P(A \cap B) + P(A' \cap B)$

It now follows that

$P(A \cup B) = P(A) + P(B) - P(A \cap B)$

Figure 7.3(a) will help to show the various disjoint sets used in the above proof but it is pointed out that it does not form any part of the proof.

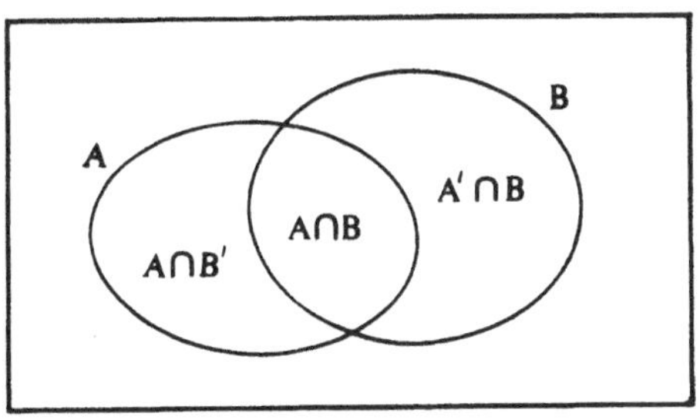

Fig. 7.3 (a)

Corollary: $P(A \cup B) \leqslant P(A) + P(B)$ which is sometimes useful.

Theorem 4: If the individual outcomes of $A \subset S$ are $A_1, A_2, A_3, \ldots$, i.e. $A = A_1 \cup A_2 \cup A_3 \cup \ldots$ then $P(A) = P(A_1) + P(A_2) + P(A_3) + \ldots$

Proof: We again apply axiom 3 to

$P(A) = P(A_1 \cup A_2 \cup A_3 \ldots)$ to get

$= P(A_1) + P(A_2) + P(A_3) + \ldots$

Theorem 5: If $K_1, K_2, \ldots K_n$ constitute a partition of S, and $P(K_1) = P(K_2) = P(K_3) = \ldots = P(K_n)$ then $P(K_i) = 1/n$.

Proof: Since $K_1 \cup K_2 \cup K_3 \cup \ldots \cup K_n = S$

$P(K_1 \cup K_2 \cup K_3 \cup \ldots \cup K_n) = P(S)$ giving

$P(K_1) + P(K_2) + \ldots P(K_n) = 1$

But $P(K_1) = P(K_2) = \ldots P(K_n)$ and we have

$nP(K_1) = 1$ and finally

$P(K_1) = 1/n$

It now follows that $P(K_i) = 1/n$

Theorem 6: If $A = K_1 \cup K_2 \cup \ldots \cup K_s$ where K_i are as defined in *Theorem 5* and $s \leqslant n$, then $P(A) = s/n$.

Proof: $P(A) = P(K_1 \cup K_2 \cup \ldots \cup K_s)$

$= P(K_1) + P(K_2) + \ldots + P(K_s)$

But $P(K_i) = 1/n$ and we have

$P(A) = s/n$

This theorem is the equivalent of that 'definition' of probability which says that if A can occur in s ways and fail to occur in $(n - s)$ ways, all of which are equally likely, then the probability of A occurring is

$$\frac{s}{s + (n - s)} = \frac{s}{n}$$

Definition 1:

$$P(A \mid B) = \frac{P(A \cap B)}{P(B)}, \quad P(B) > 0$$

Definition 2:

$$P(B \mid A) = \frac{P(B \cap A)}{P(A)}, \quad P(A) > 0$$

Theorem 7: $P(A \cap B) = P(B).P(A \mid B)$

Proof: This follows directly form *Definition 1*

Theorem 8: $P(A \cap B) = P(A) . P(B \mid A)$

Proof: This follows directly from *Definition 2*.

Definition 3: A and B are independent if and only if
$P(A \cap B) = P(A) . P(B)$

Theorem 9: If A and B are independent and $P(B) \neq 0$,
then $P(A) = P(A \mid B)$

Proof: Since A and B are independent
$P(A \cap B) = P(A) . P(B)$
$P(A \cap B) = P(B) . P(A \mid B)$ (*Theorem* 7)
Therefore $P(A) . P(B) = P(B) . P(A \mid B)$
Giving $P(A) = P(A \mid B)$

Theorem 10: If A and B are independent and $P(A) \neq 0$,
then $P(B) = P(B \mid A)$

Proof: Similar to the proof of *Theorem* 9.

That then is how probability theory begins when developed axiomatically. For further developments the reader is advised to refer to books that deal specifically with this topic.

Exercise 7

1. Prove that $P(A \cup B \cup C) = P(A) + P(B) + P(C) - P(A \cap B) - P(A \cap C) - P(B \cap C) + P(A \cap B \cap C)$. Extend this result to four sets.

2. Given A and B are subsets of an outcome space S and represent independent events, prove that (a) A and B' are independent (b) A' and B are independent (c) A' and B' are independent.

3. Prove that $P(A \cap B \cap C) = P(A)P(B \mid A)P(C \mid A \cap B)$ where A, B, C, are dependent events.

4. Given $B_1, B_2, \ldots, B_n$ form a partition of S and $P(B_i) \neq 0$ for all i, then prove

$$P(A) = \sum_{i=1}^{n} P(B_i)P(A \mid B_i).$$

5. Construct a situation where A, B and C are subsets of an outcome space S, $P(A \cap B) = P(A)P(B)$, $P(A \cap C) = P(A)P(C)$, $P(B \cap C) = P(B)P(C)$, and A, B, and C are not independent. Hence show that for independence the further condition $P(A \cap B \cap C) = P(A)P(B)P(C)$, (together with the other three) is necessary.

6. Prove (a) $P(A \cup B) \leqslant P(A) + P(B)$ (b) $P(A) \leqslant P(A \cup B)$

7. Prove $P([A \cup B]') = P(A' \cap B')$

8. If B_1, B_2, and B_3 form a partition of an outcome space S, where $A \subset S$, prove $P(A) = P(A \cap B_1) + P(A \cap B_2) + P(A \cap B_3)$. Extend the result to a partition consisting of n subsets of S.

Kolibri 360 GmbH
Ferdinand-Jühlke-Straße 7
99095 Erfurt, Deutschland
produktsicherheit@kolibri360.de